EUROPRENEURS

HERBERT A. HENZLER

EUROPRENEURS

★

THE MEN WHO ARE SHAPING EUROPE

BANTAM PRESS

LONDON · NEW YORK · TORONTO · SYDNEY · AUCKLAND

TRANSWORLD PUBLISHERS LTD
61–63 Uxbridge Road, London W5 5SA

TRANSWORLD PUBLISHERS (AUSTRALIA) PTY LTD
15–25 Helles Avenue, Moorebank, NSW 2170

TRANSWORLD PUBLISHERS (NZ) LTD
3 William Pickering Drive,
Albany, Auckland

Published 1994 by Bantam Press
a division of Transworld Publishers Ltd
Copyright © 1994 McKinsey & Co., Inc.

A catalogue record for this book is available from the British Library.

ISBN 0593 035224

Typeset in 11/13pt Times by
Chippendale Type Ltd, Otley, West Yorkshire.
Printed in Great Britain by
Mackays of Chatham, Chatham, Kent.

Contents

Foreword

The completion of the English-language version of this book coincides with the spread of disenchantment about Europe and its future prospects. A mixture of aversion to supranational central governments and to the costs of Brussels bureaucracy prompted the Danes to say 'no' to Maastricht in June 1992 before saying a mild, qualified 'yes' a year later. The French barely managed a faint 'oui'. It is small comfort to find that the 'yes' vote was significantly higher in the younger generation and in Alsace, the historical neighbour of the Germans. The Germans, after a qualified 'yes' by the Constitutional Court in October 1993, hold the record of being the last member state to put ratification into effect. This 'yes – but' leaves some scope for later decisions on how European the Germans can, or want to, be.

The Europe of today lacks two things: visionary political leadership and direct political pressure from outside. While its political leaders work on the implementation of the Maastricht treaty, disappointing levels of public support for the treaty, as reflected in a series of opinion polls, shows that they have often forgotten to tell their voters what benefits Maastricht could bring them – a criminal omission in the age of communication. As a result, the concept of a united Europe suddenly seems much less attractive to the citizens of the European Community at a time when would-be entrants are clamouring to join.

The lack of direct external political pressure has allowed the Europeans the luxury of disagreeing among themselves on the Gulf War, playing an unseemly waiting game as tragedy in former Yugoslavia unfolds, hesitating on reconstruction aid for Eastern Europe, and practically dropping the North–South conflict from their agendas. We can only hope that this European 'hang-fire-ism' will soon be overcome and that vigorous political action will take its place.

Largely ignoring this political inertia, however, European corporations have set an example of dynamism and initiative. Sparked by an emerging generation of fifty or more 'Europreneurs', all outstanding leaders of large corporations, and supported by the energies of hundreds of owner-entrepreneurs in their mid-sized companies, a level of energy was generated in the second half of the Eighties not seen in such pan-European form for many years. It is true, however, that in the course of the overall world economic recession of the early Nineties many European companies face massive restructuring tasks, involving substantial layoffs of people and pruning of product lines. It seems that this restructuring process is well under way.

My objectives here have been to retrace that earlier surge of energy and to describe its sources. I have not attempted – or intended – a scientific analysis, but a general observation of the patterns of success. What makes these Europreneurs different? In what way do they lead their companies? Is there a specifically European management culture? What role is played by the mid-sized companies, the traditional backbone of European industry? Finally, I wanted to assess whether the European success model that has so dominated the continent's economic progress during the past decade can survive in the face of these upcoming challenges.

Some readers may feel many of my observations are too optimistic. But I am convinced of the intrinsic strength of European entrepreneurs and I know that they do, indeed, stand a very good chance of coping successfully with major challenges that are facing them now and will face them in the future.

In writing this manuscript I have received invaluable support from my McKinsey partners – especially my colleagues in the European offices – in the form of one-on-one discussions, meetings and comments. I should like to extend my warmest thanks to all of them. I should also like to thank Christel Delker for her editorial work, and Alan Kantrow and Patrick Tanghe for their valuable contributions of economic history and research. Finally, I also would like to thank my secretaries, Roswitha Frenzel and Gisela Ludorf, who kept the pressures of my day-to-day work firmly under control and thus enabled me to find time for this book.

Munich, October 1993

I

At a Turning-Point

Whenever Europe and its future are discussed, opinions diverge as widely as moods. At the beginning of the Eighties, Henry Kissinger feared that Europe was abdicating its traditional leadership in political, cultural and economic development. Barely ten years later, Hans-Dietrich Genscher, then Foreign Minister of a newly united Germany, seemed perfectly justified in his diagnosis of Europe's markedly successful 're-entry into history'.

As we approach the mid-Nineties, there appears no end in sight to such divergence in views. No sooner had Francis Fukuyama proclaimed the end of ideology, even of history itself, with the end of the Cold War, than the shades of the past started to catch up with us again: 1992 has not brought a unified Europe in economic, let alone political, terms. Together with Europe, the United States, traditional seismograph of future economic trends, is still in the throes of a recession. Japan's economic doldrums show little sign of ending. Europeans in particular, who had the most to hope for from the end of the Cold War and the opening up of Eastern Europe, seem to be losing their confidence in political stability, social harmony and economic growth.

Is it too much for us to cope with? Supported by a seven-year boom, we have put off solving structural problems. Are they catching up with us at last? Are we so preoccupied with the political and social crises of the Nineties that our collective and individual entrepreneurial ability has atrophied? Has Eurosclerosis returned and taken on a new, intransigent form?

I believe that we are now at a turning-point. I also believe that we have grounds for cautious optimism. At the same time, however, I am certain that success will not come of itself. There is an urgent need for us to understand, maintain and develop our specifically European strengths. Evidence can readily be found for the reality of this turning-point, as signalled by the accumulation of 'historic' hours, days, and events since 1989. But the signals are also to be seen in the remorseless catalogue of problems that have beset the region's economy, the engine of all its other hopes: consistently low growth rates; unemployment stuck at around 10 per cent; stubborn budget deficits driven by a mentality that takes subsidies for granted and protects vested interests; productivity and innovation that lag in major areas of the economy; the lack of cost orientation in almost all public institutions; and increasing competition on price and quality from Asian producers. And all these problems come at a time when there are already unprecedented financial burdens stemming from Eastern Europe's collapse and the need for reconstruction, from the growing threat to the environment, from regional conflicts, and from the pressures of immigration.

The next few years will tell the tale. They will determine how Europe manages its turning-point. Those same years, moreover, will see a generational change in much of the industrial and political leadership. Like it or not, Europe will have to change to meet its problems and to take advantage of its opportunities in the world economy. Passivity will inevitably lead to a decline in competitiveness, standard of living and, more seriously, to a collapse back into endless national, regional and local squabbles. 'Europe' will have been lost.

Grounds for Optimism

Less obvious, perhaps, are the reasons for my optimism. First, of course, there is our experience with the European 'economic miracle', now more or less taken for granted by the general public. The real miracle is not so much the economic growth from the mid-Eighties onward, but the fact that we have a European – or, to be more precise, a 'Europeanized' – economy at all. Viewed against the background of twentieth-century economic history, that development was by no means guaranteed. Other outcomes were possible, other approaches conceivable, and serious attempts were made to implement them. Thus, at the beginning of the century there was a polarization of the European national economies into self-sufficient colonial systems (the British Empire, for one) and power blocs (the Central Powers), which dealt with one another on the basis of opportunistic, mercantile export policies. In one view, the First World War was itself an inevitable clash between increasingly incompatible economic systems.

After 1918, the victorious Allied powers attempted to exclude Germany from the system of Western European economies in a manner comparable to the self-sought macro- and micro-economic isolation of the emergent Soviet Union. Later, economic activity was effectively bundled

into national spheres of influence. In the end, it took a
second world war and a cold war to convince Western
Europeans that such models of development were not the
way to go.

As recently as 1987, the American author Stuart Miller
claimed – in *Painted in Blood*,[1] a book about Europe with a
title rich in associations – that Europeans could be understood properly only if you considered that the current
coexistence of nations was built on a history more scarred
by wars than that of any other continent. In his view, the
historical need for defence shaped the way Europeans think
and how they deal with each other. For 250 years, war and
peace followed one another in rapid succession; generations
sequentially built and destroyed all they possessed in the
blind rage of conflict. When one generation passed, it not
only handed down damaged national assets, but also a deep
mistrust of its enemies. Hereditary enmities became deeply
ingrained.

The path Europe took to correct the mistakes of its past
is the second reason for optimism today: Europe has always
made the most impressive advances in its political and economic position in situations of crisis or latent danger. The
EEC and later the EC, new organizations focused squarely
on economic objectives, were founded – and expanded
from six members to twelve – as a clear response to the
perceived inadequacies of earlier economic and political
arrangements.

The key events *en route* included:

☐ The European Coal and Steel Community, the first of the
three European Communities, was formed in 1951 to
solve the supply problems of all its member states during

[1] Stuart Miller, *Painted in Blood, Understanding the Europeans*, Atheneum,
New York 1987.

post-war reconstruction and to place the redeveloping national coal and steel industries under joint control. Adenauer's, Monet's, Schuman's and de Gasperi's visionary intention was that, once these industries were integrated, war between the participant countries would no longer be possible. The European Atomic Energy Community (Euratom) was founded in 1957 with similar objectives.

☐ The European Economic Community initiated by the Treaty of Rome on 1 January 1958 was founded against the background of the smouldering Berlin crisis and the dissolution of European colonial rights in Africa and Asia. The creation of a common market for industrial and agricultural products and a common trade policy towards other countries was intended to strengthen the debilitated democracies' powers of resistance in the East–West conflict and to create the economic climate for political integration at a later date. The abolition of regulatory restrictions on the traffic of goods and capital in Europe and the growing defences against outside countries created favourable environmental conditions for the expansion of national industries. During the Sixties, the Europeans were thus able to reduce their disadvantage against the overpowering US competition. The natural strengths of German capital goods producers, French and Italian consumer goods companies, and British banks and insurance companies, favoured the growth dynamics of the entire community. The law of comparative advantage worked well among the individual national states.

☐ The external threats posed by the collapse of the Bretton Woods system of fixed exchange rates and the oil crises after the Yom Kippur War speeded up the transition from

the EEC to the EC, and pointed the way to European
Political Union. The entry of Great Britain, Denmark
and Ireland (1973) and, subsequently, Greece (1981), and
Portugal and Spain (1986) lent the EC new political significance. Access to North Sea oil, a long-term gas treaty
with the Soviet Union and the expansion of nuclear
energy reduced dependence on Arab oil supplies.

☐ In 1985, in response to waning growth, a lagging position
in the technology race, and the widespread advance of
low-cost Asian vendors, EC members adopted Jacques
Delors' proposal to create a single European internal
market. The concept of 'Europe '92' was accompanied by
an easing of regulation and a supply-oriented economic
policy at the national level. This industry-friendly policy,
in which Margaret Thatcher led the way from 1979 onwards, was pursued to varying extents and with varying
objectives in mainland Europe by Helmut Kohl, François
Mitterrand, Felipe Gonzalez and Giovanni Spadolini in
the Eighties. It gave an enormous boost to industrial
vitality.

The overall historical pattern here is that solutions have
grown more and more 'European' from crisis to crisis –
that is, less dependent on support and stimuli from outside
Europe, as well as less individually 'national'. The history
of post-war Europe, thus, is the story of a step-by-step
reduction in the over-dependence of European national
economies either on the US or on the Arab oil cartel,
coupled with a steady rise both in economic performance
and in the general welfare of broad sections of the population. At the same time, with the elimination of many
nation-specific regulations and the development of large,
efficient markets, the role of 'European' companies and
industries – as opposed to simply national ones – has

steadily increased. That seems particularly encouraging in view of the growing strain on government institutions in all European countries.

In the immediate post-war period, the first imperative for every Western European economy was that of national reconstruction. Construction was the dominant industry in every part of the region. Manufacturing dominated the value-added chain of all industrial companies, and there was a buyer for every product.

The most significant factor in post-war Europe was its orientation toward the US – the superpower that protected Europe from the westward expansion of the socialist bloc through 'containment' and, through the Marshall Plan, sustained the day-to-day functioning of the mainland European economies. It seemed as though Goethe's envious words, 'America, you are better off,' also applied to the dynamic American economy. Alexis de Tocqueville, the far-seeing French constitutional lawyer, admired America's democratic foundations as early as 1835. He predicted that its specific Anglo-American order of society, the relationship of individual states to the Federal government, the powers of the judiciary, its political parties, its democratic government, the moderation of the tyranny of the majority, and its turbulent yet homogeneous society would give the US a society superior to the aristocratically-based social orders of Europe. In contrast to Europe, major corporations gained huge significance there and the role of the state appeared secondary. Industrialization was pursued with much greater energy than in Europe. The US recovered from the world economic crises of the Twenties faster than the European countries. After the Second World War it was the world's absolute economic leader, safeguarding the survival and recovery of the Old World. The Europeans built an export economy on the foundations of the strong dollar. West Germany's exports, for example, increased by 358 per cent from 1950 to 1960 to over $16 billion, accounting for 23.6 per cent of GNP.

Direct investments by US companies poured into Europe during the Fifties. The Americans built 'insider' positions in such important areas as the oil industry, automotive production, and consumer goods. Apart from the injection of capital, Europe thus gained the technological know-how and management practice it needed so urgently. American direct investments in Europe grew from $1.7 billion in 1950 to $6.7 billion in 1960. In the Sixties, however, danger signs appeared. The migration of European professionals and specialists to US universities and the laboratories of US industry became a disquieting 'brain drain'. European culture, that rich heritage of the centuries, seemed to be swamped by consumer durables, books, films, and pop idols from across the Atlantic. Americanisms took possession of European languages in full force. It was almost like an advance confirmation of Paul Kennedy's later arguments about the congruence of political, cultural and economic power.

Europe's self-doubts grew. The superiority of the US appeared more and more of a threat, but also an example to follow. The management beliefs and techniques that were apparently responsible for the success of the US industrial machine were things to emulate and to learn. How far would European industrialists have to follow the example of their US colleagues? Had not the major US companies solved the organizational complexity problems of the post-war environment by aggressive divisionalization? Who knew more about divisionalization than the people at the top of General Motors? In consumer goods, the strongest players relied on a highly developed system of product managers. Where could you learn more than from Procter & Gamble? Wasn't portfolio planning the key element of the most progressive strategies? Where was that done better than at General

Electric? Were more interdisciplinary product development teams the order of the day? AT&T had developed them to perfection. Did a company want to set up a truly international organization structure? All roads led to IBM.

For European managers grappling with the challenge of reconstruction, the list of America's 'first' and 'best' companies was as long as it was discouraging. Even in 1970, the *Fortune* 100 largest companies in the world included no fewer than 64 US players; the Top 450 contained 255 companies of American origin. They shaped innovation in management theory and practice. They also determined what would be on the programme of executive training courses and in MBA classrooms in the United States. And that decided what was taught elsewhere. Virtually every new idea that arose – new applications in information technology, matrix organization, profit centres, creative marketing, and so on – developed first in the US, was discussed first in the US business press, and was taught first in US business schools. Management consulting, a profession established generations back in the US, was exported to Europe in the mid-Sixties, where it helped pass on to European companies the basis of American management know-how. Europe's goal was simply not to be left too far behind. At least, that was the way it seemed.

In reality, the 'American challenge' – favoured for many years on the investment side by a prohibitively high dollar exchange rate – had lost a great deal of its momentum even before Jean-Jacques Servan-Schreiber's famous book thrust it into the limelight in 1967.[1] In the period from 1960 to 1970, the US share of GNP in the OECD countries fell from 59 to 43 per cent; the share of the US in OECD foreign trade declined from 25 to 20 per cent of

---

[1] Jean-Jacques Servan-Schreiber, *Le défi américain* (The American Challenge), Paris 1967.

exports, and from 21.4 to 20.1 per cent of imports. A more dramatic slump took place in currency reserves: in 1960 the US still held 32 per cent of the IMF's currency reserves; in 1970 that share had fallen by half to only 15.6 per cent.

But imitation, once it becomes a habit, is hard to shake off. When the uncontested intellectual, moral and economic dominance of the US began to disintegrate during the oil shocks of the Seventies and after the Vietnam War – and when the US gave itself up to a soul-searching process under Jimmy Carter – the Europeans' initial response was to look for models elsewhere. What could they learn from the Japanese, who were just at the beginning of their triumphal progress based on export strategies, an obviously MITI-influenced industrial policy, and the loose yet rigorous organizational form of the Keiretsu for major industrial groups? Innumerable experiments with these methods – quality circles, kanban, just-in-time, ringi decision-making processes – rarely produced truly 'Japanese' results for the Europeans. Consequently, they began to bombard them-selves with an endless succession of penetrating questions – questions asked from the point of view of the eternal laggard, trying to emulate the first mover's example. Not a particularly promising angle. In any case, none of this interest in successful foreign models could prevent them from dropping further and further to the rear. Europe's de-pressing loss in world market share told its own unequivocal tale.

European export-driven strategies lost their effectiveness after 1973 with the collapse of the Bretton Woods system. What growth there was stemmed largely from trade within the European Community, the largest trading bloc in the world. EC exports of industrial products to countries out-side the Community between 1973 and 1981 lost market share in five out of six major sectors (Diagram 1).

European Decline in World Markets

Percentage share of EC companies in world exports* of
industrial production

Per cent, 1973 and 1981

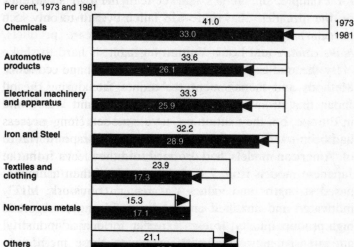

	1973	1981
Chemicals	41.0	33.0
Automotive products	33.6	26.1
Electrical machinery and apparatus	33.3	25.9
Iron and Steel	32.2	28.9
Textiles and clothing	23.9	17.3
Non-ferrous metals	15.3	17.1
Others	21.1	25.3

* Excluding exports between EC countries
Source: International Trade (GATT), McKinsey analysis

© McKinsey & Company, Inc.

Diagram 1

Neither American nor Japanese management methods,
uncritically adopted, were the solution. Indeed, the Japanese success formula did not even work for its inventors
in every case: entry as a low-cost supplier into low-price
mass markets, followed by a step-by-step move into higher
value-added segments, may have given them impressive
international market share in cars and consumer electronics. But it failed in industries where highly-developed
application engineering and system solutions were required
– that is, in precisely those industries (such as project engineering, telecommunications and transport systems) where
Europeans tended to have a competitive advantage. Besides, by this time European success models had emerged

as well. They were still few in number, but high in impact:
Nestlé's huge success in the Japanese instant coffee market,
for example, or Wella's market leadership in shampoos,
or the decades of world-wide success enjoyed by such
French luxury goods as champagne, haircare products,
haute couture and Louis Vuitton luggage.

By the mid-Eighties, there had been a change of mood.
Methods and management techniques from the US and
Japan that promised direct benefits still found a welcome
in Europe, but the fixation on success models from overseas
had been overcome. On a scale of 1 to 10, the importance
of 'American models' had dropped from, say, 9 to 5, that of
Japanese models from 7 to 4. The stock of natural, home-
based strengths and values was rising: teamwork, highly
motivated and qualified employees, solid engineering and
high product quality, foreign experience, local adaptability,
and intensive networking with customers, suppliers and public administration. You could practically see Schumpeter's
entrepeneur reawaken and go into action – often in the
person of a newly appointed corporate leader.

True, there was no European Bill Gates, John Sculley
or Gene Amdahl. Nor a European Nintendo. And while
athletic shoe newcomer Nike ran up sales of over $3 billion
on the West Coast of the US, the former German world
market leaders, Adidas and Puma, lost both market share
and their independence. But there were new faces and new
energy in Europe: Bernard Arnault of LVMH in France,
Anton Dreesman of the Dutch retailing group Vendex,
Silvio Berlusconi of the Italian Fininvest Group, Stephan
Schmidheiny of the Swiss Schmidheiny Group and Reinhard
Mohn of Bertelsmann in Germany.

This new self-confidence and self-assurance was undoubtedly partly the cause and partly the effect of the energy surge
emerging from the run-up to the EC single market. As we all
know, nothing succeeds like success, and success appeared

Strong Recovery after Years of Eurosclerosis

Growth in real gross domestic product
per cent per annum (average)

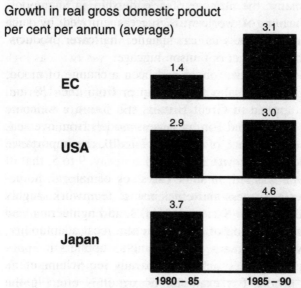

Source: OECD, 'Main Economic Indicators' 1992 © McKinsey & Company, Inc.

Diagram 2

to be showing that the Europeans were, at last, doing things right. After the slump in the early Eighties, Europe enjoyed an explosion of economic vitality between 1985 and 1990. All over Europe, real gross domestic product was growing again by an average of 3.1 per cent per annum – more than twice as fast as in the previous five-year period. This meant that, in comparison with the rest of the Triad, Europe showed the strongest growth-rate recovery (Diagram 2). Seven and a half million new jobs were created in these five years, as against only nine million in the entire previous decade. Exports grew on average by 4.7 per cent per annum, with significantly higher figures in some key industries: 12.4 per cent in cars, 11 per cent in mechanical engineering and chemicals.

At the same time, over 60 per cent more patents were applied for than in the years from 1975 to 1980.

In Germany, the number of new businesses founded in 1988 was around 80 per cent higher than in 1980, and the percentage of business failures significantly lower. No wonder that the industrial optimism indicator was twice as high as in 1985. In France, too, there was a substantial increase in new businesses, sales figures and profits in this period. The same applied to Great Britain, the Benelux countries and Italy. Throughout Europe, economic performance and, with it, the confidence of consumers and business people in further economic growth improved.

The boom was fed, in some cases, by amazing improvements in effectiveness and efficiency in companies such as British Steel, Usinor-Sacilor and ABB, and by the climbing world market position of companies like Airbus Industries, Electrolux and Siemens. Between 1985 and 1991, many European companies achieved soaring improvements in sales and profits. For example, Glaxo, BSN and L'Oreal more than doubled their sales and saw double-digit increases in their annual profits (Diagram 3). The share of European companies in the world-wide 'Top 100' rose from twenty-seven in 1970 to forty-five in 1990 (Diagram 4). And this change occurred, for the most part, independently of exchange-rate movements.

All in all, Eurosclerosis looked like distant history. And today, a few years into the Nineties? It seems to me that preoccupation with moods and signs of decline tend to cloud our sense of reality – and, more importantly, of the need to act.

Surge in Growth of Leading European Companies

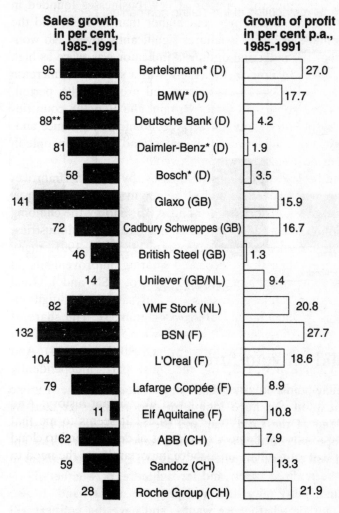

Sales growth in per cent, 1985-1991		Growth of profit in per cent p.a., 1985-1991
95	Bertelsmann* (D)	27.0
65	BMW* (D)	17.7
89**	Deutsche Bank (D)	4.2
81	Daimler-Benz* (D)	1.9
58	Bosch* (D)	3.5
141	Glaxo (GB)	15.9
72	Cadbury Schweppes (GB)	16.7
46	British Steel (GB)	1.3
14	Unilever (GB/NL)	9.4
82	VMF Stork (NL)	20.8
132	BSN (F)	27.7
104	L'Oreal (F)	18.6
79	Lafarge Coppée (F)	8.9
11	Elf Aquitaine (F)	10.8
62	ABB (CH)	7.9
59	Sandoz (CH)	13.3
28	Roche Group (CH)	21.9

* Figures for 1986-91 due to change in law on financial statements, and for 1987-91 for Bertelsmann
** Balance sheet total

Diagram 3

Rise of European Companies in World Rankings

Regional distribution of top-selling companies, per cent

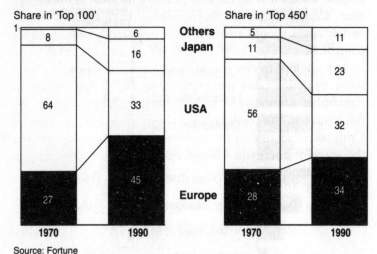

Source: Fortune

© McKinsey & Company, Inc.

Diagram 4

Build on your Strengths!

Turning-points are, by definition, transitory. Whether Europe can exploit the huge long-term opportunities created by the end of the Cold War and the opening up of Eastern Europe will be decided within a very few years. The answer will depend on whether Western European unification will be realized wisely and far-sightedly, or whether short-sighted, petty misgivings will gain the upper hand. It also depends on whether we want – and have the political will – to provide aid systematically and intelligently to the less favoured parts of the world, such as Eastern Europe, or the less developed countries of the Southern hemisphere, even at the cost of a real sacrifice in our own current prosperity.

Europe has proved that it can master crises and challenges. Today it is faced with possibly its greatest challenge ever. Concentrating on the strengths that helped it out of earlier crises should also bring the tasks of the future under control.

Any attempt to categorize these strengths, stick labels on them, or define cause and effect, is bound to give rise to innumerable alternative views. No rough simplification can do full justice to the multi-layered nature of events. However, I will take that risk – primarily because I am convinced that the surge of energy in Europe during the mid-Eighties and after brought out some less obvious European strengths. It is vital to nurture these largely underestimated strengths and bring them to bear as vigorously as possible. The following is a roll-call of examples:

Eurocapitalism. Different though the varieties of European capitalism in individual countries may be in superficial detail, they share an underlying structure that is distinctly different from that of American and Japanese capitalism. What sets the Europeans apart, giving them 'unity in variety', are social fabric and economic success factors. As an American colleague of mine once noted, 'Unlike Americans, most Europeans evidently have the feeling that they are all in the same boat. Unlike the Japanese, there is a very mixed bunch on board that boat.'

In the current situation, our European variety of capitalism carries both advantages and risks. Since the mid-Eighties we have seen that connecting the forces of politics and industry, encouraging active initiatives by statesmen and industry leaders, and seeking constructive participation of various social groups in the development process have generated a higher quality of life and an increase in general prosperity. At the same time, the impression is growing that vested social rights and the thicket of bureaucratic rules and regulations have already gone beyond their optimum – and possibly even their limits of affordability. Eurocapitalism will now have to prove its strength by the extent to which it can shift the focus of attention from the distribution to the creation of wealth.

Entrepreneurial personalities. The last decade, in particular, has seen a generation of 'Europreneurial' managers emerging strongly at the head of major European companies. They have taken European industry forward in an enormous surge of energy and thrust their companies more than ever into pan-regional and even world leadership. And they have advanced and expanded the role of the entrepreneur. Much the same applies to the strong group of medium-sized companies – equally important, from my point of view – which is characteristic of all European countries. Its dominant role has no counterpart in the US or Japan. A strong technology base, a rich store of inventiveness and, last but not least, dynamic entrepreneurs – often owners – at the top have taken some of these companies to world-wide leadership in profitable niches.

In future, all these entrepreneurs will have more demands than ever made on them, especially since entrepreneurial talent is an extremely scarce commodity in the face of emerging international opportunities for expansion. Because a new generation is due to take over soon in many companies, it is important to train up high performers and committed individuals to step into the present managers' positions when the time comes.

Management culture. Many of the outstanding European companies are *de facto* led by a management team with extensive technical know-how and a clear long-term orientation. Together, these traits form the breeding ground for concentrating on value to the customer and building supplier and customer relationships of many years' standing. Functional departments, business units, and even foreign subsidiaries, are managed 'at arm's length'. Generally well-qualified and highly committed staff at all levels have wide-ranging rights of consultation or decision-making. In their external relations, these companies regard themselves as 'corporate citizens', with an obligation to take on social and, increasingly, environmental responsibility.

There are genuine competitive strengths here. They will become all the more important as external challenges increase and companies have to cope with growing complexity both inside and outside. For these strengths are needed to bring about the changes that will become more than ever the determinants of success: changes such as the flattening of hierarchies, extensive delegation of responsibility, and working within international networks.

What I have put down on the following pages about these 'European' strengths and challenges are mainly personal observations. They are not intended as a substitute for either scientific analysis or comprehensive statistics. However, long years of experience in all the industries and areas touched on, as well as many discussions with leaders of industry and politics in the Europe–US–Japan Triad, have convinced me that Europe does possess strengths which should give us grounds for cautious optimism.

II

Three Capitalisms

Capitalism, born in Europe, is now probably its most successful export. At any rate, the US and many areas of the Japanese economy have been the site of its most vigorous development over the last fifty years. It takes widely differing forms in these two countries, but plays a far greater role in determining the social fabric than in any of its European homes.

The comparatively moderate form of European capitalism is undoubtedly due in part to the need for reconstruction after World War II. This gigantic task could be achieved only with government support. The state played supplier (both as an entrepreneur and through share ownership in a variety of industries) and customer for up to 50 per cent of Europe's gross national product. That influenced the form capitalism took, as did the boom in demand at home and abroad, which ensured that everything Europe could produce would find a market, even without sales efforts, let alone marketing tools. The subsequent years of Eurosclerosis, when floating exchange rates and oil shocks curbed the soaring domestic and export growth, also had a major influence. 'Zero growth' and the protection of vested social interests became familiar concepts.

But another experience common to all Western Europeans probably had the deepest impact: the potential for evil that can build up when extreme differences in wealth bring social tinder to the flashpoint. A determination to prevent such occurrences in the future was, perhaps, the strongest bond leading to the emergence of a distinctive 'Euro'-capitalism. Above all, it produced what is probably the most striking peculiarity of Eurocapitalism: its strong social component.

Today, understanding the varieties of capitalism in the three regions of the Europe–US–Japan Triad seems to me easier – but also more important – than ever before. Easier, because after the decline of socialism discussion on the subject seems to have advanced several steps. More important, because each form of capitalism needs to develop further if it is to find answers to today's most pressing problems: population explosion, poverty, preventive health care, and so on. As variations in the capitalist model emerge more clearly, the internal conflict between them is more readily apparent. Assuming we are at the turning-point discussed above, the issue of whether Europe's specific economic model and managerial approach are strong, flexible, balanced and entrepreneurially dynamic enough to take us through the coming years successfully, becomes a pressing one.

This issue is not about whether one of the three 'systems' is basically superior to the others. It is about whether a particular model adequately meets the specific needs, conditions and demands of its society better than any alternative. To obtain a reliable answer, the characteristics

of the three variants have to be examined as impartially
as possible and their underlying game rules identified. In
addition, the nature of the fault lines currently emerging
in the European system in particular, as well as the prospects for dealing with them, have to be reviewed.

The Characteristics:
Handling Inequality

The demands of the future will not respect geographical
frontiers. In all the regions of the Triad, companies and their
leaders are – and will continue to be – confronted with almost
identical challenges. Also, free markets, private ownership,
private investment decisions, comparative advantage, and
a supportive legal structure are capitalist principles of
universal validity. What varies from region to region is
the availability of human and financial resources, the constraints on corporate management teams, and the criteria
by which they are judged. Notwithstanding its historic
victories over centralized economic structures, capitalism
itself wears many different faces.

In the United States, for example, an unrestricted free-
market economy and individual performance are the quin-
tessential models. Collective solutions to social problems are
not all that well regarded (Diagram 5), and institutions such
as industry associations, works councils, public authorities,
in part even trade unions, do not play a significant role in the
everyday running of private companies. Corporate executives are far more concerned with quarterly results, trends
in stock prices, and the public image of their companies.
As a rough generalization, when stock prices are rising,
American top managers can do more or less as they please.
It is no coincidence that their relative standing and income

Individual and Collective Solutions

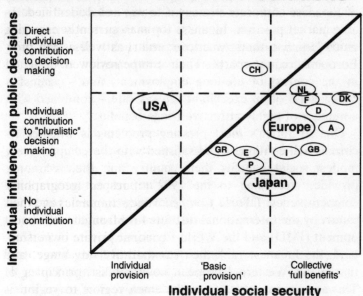

Diagram 5

reflect stock value. By general consent, profits should benefit investors, who provide the capital. 'Shareholder wealth' is, consequently, the widely recognized yardstick of management performance. Share options as a popular component of top management compensation also lend this corporate objective a considerable personal relevance.

By contrast, Japanese capitalism is much less individualistic. It is also aimed at private profit, but it is primarily the company or the Keiretsu – the group – that benefits from growing revenues, not so much the dividend-earning investor. Japanese managers are expected to use profits to finance corporate investments, not to distribute them to stockholders (who traditionally earn their money from

rising stock values) or to employees. The foremost objective
of Japanese corporate strategy is to win and defend sustainable market position. Japanese top managers normally earn
much less than their American, and slightly less than their
European, counterparts. Their compensation is designed
in the context of life-long employment, and – against a
background of an exorbitant top tax rate – combined with
a number of highly attractive fringe benefits.

One of Japan's most pressing problems is whether its
citizens will continue to be satisfied with the comparatively
modest social benefits their country and their economy
provide. According to the 1992 report on international
competitiveness (*World Competitiveness Report*), published
jointly by the International Institute for Management Development (IMD) and the World Economic Forum in Switzerland, the Japanese rank their standard of living lower than
that of all Western European countries except Portugal.
This assessment comes from the employees of major international companies, not from workers in third-tier suppliers
or small businesses, for whom low wages and insecure jobs
are the natural consequences of the fierce competition in
the Japanese domestic market. Considering that ex-Prime
Minister Miyazawa recently set an example by taking a
two-week holiday (the vast majority of Japanese get by
on one) as part of a 'spoil-yourself-more' movement, and
that over ten million Japanese have been going abroad in
one year, changes in social behaviour are definitely in the
wind. However, in recent years there has been practically
no trace of a class struggle in Japan. More than 90 per cent
of Japanese people see themselves as middle-class, although
many live in cramped conditions and spend hours commuting to work crammed like sardines into crowded trains.

The homogeneity of the population has so far made it
largely unnecessary for the economic system to balance
conflicts of interest. Europe does not share that kind of

comfort. In practically every country where it operates, the European form of capitalism has been shaped by the social burden of creating or maintaining unity in diversity. Social and ethnic groups with different cultural heritages, national movements, political splinter groups, religious influences, historical divisions and class differences have all had to be taken into account in politics generally, social policy and industry. Historically, the 'contract between generations', like the social contract, was a European invention.

Western Europe, the region where all these things are happening, is a conglomeration of tensions and conflicts. It has never enjoyed a unified culture, constitution or ideology. The yoke of central pretensions to leadership – whether under King Gustav II Adolf of Sweden in the Thirty Years' War, Napoleon, or ultimately Hitler – has always been cast off. There has never been a homogeneous population. Nor a mass declaration in favour of 'one Eurocapitalism'. Nor a general consensus about its advantages compared to other systems.

Capitalism in Europe is not the product of joint decision-making or of a unified policy. On the contrary, it grew step by step over time, often out of very different motives. It is a patchwork composed of thousands of poorly-matched pieces. The differences are everywhere. Labour costs vary dramatically from one country to another: the weighted average of $17.50 per hour calculated for its manufacturing industries in 1990 is made up of figures ranging from $23.40 in Germany to $4.40 in Portugal. Labour legislation, social security, and the extent of trade union organization show similar variations. In addition to the great differences between the countries, there are also differences *within* individual countries. It is rare for the per capita income of a country to vary by less than a factor of two between its richest and poorest areas. Taking the average of the twelve EC countries as 100, the poorest region of France

Considerable Wealth Differentials in Europe

Highest and lowest regional figures

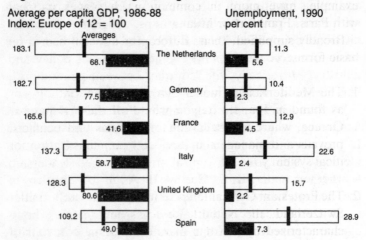

Average per capita GDP, 1986-88
Index: Europe of 12 = 100

Unemployment, 1990
per cent

Source: Commission of the European Communities: The
Regions in the Nineties, 1991

© McKinsey & Company, Inc.

Diagram 6

earned a GDP of 42 per capita between 1986 and 1988; the
richest, 166. Great Britain ranged from 81 to 128; West
Germany from 78 to 183. Unemployment figures varied
among EC regions from 2.2 to 28.9 per cent (Diagram 6).

Management responsibilities and practices also vary.
Thus, Scandinavian companies typically operate on a much
smaller scale and less globally than do French or German
firms. In France, the government holds a majority stake in
a number of large industrial groups; President Mitterrand
has positioned himself as the top industrial politician of the
nation in many public speeches. Great Britain endorses the
general European view that the whole of society should
participate in industry's profits: Margaret Thatcher was

one of the most important advocates of having every Briton share in the fruits of capitalism. Yet the style and orientation of the country's financial markets, for example, have more in common with New York than with Paris, Frankfurt or Milan.

Broadly simplified, then, Eurocapitalism comes in three basic forms:

1. The Mediterranean model, with a dash of Catholicism, as found in France, Italy, Spain, Portugal and parts of Greece, where a high level of government participation prevails and management is closely linked with the political system.

2. The Protestant Germanic model found mainly in Germany, Switzerland, the Netherlands and Scandinavia. This is characterized by a strong private industrial base, a substantial degree of social consensus, and co-operation between management and government as a customer, but not on the operational side.

3. The British model, which has come very close to the American private enterprise model, with a strong service and consumer goods sector and a government eager to free itself from the social burdens of the past.

Despite this breadth of variation and internal diversity, the different types of Eurocapitalism have a key factor in common: a combination of social individualism with efficient collectivism. The fundamental difference between Eurocapitalism and the forms dominating the economies of North America and Japan does not lie primarily in the details of outward appearance; of greater significance are the underlying convictions. Meaning, in particular: is inequality accepted, ignored, or moderated?

In Japan, notwithstanding the perceived homogeneity of Japanese society, there are still serious social and economic discrepancies – for instance, between the Keiretsu and supplier companies. The economic system has managed to ignore them so far, since thousands of small Japanese companies, often family firms, still accept them without complaint.

In the US, on the other hand, with its cult of individualism, the economic system is not required to keep a close lid on inequalities. The idea of unlimited opportunities, the fairy-tale rise from dishwasher to millionaire, is still deeply rooted. A recent survey showed that the vast majority of Americans are in favour of abolishing capital gains tax. The fact that today this would benefit only the rich and mega-rich is secondary; tomorrow, John Doe might be one of them himself and so would profit from it as well. In other words, as long as the game remains fair, differences in income are accepted. Even during Roosevelt's New Deal and Johnson's Great Society, no-one – apart from extremists on the edges of the political debate – called on the government to absorb what it could of the effect of market forces. Since then, particularly during the Reagan and Bush administrations, the gulf between rich and poor has continued to widen. Recently, Romano Prodi, former head of the IRI and now a professor at the University of Bologna and a great admirer of America, reported that his students came back from the US shocked at what they regarded as a loss of social conscience: a disturbing new willingness to accept such problems as homelessness, poverty and illiteracy with indifference as inescapable facts of life. He said that such problems had also existed fifteen or twenty years ago, but then there had been a public sense of responsibility, an ethically-motivated willingness on the part of the people to seek practical solutions.

Only the Europeans have set themselves a twofold task:

creating and sustaining an efficient economic system that upholds a multi-faceted social and cultural heritage and, at the same time, does not allow the gap between rich and poor to become too wide. In contrast to North American capitalism, Eurocapitalism is bound to the terms of a social contract supported by the vast majority. In contrast to the Japanese model, it is highly pluralistic and aimed at protecting the basic needs of all sections of the population.

The delicate balancing act – the creation of conditions for decent growth rates and adequate profits on one side, and a relatively balanced distribution of income and a comfortable standard of living on the other – means, in practice, that Eurocapitalism has to find the golden mean between trade unions and employers, citizens and governments, the more and the less privileged, the older and the younger generations, and between once-hostile neighbouring countries. In addition to the trade-off between social obligations and the interests of private enterprise, there is increasing concern for striking an environmental balance. Western Europe is more environment-conscious than either of the other Triad regions. All European countries have Ministries and Offices of the Environment; companies increasingly regard environmental protection as a business opportunity and a responsibility. Just witness the recycling offers of European car manufacturers, the first-ever Environment Division at Volkswagen, and the international commitment of entrepreneur Stephan Schmidheiny.

This commitment to balance means, in turn, that the implicit social contract needed to give legitimacy to any economic system is more complex and multi-faceted in Europe than elsewhere in the Triad. It places greater restrictions on entrepreneurial activity, both in letter and spirit. It prevents the majority from being too greatly neglected for the benefit of the minority. It also prevents the minority from forcing its values on the majority. In our mixed society, we are all in the same boat. The passengers and the crew are the same.

This social contract gives pluralism room for manoeuvre, but also limits the range of its economic consequences. That is, it puts a social conscience in place in the form of laws, regulations, and policies on social insurance, co-determination and labour legislation. None of this means, of course, that Eurocapitalism has put an end to poverty or achieved an even-handed distribution of wealth. True, the percentage of people living in poverty in the US is said to be twice as high as in Germany and one and a half times as high as in France. However, if the poverty line is drawn at around half the average living costs for one adult, around 15 per cent of the population of Spain, Greece and Great Britain, 9–12 per cent in France and Italy, and roughly 7 per cent in Germany live below it (Diagram 7).

At the same time there is a whole range of EC aid programmes – particularly the European Regional Development Fund – aimed at wiping out this imbalance. Neither of the other Triad regions treats the reduction of poverty as so explicit a goal or spends as much money on it. Moreover, this goal is supported by a broad majority consensus. Europe really does talk and think about solidarity, the 'contract of the generations', and equitable economic living conditions. One result is that the traditional social fabric is still intact in Europe, although current developments in Eastern Europe will certainly put it to the test. Such intactness translates into a high quality of life in general, which is indicated by, among other things, low crime rates, relatively low drug abuse, and relatively low divorce and suicide rates. (The occurrence of criminal acts and the imposition of prison terms are two-thirds below US levels – though still fifty times higher than in Japan. But Japan has the major advantage of a homogeneous society,

The Persistent problem of poverty

Share of population below poverty line,* 1991
per cent

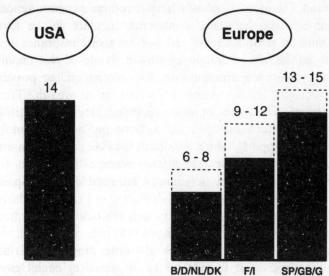

* 50% of average living cost of an adult (for USA defined as
$6,932 per person p.a.)

Source: Eurostat 'European Social Policy' 1991, US Bureau of
the Census, McKinsey/estimate

© McKinsey & Company, Inc.

Diagram 7

and the doubtful privilege of a Mafia that profits from law
and order.)

Western Europe also leads in the provision of health
care. The great majority of the people – from 61 per cent
in the Netherlands to 100 per cent in Great Britain and

Sweden – enjoy public health insurance. In the US, by contrast, the only comparable institution is the 'Medicare' programme for people over the age of 65; a major motivation behind President Clinton's health reform programme, no doubt, is the fact that at the turn of this decade over 31 million people, nearly 13 per cent of the population, had no health insurance of any kind. In Japan, public health insurance protects only 45 per cent of the population.

The social effects of unemployment, still a key problem in Western Europe, are at least partly alleviated by financial support, which at about $4,000 per person per year far exceeds the comparable sums of $2,000 in the US and $900 in Japan (figures adjusted for purchasing power).

These data and many others demonstrate a simple fact: Western Europe puts more funds into improving the living standards of its people than do the other legs of the Triad. In the process, it spends up to 30 per cent of its gross domestic product on social benefits, financed directly by higher taxes and indirectly by higher prices. In purely theoretical terms, this approach is neither better nor worse than others; it is simply different. It would not necessarily fit well with American culture and its celebration of unbounded individualism. For Japanese culture, which has no past experience of universal welfare, it would represent a quantum leap in aspirations.

Years ago, when the discussion on Eurosclerosis was rising to pathological heights, many Europeans reverted to their artistic and cultural heritage, which seemed to be their last source of competitive advantage. But this cultural heritage has also made Europeans address tasks felt to be the responsibility of society as a whole. And these aspirations, in turn, determine both the objectives and the game rules of Eurocapitalism.

The Game Rules: Co-operation before Confrontation

Maintaining the delicate balance championed by Euro-capitalism has its price. Labour laws and legal regulations on company closure are strict, pension and benefits legislation is firmly anchored, the social net – for example, in the areas of health care, education and training – is close-woven and accessible to all. It is no coincidence that the government's share of gross domestic product is between 45 and 55 per cent in most European countries – and only half that amount in Japan and North America. Nor is it surprising that industry carries higher-than-normal social costs: Western Europe's labour costs and ancillary costs for social contributions, holiday pay, old age pensions and training are the highest in the Triad. In 1990, when labour cost an average of $17.50 per hour in Europe, it only cost $16.00 in Japan and $15.00 in the US.

Annual holidays, public holidays and sick days reduced the effective number of hours worked in Europe to an average of 1,672 in 1989, compared with 2,142 in Japan and 1,996 in the US. (Paid holiday accounted for 10.1 per cent of labour costs in Europe, while the comparable US figure was only 7 per cent.) In addition, Europe, with its powerful trade unions, lost an average of 257 days per 1,000 workers per annum through strikes between 1980 and 1988, compared to 120 in the US and eleven in Japan. Although the figure dropped in 1989, 191 days of industrial action per 1,000 workers were still recorded, compared to 170 in the United States and five in Japan. Overall, every European worker is absent on 54.4 working days per year. The equivalent is 30.1 days on average in the US and 29.7 in Japan.

In all this, Adam Smith would hardly recognize his free-market economy. Where all transactions are voluntary arrangements between freely contracting parties, cost factors tend to decide business loyalty. In the Western Europe of today, however, social values put a premium on development and maintenance of good, long-term relationships between suppliers, producers and the trade, as well as between employers and employed. Costs are often less crucial than the stability of relationships.

Employees are not regarded here as neutral factors of production, nor do they perceive themselves as such. They are – and are seen to be – 'co-workers' who make a significant contribution to company profit. Blue-collar workers at Daimler-Benz take it for granted that they are middle-class individuals who have every right to a Mercedes in their driveway. Traditionally, their work ethic is strong and identification with the company is high.

Suppliers and distributors are not opponents trying to grab an ever-larger piece of a limited profit pie for themselves. Instead, all parties are more likely to pursue common objectives in fair co-operation. This is because they see themselves as sharing largely the same economic fate. In German mechanical engineering, for example, according to a new McKinsey study, the top companies have an average of only about 900 suppliers, half as many as less prosperous firms. The best companies, also, are more likely to entrust their suppliers with the quality control for the parts supplied. In a similar vein, the state is accepted as a partner closely involved in business and industry. Above all, however, some sacrifice of efficiency and profit is widely accepted in Europe as the price of general social cohesiveness.

In many cases, European managers think of themselves as the natural partners of politicians and civil servants in matters of national economic development. Like these groups, they think about how history will see them. American managers, by contrast, are concerned, first and foremost, with ways to improve their own companies' performance. Japanese managers, despite the fierce in-fighting of domestic competition, concentrate on promoting the performance of 'Japan, Inc.' abroad. Europeans occupy a middle position here. In addition to their responsibility for their own business, they explicitly regard their companies as an integral part of the countries, regions and communities in which they operate.

The European conviction that industry could – and should – serve the interests of the state grows out of a long history of mercantilism. When modern big business developed in the latter part of the nineteenth century, the relationship of industry to government was much less antagonistic in Europe than in the US. According to Alfred Chandler,[1] this was partly because the administrative apparatus of the modern state had reached maturity in Europe long before industry had, and the state had a decisive influence on all areas of life. According to an old saying, the Bavarian civil servant had a duty to no-one bar his king. The same applied to his colleagues in other places. As a result, the development of industrial institutions did not pose a threat to government or to government officials. The opposite was true in the US: industry developed to its full power before the state – an imbalance that contributed heavily to the mistrust and even open hostility that still characterizes the mutual attitudes of government and industry.

There are certainly tensions in the European model, but they developed more from a mixture of civil service élitism and the prejudices of a class-conscious society towards industry. Remember, for example, the anti-business mind-set of the big English landlords or the Pomeranian 'Junkers' of the nineteenth century. But such distrust never attained the

[1] Alfred D. Chandler, Jr, *Scale and Scope, The Dynamics of Industrial Capitalism*, Harvard University Press, Cambridge, Mass. and London, 1990.

poisonous heights reached on the other side of the Atlantic
when the voice of the people was first raised against the
trusts in the decades following the American Civil War.

The moderation of opposites created stability. The price,
such as it was, was ultimately paid by consumers. It was
not without cause – nor for the first time – that voices arose
during the deregulation and privatization wave of the mid-
Eighties onwards blaming an excessively close relationship
between politics and industry for the inefficiency, sluggish
innovation and poor service of European industry. Trying to
get an itemized telephone bill in Europe is still a nightmarish
experience. In Germany, France and Italy, where the supervisory bodies for mail and telecom and for the railways
are composed in part by suppliers, these suppliers' prices
drive up the costs to the customer. The fact that consumers
in different countries pay different prices for the same
products and services is currently much under discussion.
There is, for example, a differential of up to 44 per cent in
the price of flights between the European capitals, and of
up to 383 per cent for rail travel. And, looking around the
Triad, a flight from London to Paris costs 50 per cent more
than one from New York to Washington.

Even though the single market in Europe aims to eliminate
competitive distortions of this kind, economic efficiency is
only one side of the coin here. Historically, government-
owned enterprises had other objectives than satisfying
the needs of customers at the lowest possible prices.
For example, their chronic overstaffing is also a logical
consequence of government employment policy. Faced with
the choice of a strong economy or social peace, Europeans
have tended to prefer social peace.

Similar motives lie behind the inevitable outcry provoked
when a major European company decides, for perfectly
understandable economic reasons, to close a long-established
production site. Whether Krupp at Rheinhausen, AEG

Olympia, Bull in Belfort or British Steel at Ravenscraig, those responsible cannot escape appeals to their social consciences and/or accusations of a breach of trust.

As a rule, the corporate sense of responsibility as a 'local citizen' is quite strong in Europe. It would be almost inconceivable to shift a corporate headquarters away from its long-standing base in the way that General Electric or American Airlines did when they moved out of New York City in the last twenty years. Arguments such as exploding office rents, unreasonable travelling times for staff, or limited opportunities to expand office space, would not be considered reason enough for such a 'breach of faith'. One might say that it took a lost war, the subsequent division of the country by an Iron Curtain, and the partition of the city, to persuade large German companies to move from Berlin to Western or Southern Germany. And even then, Berlin often remained the nominal headquarters of the company, not just for tax reasons.

Their identification with the common good reflects the fact that, in many areas of life, European companies have adopted a role that goes far beyond strictly economic or business objectives. In such matters as maternity leave, social benefits, or the social integration of minorities, they have increasingly taken up responsibilities that, at one time, would have been assigned to the churches or other social bodies. In effect, a hard choice between the extremes of economic logic and social advantage is rarely needed, for corporate practice can normally take incremental practical pressures in its stride. It is still generally valid that sacrifices in economic performance are to be accepted as long as such social burdens remain within tolerable limits, and if they help create the desired social stability and quality of life. Who, after all, would willingly do without the immediate, concrete benefit of 70 per cent-subsidized theatre tickets or a free university system simply because their removal would indirectly ease the strain on the industrial 'locomotive' of the country? Or because German, French and Dutch products would become more competitive in international markets? Even the high subsidies for local public transport systems are considered justified by many Europeans because the facilities provided are much nicer than in the US and much less crowded than in Japan.

But doubt is spreading. Even Europe is now faced with the question of whether – and for how long – such support, for instance to structurally weak areas like steel, coal or agriculture, can and should continue to be guaranteed. The controversy on this point is one of the major fault lines threatening Europe's stability in the years ahead.

Fault Lines: Testing the Ability and the Will to Bear, Share and Change

Social peace does have its price. But at what point does it begin to affect international competitiveness and, thus, the ability to sustain such peace? As the European single market takes shape, as the borders between EC and EFTA vanish, and as the wider European economic area begins to emerge, outsiders are increasingly voicing fears that Europe will withdraw behind protectionist walls and turn in on itself. Although this concern cannot be dismissed entirely, it is easily exaggerated. There is another risk, however, that deserves much greater attention: the gradual decay of the social contract that has supplied the stable foundations for Europe's impressive development during the post-war period.

The desire to build protectionist bulwarks will inevitably be constrained by the realities of competition in a truly global market. Although there are likely to be some local conflicts and confrontations, strong counterbalancing forces exist in the attitudes and policies of senior corporate management. They know that, now more than ever, it is essential for Europeans to remain a vital part of an integrated international know-how transfer system. After all, they have traditionally been the most energetic international traders in the world: more than half of world trade occurs in Europe. By contrast, there are no such 'natural' forces at work strengthening or revivifying the social contract. If social inclusiveness is to be preserved, a targeted effort must be made to find new tools to do this.

It seems to me that the risk is not whether we Europeans will turn inward too much, but whether we will *turn inward enough*. I fear we will not pay serious enough attention to such questions as: can the European economy continue to function on the basis of the present social contract, if droves of economic refugees pour in from Eastern Europe or North Africa? Can it create sufficient wealth to sustain its closely-woven social safety net? Can it cope with changing demographic conditions as its population ages and more and more funds are needed to finance health care and pensions? Can it offer the younger generation the incentives needed to keep them integrated within the existing social order?

The fault lines that could block the satisfactory resolution of these questions are already beginning to form. They fall into three broad categories. First, *social overhead costs*, now at the limit of tolerance, have been stretched to breaking point by the huge new challenges of Eastern European reconstruction and the refugee problem. Then there is the temptation of traditional economic contributors to *back away from their voluntary support for all social groups* and, instead, to create a patchwork of enclaves of privilege, surrounded by the envy of those excluded. Finally, *lack of adaptability* in facing inevitable economic and technological change – a weakness possibly aggravated by one of our traditional strengths, the tendency toward stability.

Social overhead. Up to now, management experience in dealing with the burden of social overhead has produced an extremely constructive discipline in Europe. It has made corporate leaders into citizens with a sense of civic duty and given them a respected position in society. It has taught them to collaborate with their governments in a way that makes sense for both sides, and to strike an acceptable balance between economic performance and social stability. But if the burden continues to grow, or if global competition demands more efficiency, the fault lines will become apparent. Industries such as shipbuilding and textile manufacturing are then likely to call for increased protectionism. Others – the chemical industry, perhaps – will come up against increased competition when seeking access to lucrative foreign markets.

Differences will also arise between individual European countries. France will probably erect additional barriers if threatened with foreigners buying 'too many' French firms or dominating key domestic markets. The same goes for Switzerland, particularly in banking with its multitude of cartels. One does not have to look far for past examples of such measures. When, for instance, the Shah of Iran wanted to buy into Daimler-Benz in the Seventies, German Chancellor Helmut Schmidt intervened. The fierce resistance in Belgium when Carlo de Benedetti attempted to take over Société Générale de Belgique in 1987 tells a similar tale, as does President Mitterrand's reaction to the news that Thomson might be willing to sell its electronics division. And as late as 1991 there was more than a hint of the same undertones in the to-ing and fro-ing between Pirelli and Continental.

The unwritten code of behaviour ruling each of these national economies comprises a wide range of expectations – for example, that prices should be raised only to a certain level, that so and so many people per year should be trained, that distribution networks and spare parts for products should be available on a long-term basis, that excessive dividends should not be paid, and that corporate actions should not contravene the values of the community at large. By following the code, companies gain legitimacy based on society-wide consensus about the ends of economic activity. That is why companies are unwilling to violate the code. But when the cost of respecting it depresses economic efficiency below a tolerable level, the laws of competition will penalize those who adhere to it. Troublesome conflicts may arise at that point.

It is quite conceivable that such strain might occur in European companies within the next few years. It is possible that frustration will spread because competitors from other regions support a much smaller social overhead and can exploit the resulting cost advantage in European and other markets. Moreover, when environmental rules and restrictions lead to a ten-year period for the building of a section of road or fifteen years for the commissioning of a new power plant, the inherent conflict between economic rationality and social considerations may flare up.

Investment flows are one indication that the volume of national and European regulation has gone beyond the optimum. It is, of course, not just the level of return that governs investment behaviour – a well-qualified labour force and a receptive market will always attract investment. But if overhead costs get too high and freedom of action too restricted, the balance gets tilted. Investment capital and companies will go elsewhere. When, for example, German companies invest a net total of almost DM30 billion a year abroad, but only DM1.9 billion of foreign capital comes to Germany, this is only in part a reflection on the attractiveness of Germany as an investment location. (Two-thirds of German foreign investments do not go into relocating production, but into coverage of foreign markets.

In important markets such as South-East Asia, German companies are still investing too little rather than too much.) But comparing the DM1.9 billion of foreign investments in Germany in 1991 with the total volume of foreign investments, which amounted to DM270 billion in the same period, does provide food for thought.

Voluntary support. All these developments may have serious consequences for economic performance and, thus, for Europe's capacity to bear social burdens. All the more so since readiness to shoulder these burdens voluntarily is declining in many areas. In the past, for example, European investors of all kinds were fairly modest in their expectations of financial return. By international standards, dividends and return on capital were relatively low and were accepted as such, possibly due to the poor functioning of Europe's capital markets. But a change is under way here. More private asset formation is becoming necessary to supplement government old-age pensions, investors are beginning to pay more attention to shareholder value, and an escalating world-wide demand for capital, coupled with the growing interdependence of the main capital markets, is fuelling competition between alternatives for investment. European companies' inclination to finance growth less through new equity or long-term debt than through retained earnings will sooner or later reach its limits.

There is also a risk that attempts might be made to master the growing burden by methods that damage the basic structure of social stability rather than strengthening its foundations. Thus, if public education fails, companies may take more and more of the responsibility upon themselves for training their young staff. If the public telephone networks and mail and transport systems no longer meet requirements, companies might set up their own. If social security and pension systems prove inadequate, companies may offer alternatives of their own. In short, corporate Europe could rapidly establish its own walled-off reservations, at high cost, within the larger communities in which it operates. It could cut itself off from its social environment, as companies in Latin America and, to a lesser extent, the US have already done. Examples of such 'isolationist' movements already exist.

A step of this nature may well be efficient. It may even become a matter of necessity for individual companies. But it will undoubtedly arouse envy and resentment among those left outside. It will jeopardize the long chain of suppliers in the countries concerned, who have traditionally been treated as valued long-term partners. And it will rip a gaping hole in the social fabric that has taken shape on the basis of post-war stability. Envy is a social canker. For many years, traditional European behavioural patterns dictated that it was wiser not to be conspicuous. It is only in the last ten years or so that Europeans have begun to apply the universally visible performance yardsticks that are taken so much for granted in the United States: securities with the best returns, managers with the largest compensation packages, and so on. That sort of thing used not to be particularly important, but the change is now perceptible.

Adaptability. The pace of change should not, of course, be overestimated. Europe has shown considerable economic and social stability through crises of all sorts, but this very fact might contain a further risk: Europe may not be adaptable enough. The phenomenon of unspoken consensus is deeply rooted in European attitudes – consensus between individualism and collectivism, between politics and industry, between social responsibility and entrepreneurial drive. The prevailing spirit has favoured continuity and evolution more than rejuvenation, renewal or even radical change. Often, the most stubborn forces of conservatism are to be found in the companies themselves. With their increasing size, many European companies have

built up steep hierarchies. This 'over-hierarchization' not
only leads to problems of effectiveness and cost; it also
means that the younger generation are not given management responsibility until relatively late in their careers.

The relationship between management and workers or
their representatives is another example of conservatism
creating negative forms of stability. This probably applies
in principle all over Europe, although the charter and the
role of the unions do vary considerably between countries:
from the rational, industry- and company-based model in
Germany, the Netherlands, Scandinavia, Switzerland and
Austria to the more politically-oriented unions in France
and Italy. (In Spain, with its trade union experience still
young, a clear picture has yet to emerge; in Britain, unions
lost much of their importance during the Thatcher administration.)

At the risk of generalizing too much in the face of such
variety, I do think the following points are generally valid
and pose a threat to European adaptability:

1. Employment-insensitive civil services increasingly take
   the lead in collective bargaining confrontations, ignoring productivity growth, scope for the distribution of
   wealth and the knock-on effects on industry performance. Looking at the overall picture, no other sector
   of the economy seems quite as strike-prone as European
   public administration.

2. Particularly in boom years, employers have been reluc-
   tant to resist excessive demands. The huge cost increases were passed on as higher prices wherever possible
   – often ignoring the longer-term structural effects on
   competitiveness.

3. European collective bargaining has rarely pointed the way

to new solutions. Innovative approaches from outside, such as a McKinsey study showing that flexible part-time work could significantly ease strains on the labour market, have met with little response.

4. Many of the conceptual blueprints of the European trade unions are more appropriate to the past than the present. In a complex world with more highly differentiated jobs, and employees wanting a multitude of different things, monolithic organizations and universally applicable wage agreements often fail to meet contemporary needs. The pressure to change, to which companies are responding with new organizational forms and principles, has provoked at best cautious reaction on the trade union side – the abolition of the 'scala mobile' in Italy, the latest Lufthansa wage agreement. That zero sum games should take precedence in worker-management dialogue over consideration of the skills needed tomorrow and the day after cannot be in anyone's interest. But still they do.

Implementing constructive change here is becoming more and more difficult in the face of the well-manned ranks of the public administration. Lack of adaptability in many European countries is partly due to the wealth of regulations imposed by local, regional and central government. New industrial zones are conceded most reluctantly, planning permission takes for ever, and produce and technology inspections go far beyond technical needs.

In the Eighties, Europe often lagged behind the other Triad countries in shifting production to newer high-technology and high-growth industries (Diagram 8). Sixty-three per cent of industrial production was in low or medium growth areas; in Japan this figure was only 59 per cent, and in America 60 per cent. In contrast to its remarkable historical achievements in science and technology, Europe now brings up the

Europeans tend to have Strengths in 'Classical' Industries

World-wide ranking of sales, 1991

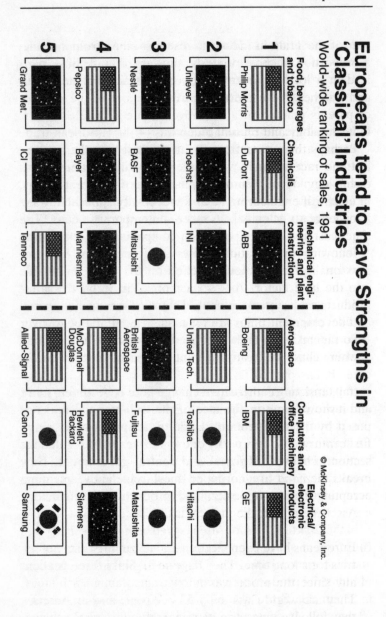

	Food, beverages and tobacco	Chemicals	Mechanical engineering and plant construction	Aerospace	Computers and office machinery	Electrical/ electronic products
1	Philip Morris	DuPont	ABB	Boeing	IBM	GE
2	Unilever	Hoechst	INI	United Tech.	Toshiba	Hitachi
3	Nestlé	BASF	Mitsubishi	British Aerospace	Fujitsu	Matsushita
4	Pepsico	Bayer	Mannesmann	McDonnell-Douglas	Hewlett-Packard	Siemens
5	Grand Met.	ICI	Tenneco	Allied-Signal	Canon	Samsung

© McKinsey & Company, Inc.

Diagram 8

rear of the Triad in industrial research and development as a proportion of gross domestic product. It has also lost its lead in a lot of classical production areas, such as clocks and watches and cameras, and it is behind in the number of patents granted in automotive engineering, electronics, biotechnology and pharmaceuticals.

Perhaps the greatest cause for alarm is that Europe has lost the race in many areas of microprocessor-dependent technology. Here, Europe had generations of experience in electrical engineering at its fingertips, but it failed to acknowledge sufficiently the changes in success factors. With time, cost and quality now of equal importance, Europeans – following their traditional ways – put plenty of effort into quality issues, little into cost, and practically none into the time factor. As a result, productivity in electronic products and systems is 30 per cent lower than in Japan and development times are twice or three times as long.

So far, all these fault lines are more hairline cracks than yawning chasms. The Eurocapitalism model is sound at the core. It has proved its strength in coping with the classic social tensions of the nineteenth and twentieth centuries, and it shows promise of mastering the comparable challenge posed by the great environmental problems of the twenty-first century. The tricky part of the journey is likely to be the section in between. Prospects are good, but only if Europe breaks the habit of ignoring or denying the risks, and starts accepting them as opportunities for beneficial change.

Assets helpful in the process could be things like these:

☐ Europeans have been model 'local citizens' in many countries for a long time. They have been thinking internationally since the modern industrial age was in its infancy. They are world-class exporters. Wherever they operate, they follow a long-term approach, not hit-and-run tactics. A certain bottleneck may arise as the historic opening up of Eastern Europe ties up a great deal of management capacity for quite some time, but the unique opportunity is well worth it. No other member of the Triad is as well placed to work fruitfully in the rising industrialized countries of Eastern Europe. And, last but not least, their international experience should encourage Europeans to turn with more vigour to such promising markets of the future as Taipei or Seoul.

☐ Even in the globalizing world market, local adaptation will continue to be important. While Europeans may well be at a disadvantage against Asian suppliers in standard products for world-wide markets, they ought to win territory wherever they can use their ability to create value to the customer – by meeting local customer preferences, adapting product design to local needs, or providing local training and development. Not offering undifferentiated commodities, but goods of superior customer value, not selling products, but supplying solutions to customer problems – these could be European success strategies of the future.

☐ Europe, with its unique combination of technological know-how, skilled labour and sophisticated customers, is in an outstanding position where project management and integrated solutions are required. European companies are, for example, leaders in the fields of environmental technology and complex telecommunications engineering. They can bring strengths to bear that will only increase in importance in future: highly developed know-how in operating the most advanced technology, e.g. in telephone networks, power plants, railways with state-of-the-art control systems, satellite operation or magnetic track systems.

☐ A strong 'old boy network' provides real stability. Long-term supplier and customer relationships, management transfers from a shared 'corporate alma mater', and shared school and university experience play an important role in many western countries. Regular meetings of top managers and Europe-wide staffing of supervisory boards strengthen the links.

☐ The long-standing tradition of partnership – fairness in relationships with customers and employees, a sense of responsibility to the community – has also ingrained Europeans with the behaviour patterns for dealing with new problems – if only in the sense that manufacturers and suppliers learn new process technologies together, or that procedures are in place for cushioning the effect of discontinuities. Maintaining common interests and multi-faceted, long-term relationships adds costs in the short term, but these are costs that will be more than paid back over time. Suppliers, customers, and employees who get backing at a critical time, will not forget it later. Within these relationships, it should also be possible to develop the annual collective bargaining procedure from a ritual with no strategic orientation to a constructive discussion of the real problems and concerns of all the parties concerned.

☐ Preparing for the European single market has entailed a learning process. It should have shown Europeans that giving free rein to the destructive spiral of protectionism serves no purpose. As recently as the early Eighties France charged all video-recorder owners an annual licence fee of 500FF and insisted that all Japanese VCRs imported into France had to pass through customs at an understaffed customs post in inaccessible Poitiers. Today, Japanese VCR products dominate the French

market, just as Japanese copiers dominate the EC market
after various attempts to keep them out.

Relapses will naturally keep on happening. Remember the controversial agreement in July 1991 to restrict
imports of Japanese cars until the year 2000 by voluntary export restrictions (without knowing exactly what
was included in the applicable volumes). Overall, however, there is a growing realization that barriers should
be lowered within the Triad. David Ricardo's law of
comparative advantage, first expounded in 1817, is attracting a growing following.

☐ Finally, even the high social burden could, in a sense,
become a strength because of the experience it brings
in coping with burdens that will probably affect our competitors in other Triad regions in the future. Demographic
developments and changes in values appear to be going
in the same direction there as here.

A conversion of American and Japanese capitalism
toward the European model is not to be expected. Nevertheless, social pressure in the US is likely to increase
very strongly in the next few years, so that social costs
– on an assumed 10-point scale – will gradually move from
their current position of 2 or 3 to 5. Japan – where
the social blessings of the Keiretsu benefit only around
40 per cent of the population, and where one week
of annual holiday, hours of commuting by train between
home and work, and extremely cramped living conditions
are normal – will probably rise from a relative position
of, say, 4–5 to 5–6.

If, at the same time, Europe could reduce its position on the scale from its current 8+ to around 6–7
by smoothing out some excesses (early pension rights,
inflexible working conditions, or excess regulations at
the local level), it would vastly improve its competitive

position. But as everyone knows, it is easier in all these areas to give than to take away. Some exceptions, as have recently occurred in collective bargaining and wage policy in Italy and Germany, or in the privatization of government-owned housing in Britain, do not yet indicate a social consensus in favour of giving up 'vested' rights. Still, on purely objective terms there should be room for such a move – not least in view of the Western Europeans' prosperity. Per capita financial assets in the old Länder of the Federal Republic of Germany, for instance, are now as high as DM53,000; per capita real estate holdings are at DM57,000; and there is DM2 trillion waiting to be inherited in the next ten years.

All in all, *the* principal problem for Europe is not simply staying on its feet under burdens of one kind or another, but the ability to push forward as quickly as possible into new areas where wealth can be generated. Europeans must prevent their stability from becoming their greatest enemy.

Then, the best years of Eurocapitalism may still be to come.

III

The Age of the Europreneurs

Boom, recovery, re-entry into history – whatever label you put on it, the dynamic development Western Europe underwent from the mid-Eighties to the beginning of the Nineties has sprung from the soil of Eurocapitalism. Its most important protagonists, the principal actors of the new Europe, are what I call the 'Europreneurs' – a group of fifty or so leading personalities at the heads of large European companies. Together with thousands of independent entrepreneurs, the owner-managers of Europe's distinctive mid-sized companies, they have unleashed an immense surge of energy and given it direction and impact.

The entrepreneurial potential of these 'Europreneurs' will also have to provide the answer to the most pressing question of Europe's future economic development: in this period of transition, can Eurocapitalism cope effectively with the turmoil on its Eastern borders, the intensification of world-wide competition, and the rapidly rising demands of its people?

My personal answer is cautiously optimistic. *Cautious*, because even the most recent past cannot be a guarantee of what will happen in future, and because the examples of vision, entrepreneurial spirit and competence described in this book are by no means the rule, but simply what I have called them, examples. *Optimistic*, because of the obvious high performance of these leaders, who rose to their companies' highest office during the mid-Eighties and have since given new momentum to organizations often set in their ways. They have created for themselves a role that – beyond corporate boundaries – has given their opinions weight in politicians' thinking, and their work an impact on the development of their countries' economies. In addition, their 'European' orientation has made them a stable element in the whole region's development toward the Europe of tomorrow.

Naturally, we cannot draw a clear and fixed line where this generation of top managers begins and ends. Some of them have considerably increased the intrinsic value of their companies without basically differing from their immediate predecessors or from previous generations. Some failed when the business climate turned inclement and fairweather sailing no longer sufficed. Others were preceded by men distinguished by an even broader, more entrepreneurial view of their managerial responsibilities. However, it is certain that Europe has boasted a remarkable group of entrepreneurial top managers in the last decade who have shaped a characteristic era in the development of the European economy.

These first Europreneurs, who all took office in the Eighties, include men like the late Alfred Herrhausen and his successor Hilmar Kopper of Deutsche Bank, Percy Barnevik of ABB, Carlo de Benedetti of Olivetti, Carl-Horst Hahn of Volkswagen, Helmut Maucher of Nestlé, Jeremy Morse of Lloyds Bank, Karlheinz Kaske of Siemens, Anders

Scharp of Electrolux, Edzard Reuter of Daimler-Benz, Didier Pineau-Valencienne of Schneider, Eugenio Coppola di Canzano of Assicurazioni Generali, Tony O'Reilly of Heinz, Alex Krauer of Ciba-Geigy, Floris Maljers of Unilever, Mark Wössner of Bertelsmann, Lo van Wachem of Royal Dutch/Shell, Rainer Gut of Crédit Suisse, and dozens more. These men are distinguished by a set of values, an international outlook, an entrepreneurial spirit, and an overall sense of social responsibility, which mark them out from their other contemporaries and from earlier generations of top managers. Not surprisingly, where they have handed over to younger successors recently, like Ferdinand Piech at VW or Heinrich von Pierer at Siemens, the new incumbents appear to be of a very similar mindset.

Despite the many differences in their careers, national origins, cultural ties, personal style, and practical management methods, the Europreneurs have a great deal in common – for example, a visionary, entrepreneurial, risk-taking, and basically statesmanlike, definition of their role. They did not take the stage as uncritical imitators and docile applicants of American and Japanese management tools, but have constructively absorbed such methods to reinforce home-grown strengths. They appear as disciples of Schumpeter, deeply convinced of the fact that progress is not achieved by small steps, but by the 'creative destruction' of the comfortable old order. They are all – from personal inclination or sheer necessity – aggressive designers of a future based on their own ideas, not the talented protectors of past advances. They understand 'Schumpeterian' destruction not so much as the shut-down or disinvestment of business activities, but more as reorientation and complete product-related renewal.

However sceptical one may be of such generalizations, this group of Europreneurs appears to be closer in spirit

and achievement to the founders of the large industrial conglomerates of late nineteenth- and early twentieth-century
Europe than to the functional managers of contemporary
administrative group headquarters, or even to the fathers
of industrial reconstruction after the war. Like that founder generation, they have re-explored the entrepreneurial
horizon, and found it open to bold new projects shaped by
their imagination and leadership. Unlike the pioneers, however, they were not given the chance to build from scratch.
Their challenge consisted, rather, of redefining the future
by renewing and redirecting large, established companies.

In their determination not to be mere administrators
and preservers but creative designers, they have set about
slimming down and shaking up their companies. They have
delegated more downward. They have reorganized communication paths and co-operation among organizational
units, cut down inflated central administration, encouraged
innovation, released the necessary funds for investment,
and pressed unceasingly for performance improvements
within their organization and in the market. And what
particularly distinguishes them from their predecessors:
they have considerably broadened the international arena
of their businesses they have a much higher public profile,
and they bring to bear new talent for coping with new
tasks.

Wider Arena

The Europreneurs' field of action, the arena in which these
top managers move, is not restricted to a single company,
industry or country. They have opened up new markets and
integrated new business areas, often through acquisitions
or mergers, and they have expanded their geographical

Cross-Border Expansion

Direct investment by EC companies abroad
bn. ECU

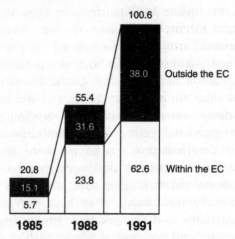

* **Estimates**
Source: Eurostat McKinsey analysis

© McKinsey & Company, Inc.

Diagram 9

presence in the way that is becoming more and more essential for global companies (Diagram 9). For the first time in many years, perhaps for the first time since the 'Gründerjahre' boom of 1870–3, the leaders of European industry have vigorously extended the boundaries of their areas of activity and have not been content just to consolidate past achievements and develop incrementally. They have occupied new market positions, and tackled the future with the power of their conviction and vision. They are becoming a role model for many other corporate leaders.

Geographically, their arena is increasingly European – no longer British, German, French, Swedish or Italian. Alfred

Herrhausen recognized early on the need to make Deutsche Bank more than a purely German institution. He strove to become a global player. That entailed, for example, acquiring the Italian portion of Bank of America, taking over Morgan Grenfell, and also creating positions for the bank in Spain, Portugal and Australia.

The Allianz Group, too, the largest European insurance company, took a major stride forward in the Eighties to become an international insurance group. New subsidiaries in Scandinavia and joint ventures with local partners in Greece, France and Spain broadened its European base. And with the acquisition of the Californian Fireman's Fund in 1991 its US market share rose from 0.2 to 1.7 per cent. Its international share of premium income multiplied by a factor of four, from 12 per cent in 1980 to 48 per cent in 1991. Despite recent losses in the insurance business, Allianz has created an excellent base for future development.

The British pharmaceuticals group Glaxo has built its international position mainly on a single path-breaking product. *Zantac*, introduced in 1981 as a remedy for stomach ulcers, became the best-selling medicine in the world within five years. Now other new developments are gaining importance, and today the European industry leader carries on its R and D in seven countries. Forty per cent of Group sales are generated by its US subsidiary, Glaxo, Inc. Under Chairman Sir Paul Girolami, a number of new markets have also been opened up via strategic alliances.

In Spain, Emilio Botín has led Banco Santander into an alliance with the Royal Bank of Scotland and has set up bases in Germany, Italy, Belgium and Portugal. At the same time, he has managed to secure its historical presence in America by direct investments in First Fidelity in the US as well as in banks in almost all the Latin American countries.

In a way, the Europreneurs' cross-border activity does follow on from a tradition. Much of European industry had very strong commitments abroad before the two world wars. The leading companies of the electrical and mechanical engineering, chemical and pharmaceutical industries have long been engaged in international business. In those early times, they often transferred large chunks of their home corporate structures and value-added chains to other countries. You only have to think of the wide network of activities of Siemens, Hoffmann La Roche, Brown Boveri or LM Ericsson – as early as the Twenties – in Latin America and Asia. After the war, these markets were served principally by exports from a domestic production base. For German companies this was often because of the loss of their foreign activities due to the war.

The leading Swiss companies, with their small domestic market and long tradition of international financial business, earn an overwhelmingly large share of their sales abroad. For example, only 2 per cent of Nestlé's sales come from Switzerland. Crédit Suisse has been doing business globally with multinational companies, institutional investors and high-income individuals for very much longer than many of its foreign competitors; the foreign share of its balance sheet total is around 52 per cent. In Germany, by contrast, for all its export orientation, the domestic market and reconstruction after the war offered so much demand that its strong international orientation to the US and Japan only developed fully in the last twenty years. Italy has been in a similar position.

Like the Swiss, the Dutch – think of Shell, Unilever and Philips – have long been 'world citizens' looking beyond national borders. Foreign business dominates their trade figures, and it is not unusual for their networks of international bases to consist of largely independent subsidiaries.

The French, with their long history of political foreign relations, also have strong cross-border traditions in their business life. In the last few years they have been among the most active players in the international mergers and acquisitions business. In 1991 alone, French acquisitions in Europe amounted to US$9.1 billion. Nevertheless, most French top-managers still come from a small number of polytechnic institutions and grandes écoles, in which analytical logic and the art of philosophical discussion are taught and practical management tools neglected. France's internationally-leading luxury-goods manufacturers are present abroad with their prestigious brands mainly through distribution activities. Typical of corporate Europeanization is the development of former flat glass and bottle manufacturer BSN under the leadership of Antoine Riboud. Now one of the largest food groups in Europe, the modern BSN was created by streamlining the company's product lines and making several acquisitions – for example, General Biscuit in Great Britain, the five European subsidiaries of US-based Nabisco, and Birkel of Germany. Similar developments can be seen at Rhône-Poulenc, Schneider, Elf-Aquitaine, Lafarge and Eaux Lyonnais.

In Spain, where post-war democracy and a market economy are still relatively new, there has not yet been enough time for major cadres of truly internationally-oriented corporate leaders to form. Even the younger and more entrepreneurial-thinking top managers have not yet managed to sever completely their traditionally protective links with the country's political forces.

In Great Britain, where the achievements of the Thatcher era challenged many deep-seated traditions, it is easy to forget that, even quite recently, business reality was strongly socialist in letter and spirit. None the less, the British are 'born internationals': their historical links with the US and the Commonwealth have no real parallels in continental Europe. Their strong sectors of consumer goods, banks and insurance include companies with a traditionally international presence. Names like BP, Unilever, ICI,

Grand Metropolitan and Reuters stand for an exemplary international orientation.

Today, the leading European companies have become 'locals' in many foreign markets. When Siemens seeks government support for imports of semi-finished goods to its subsidiaries in Florida, its 30,000 American employees give the company a strong base from which to influence decisions in Washington. When the company needs approval for special imports to its Brazilian factories, its 16,000 Brazilian workers offer an impressive argument. Similar examples are LM Ericsson, whose Teleindustria Ericsson SA employs 3,000 people in Mexico, or Royal Dutch/Shell with 1,200 employees in six subsidiaries in Indonesia alone.

The role of geographic borders is becoming less important. The generation of the founders knew it, and their modern descendants seem equally well aware of it. To them, it is more important to use technical and management skills wherever they find them. This is particularly true of research and development. Hoechst, for example, has concentrated almost all its genetic research in the US, and not just because of the easier legal situation. Electrolux has a research laboratory in Finland, a development centre in Sweden, and a design group in Italy. Design at IBM is done all around the world – and sometimes all around the clock – since the company uses satellite links to distribute work to its facilities in Europe, America and Japan. Daimler-Benz's commercial vehicles division has foreign Centres of Competence: medium-duty trucks are developed at Freightliner in Portland, Oregon, heavy-duty trucks at Mercedes-Benz do Brasil, and special buses at Otoman in Turkey.

But arena expansion is not limited to the geographic dimension. In Germany, Edzard Reuter saw the need to liberate automotive manufacturer Daimler-Benz from its single-business vulnerability to cyclical ups and downs, and to recognize the growing importance of electronics by formally implanting such know-how in his company. In a few short years, he laid the foundations for an integrated, technology-based group with electronics, aerospace and information-technology sectors in addition to its traditionally strong automotive business. The 100-year-old automotive group was given a new management structure with a management holding company at the top and four relatively independent divisions: Mercedes-Benz for vehicles, DASA for aerospace products, AEG for electrical engineering and DEBIS for information systems. But the move also included entering an unusually comprehensive alliance with the Mitsubishi Group in Japan.

Mark Wössner of Bertelsmann changed his company's regional arena by widespread acquisitions in the US, which now account for over 20 per cent of turnover, and by entering the private television business with RTL. The one-time German media company with a few overseas bases has become a global player. Hardly a major change occurs in the European and American media business without Bertelsmann being involved.

In Belgium, Gérard Mestrallet, CEO of Société Générale de Belgique, the largest Belgian financial and industrial holding company, has concentrated on reviving his company and making it fit again to compete in Europe and at the global level. John Goossens, CEO of Alcatel Bell Telephone, the Belgian subsidiary of the Alcatel Alsthom telecommunications group, has pressed his company to become more streamlined, more flexible and more customer-oriented, as well as pushing the development of new markets through joint ventures in China, Russia, Mexico and Turkey. Philip Bodson, CEO of Tractebel, a privately-owned group which controls 95 per cent of electricity generation in Belgium, has ensured that utilities look beyond their own country and make preparations for the upcoming opportunities provided by Europe's single market.

Similar developments are to be found in practically every country in Europe. In the United Kingdom there is Ian MacLaurin of Tesco, who gave his company a new direction and repositioned it outside the discount segment. Having tripled sales and doubled profits within a few years, Tesco is now the second-largest grocery chain in Great Britain after its main rival Sainsbury, with a strong image of quality, modern architecture and store design, as well as innovative product development and logistics. Of its current approximately 400 supermarkets, twenty-four were opened in one fiscal year.

Or take Sir Christopher Hogg, a Harvard MBA, who got rid of poorly performing divisions at Courtaulds and made the company's textile interests into a separate company. Or Sir Owen Green, who – initially as Managing Director and then as Chairman – made BTR into one of the most successful industrial conglomerates in the country, with impressive results in such supposedly unattractive businesses as valves, radiators, automobile carpets, rubber articles and building materials.

In Switzerland, Rainer Gut has split Crédit Suisse into two branch networks for private and corporate customers. He has also given his company an important role in the US by taking over the First Boston Corporation. In Sweden, Pehr Gyllenhammar made Volvo famous for the introduction of new production technologies and new forms of work organization that get away from the conventional conveyor-belt. Internationally, he forged direction-setting links with Renault and Mitsubishi.

Percy Barnevik, also of Scandinavia, has created one of the world's leading electrical engineering and civil engineering companies since combining the Swedish company Asea and the Swiss Brown Boveri into the international ABB

Group in 1988. Barnevik became a pioneer in the development of a truly global organization structure: a tiny corporate centre (with no more than around 100 staff) co-ordinating world-wide activities of sixty-five business areas and 1,100 local companies with 4,500 profit centres. And that organization, widely viewed as exemplary, has undergone another round of streamlining and adjustment just five years after its inception: in 1993, three regional groups assumed responsibility for Europe, the Americas and Asia respectively, reflecting the Triad structure of global business. At the same time, the group's product segments were reduced from six to four, the number of business areas to fifty, and the newly formed Group Executive Committee is down to eight members compared to twelve on the old executive board.

In a similar vein, Leif Johansson of Electrolux has bundled acquisitions like Zanussi, White Consolidated, and over 100 other companies into a group feared by competitors throughout the world. Anders Scharp, the company's Chairman, had previously laid the foundations for global leadership by reorganizing the complex network of its international research and development activities. Björn Svedberg has secured independence and world-wide competitiveness for LM Ericsson by taking a leading role in the development of digital-switch engineering, going full-force into mobile telephone systems, linking up with Northern Telecom, expanding the company's traditionally strong positions in Mexico, Brazil and Venezuela.

The list of Europreneurs, by no means exhaustive, goes on. In Holland, for example, Lo van Wachem, CEO of Royal Dutch/Shell, has diversified into engineering and chemicals. Floris Maljers, CEO of Unilever, has made fundamental changes in world-wide organization and business unit mix and has significantly reduced the size of the central administration – all without depressing current profits. In Italy, Carlo de Benedetti – despite recent difficulties – has transformed a minor typewriter manufacturer into a successful international electronics company. The textiles empire created by Pietro Marzotto has now, with the recent acquisition of BOSS in Germany, become the largest men's fashion manufacturer in the world. Enrico Randone and Eugenio Coppola, CEOs past and present of Assicurazioni Generali, have built one of the most successful insurance companies in the world, with dominant positions in France and Spain, through careful leveraging of new products and effective marketing.

With so many things in common and with so little relevant experience transferable from the past, it is no wonder that these entrepreneurs are seeking more interaction with one another. A wide range of formal and informal groups and functions provide the opportunity. Changing constellations of the group of Europreneurs meet on numerous occasions – the Bilderberg Conference, the European Business Round Table, *Financial Times* and *Economist* Conferences, the Tonbach Circle, Bergedorf Talks and others – as both participants and speakers. Unlike the traditional old boys' networks covering individual countries or industries, these leaders who have come to know and esteem one another have different business and national backgrounds, but face similar challenges.

An example of such European networking is the Stuttgart International Top Management Conference – also known as the 'Management Summit'. Fifteen European top managers were first invited to the Stuttgart Ministry of State in February 1988 to attend a forum under the aegis of Alfred Herrhausen and Lothar Späth, with a programme arranged by McKinsey & Company. Names like André Leysen, Peter Wallenberg, Floris Maljers, Rainer Gut, Helmut Maucher, François-Xavier Ortoli, Edzard Reuter and Romano Prodi gave the meeting an important European flavour from its inception. The timing could not have been better. Shortly before, the dollar had fallen to an historical low of DM1.51, and it had only been a few months since the 'Black Friday/Monday' on the American and European stock exchanges. In the face of the explosive growth in international finance flows, corporate leaders were wondering if world economic conditions had changed for good and what experience could be transferred from other companies. McKinsey papers about Japanese globalization strategies, American savings and loan problems, and world economic trends, formed the basis of a stimulating discussion.

As one of the organizers of this first meeting, I felt the confidence and self-assurance of these European leaders. An impromptu poll by Alfred Herrhausen revealed that none of the top managers present intended to reduce his investments because of the world economic problems; on the contrary, they were planning to raise them by 10 per cent. (Future events showed that they actually went ahead with these plans: the first group of 'Stuttgarters' invested a total of DM38 billion in 1988 and DM44 billion the following year.) At the closing press conference, Alfred Herrhausen made a plea for world-wide economic interdependence *and* entrepreneurial responsibility in designing the Europe of tomorrow.

Such meetings continued in following years, with McKinsey as programme manager, under the leadership of Edzard Reuter, who took over in 1990 after the death of Alfred Herrhausen. When twenty-five European top managers discussed global economic developments and the new conditions in Eastern Europe in 1991, a press comment said: 'It was like a class reunion.' The participants, too, felt themselves to be a group with common concerns and convictions, demonstrated by their 'Stuttgart Declaration of World Economic Interdependence', adopted on this occasion and discussed in the concluding press conference (see Appendix, page 289).

Each of these Management Summits has shown the Europreneurs' great need and readiness to exchange advice and experience. The twenty to twenty-five top managers meeting here probably have more to say to one another – and to their political leaders – across industry and national boarders than any generation of managers before them. Their network does not stop here, however, but is continued, for instance, in broad-based cross-memberships on each others' supervisory boards. Against this backdrop, it is no surprise that European top managers act as the spokesmen of European industries versus the Brussels authorities on topics such as managed trade or unfair competitive practices. It seems natural for Peugeot chief Jacques Calvet to give his German colleagues public moral support in the face of a threatened strike, as happened in the spring of 1992. This and other examples – undoubtedly also nurtured by increasing similarity of media consumption (the *Financial Times* and the *Economist* are standard reading) – signal the fact that a European top manager cadre is forming, a cadre that thinks, speaks, and increasingly acts, alike.

Perhaps the most amazing thing about these new Europreneurs is the fact that they have grown up, for most of their careers, in companies imbued with a fairly lethargic culture. Thus, they have often had to break with rigid traditions, conceptual patterns and management practices in the face of the growing challenge of Japanese competitors, more and more unstable exchange rates, and more and more rapid technical progress. For many years when Karlheinz Kaske was a member of Siemens' management board, he supported the company's traditional rejection of acquisitions: the very idea of taking over a strange company was a violation of house style. Some years later, however, when at the helm as CEO, he initiated a major acquisition strategy. An unsuccessful attempt to acquire Allen Bradley of the US merely spurred management on: within a few years, just under 15 per cent of sales was acquired in the form of GTE-Übertragungstechnik, ROLM, Plessey and Nixdorf. Allianz, Lloyds Bank and Schlumberger are similar examples of unaccustomed international acquirers.

It is part of the European picture that the corporate chiefs of today rarely have strained relations with the previous generation, despite the fact that some of them have departed significantly from their predecessors' programmes. It seems to be widely accepted that new times not only bring forth new men, but also call for different management techniques.

Many of the corporate leaders referred to here perform the function of a 'locomotive' in their industries, their regions, and also in the national and European context. Deutsche Bank, Bayer, Mercedes-Benz and Siemens rank as the undisputed leaders of their industries. The same applies to Philips (Holland), CGE (France), BSN (France), Fiat (Italy), LM Ericsson (Sweden), Nestlé (Switzerland), and Unilever (Holland and the United Kingdom). New management techniques are often introduced by these leaders, then tested and often adopted by other industry players. (As the head of one German regional bank commented: 'If Deutsche Bank is organized that way, there must be something in it.')

The influence of these leaders on other companies – through customer and supplier relations, the granting of loans, positions on advisory boards and boards of directors, as well as published comments – is considerable. Just consider, for instance, the volume and profit improvements of the major German banks, British consumer goods manufacturers, or the French insurance companies and luxury goods manufacturers.

Visible Public Role

The new Europreneurs are much more in the public eye than were their predecessors. As entrepreneur-statesmen, they have added their counsel and their influence to discussions on matters of economic policy, law and their own industries. National and supranational debate would be inconceivable now without them: EC, G7 or GATT; Helmut Kohl's Chancellor's Circle, John Major's Prime Minister's Round Table; the Bilderberg Conference, and the European Round Table in Brussels composed of forty-five European industry leaders under the presidency of Jérôme Monod.

Stephan Schmidheiny's Business Council for Sustainable Development played a prominent role at the environmental summit in Rio de Janeiro. The Council, made up of forty-eight top managers from companies such as 3M, Ciba-Geigy, Volkswagen, Dow Chemical and Mitsubishi, works on behalf of the UN on a global business perspective for environmental protection. Schmidheiny himself has stimulated environmental discussion world-wide with his recent book.[1]

In Germany, former Bayer CEO Hermann-Josef Strenger was a strong champion of environmental issues and made it very clear what his industry and his company could and would have to do in this area. Marc Moret of Sandoz has also made a commitment on these issues since the 'Rhine incident' in 1986, when leaks from the company's premises caused large-scale toxic pollution of the river. Daniel Goeudevert of VW and Eberhard von Kuenheim of BMW have for years expressed their concern about the future of the motor car in the already over-crowded cities of Europe. Edzard Reuter of Daimler-Benz pointed out the possible negative impact of cars on the environment years

[1] Stephan Schmidheiny, *Changing Course*, MIT Press, Cambridge, Mass., 1992.

ago. Recently, of course, the European single market and the huge problems in Eastern Europe have moved to the forefront of industrialists' public statements.

Any CEO or 'spokesman of the board' of a large, established company increasingly has to play the role of industrial statesman. With left-wing economic ideologies and their defenders called in question by historical developments, the Europreneurs – at home and abroad – have more than ever emerged as the outspoken champions of a *de facto* social market economy. They have realized that the public interest in industry, as well as the linkages of industry with practically all areas of life, are much too important to be left solely in the hands of politicians, employers' associations or union officials. In spite of initial difficulties in finding an audience, their comments on the important issues of society are now considered indispensable. Their voices are being heard – and listened to.

This public presence also gives the Europreneurs' generation more in common with their elders around the turn of the century than with the generation immediately before them. Men like Siemens, Krupp, Thyssen, Bosch, Boveri, Leverhulme, Mond, Nobel, Thorn and Wallenberg were also public personalities. By contrast, in the immediate post-war period who were the men who created the German 'miracle'? Who remembers their names? The company names, yes, but hardly theirs. The men at the top remained largely invisible. Some top managers did appear in public fairly frequently: Abs of Deutsche Bank, for example, or Winnacker of Hoechst, or Pferdmenges, who was an adviser to German Chancellor Konrad Adenauer. But most remained in the background. The companies were important, not the men behind them. Even the media took no great interest in them. At the end of the Fifties and the beginning of the Sixties, I worked for four and a half years for Deutsche Shell AG. I did not know the names of the

men at the top of Deutsche Shell or of Royal Dutch/Shell
or Shell Transport and Trading, either then or later. You
just never saw them.

This state of affairs remained virtually unaltered up to
the end of the Sixties. When it did change, it was not
in a way that directed the spotlight on the little-known
figures behind the institutions. The differences were based,
rather, on a fundamental change in social attitudes. People,
particularly young people, had already forgotten the worst
of the post-war hard times and, to a large extent, also
the great achievements of reconstruction. Instead, a flood
of questions arose about the performance-oriented and
materialistic society into which Germany, France and the
other European nations had developed. Was it possible to
reconcile economic activity – and, in particular, private
enterprise – with democratic values at all? What impact did
industry have on the environment? Was there no alternative
to a performance-oriented society? If losses were distributed
over society, why were profits privatized? The captains of
industry still stayed in the background. They had never
needed public relations – never learned how to go about it.
But in the face of such questions, their companies began
to lose the esteem of the public. Their achievements had
come to be taken for granted, and the image of industry as
a wealth-creating institution lacked social appeal.

All over Europe, the younger generation rebelled – most
dramatically in the 1968 revolts in France and Germany –
against the cold logic of an 'economic rationale' in whose
name weapons could be delivered to crisis areas, dubious
political regimes supported, new products tested by animal
experiments and workers turned into human robots. In
the face of so much contempt, many of the traditional
accords went by the board, and old truths were subject
to doubt. Should society be based exclusively on performance, whereby lesser achievers irrevocably fell by the

wayside? Was a 'two-thirds' or 'three-quarters' society taking shape, in which growing prosperity was achieved for many at the expense of leaving a significant fraction of their fellow citizens behind? Was it right to make profit the sole yardstick of economic performance? Was economic performance important at all?

However, in the mid-Seventies, with the effects of the first oil price shock on the European economies barely digested, the picture changed again. With the dominance of socialistic-oriented governments, public opinion now saw industry as a milk cow that could be made to yield more – if more were needed to support social needs. Opinion polls in many European countries repeatedly showed that most ordinary citizens considered that quite acceptable: the *vox populi* held the extremely vague but deeply rooted assumption that corporate profits were constantly between 30 and 40 per cent. Redistribution of wealth seemed perfectly logical under the circumstances.

The top industrialists kept out of the public eye and the public debate to a large extent. But they knew how the public judged them. Besides the fundamental change in values, arms supply scandals, cases of corrupt political donations and publicly-discussed tax frauds contributed to the further impeachment of their already-damaged reputations. Searing press reports about the escapades of the young Krupps and Flicks matched the public image. The whole economic system to which they belonged had become extremely suspect.

The changes in top managers' prestige in society also had a significant impact on who went into management to make it their life's work. At the turn of the century, the best and most talented young men in Germany and most other European countries went into the armed forces. A man serving as an officer in the Prussian Army enjoyed the highest respect. Remember, at the beginning of the First

World War, the whole of society in Germany and France –
from the extreme right wing to the extreme left – was deeply
convinced of the need to go to war. In such an environment,
a military career was a first, and much admired, choice.
After the First and particularly after the Second World War,
most new professionals in Germany wanted to join the civil
service. In some regions, such leanings had deep historical
roots: in Bavaria, for example, there was a tradition going
back hundreds of years that the best law graduates went
into government service. In times of high uncertainty, a
government post was a sure thing. Even the angry young
men of the '68 generation did not strike out as professional
revolutionaries as they grew older. And they rarely set up
their own alternative companies or sought jobs in dependent
positions in private companies. They went into the civil
service. This partiality for security was actually so strong
that Rudi Dutschke, the idol of the '68 revolt, spoke of it
as the 'march through the institutions'.

In the early Eighties, however, the picture had changed
again. A survey of the subjects taken by the best students
and the professions they entered afterwards would have
shown that they entered industry. The armed forces had
lost all their attraction. So had the civil service. In Germany
in particular, the government was so obviously prey to a
multitude of special interests that it had lost its charm as
an arena for achievement of the best and the brightest.
Freedom of action, the chance to break down barriers,
was non-existent. Besides, the government apparatus had
by this time become so inflated that there was very little
room for rapid promotion. The surplus of teachers (a branch
of the civil service) in Germany is still well remembered.

This turn of the tide in career preferences happened, of
course, at different speeds and in different ways in the
different countries. In Germany, with its strong tradition
of skilled trades, management was seen primarily as an

extension of engineering and was accordingly dominated by the technically-minded. In France, where the civil service was more in the limelight, management was a kind of bureaucracy, inspired by the graduates of the grandes écoles. In Great Britain, where the cult of the gentleman still held, management was seen as a kind of disciplined dilettantism. In the consumer goods business and in financial institutions, the principle of 'play at work' and 'work at play' was followed with great success. But wherever you turned, management was now the preferred choice of career.

If, at this point, the new generation of top managers broke with the tradition of silence and quite deliberately entered the public arena, it was not primarily in an attempt to win personal fame. Making the front covers of business magazines was not the aim, although the number of business publications has tripled in the last ten years in most European countries. It was, rather, the new demands on the leader's role that made this step on to the public stage appear necessary. Practically all these men were still at school at the end of the war. They had seen with their own eyes what it took to rebuild an economy destroyed by war: complete dedication, hard work and boundless energy. They had a low opinion of financial conjuring tricks and of dubious and enormously risky speculation. They had a low opinion of products which had no sound technical foundations. They had a low opinion of conspicuous waste of any kind. And they had no respect for a lack of respect for the worker. The past had taught them that economic survival was the result of joint efforts.

Basic consensus on goals, joint efforts and a balance of interests – this was the recipe for long-term economic prosperity. Even in hard times. As Toni Schmücker, popular chief of VW in the mid-Seventies, once said: 'In my time as the CEO of Rheinstahl, I was forced to let more than 30 per cent of the whole workforce go. Without the constructive support of the works councils, the trade unions and the local administrations, this would not have been doable.' Such co-operation, however, required communication in a way previously unknown – in particular, communication with the unions and the works councils. In the process, a relationship developed that was basically founded on partnership. Industrialists, and the public in general, had a growing respect for their responsible trade union counterparts.

Probably even more important was the fact that these men witnessed from front-row seats how many of their predecessors' strategic plans were overturned by rapid changes in exchange rates, protectionist actions by various governments or unfair competitive practices. If corporate leaders were to be effective, they now had to speak out in public debate and make responsible contributions to current issues. Moreover, other groups in society were stating in no uncertain terms what they expected of industry. The consumer movement and the environmental protection movement had their say; product liability, preventive responsibility and responsibility for knock-on damage in the widest sense formed the basis of more and more concrete demands. The unions were making their attitudes on holiday, new working arrangements and redesigned working hours more and more public. And political leaders, as always, had their own opinions and suitable platforms from which to voice them.

It was, therefore, high time for top industrialists to abandon their reserve as well. The corporate world had to be more strongly represented in public – and represented well.

New Talent for New Tasks

The Europreneurs, thus, have to some extent been forced into their new direction-setting role by the environment they were born into and by the times in which they now live. The individual European markets are simply too small, technological change too fast, competition too intense, corporate organization too complex, for it to be otherwise. Political structures are opening up and nation states declining in importance. But all this still does not explain the originality, the courage, the energy and the creativity of this generation of top managers. Nor does it explain their often drastic breaks with the type of management current in Europe for decades.

A fuller explanation lies partly in the historical context that shaped the Europreneurs' apprentice and journeyman years. They have lived through the substantial dependence of industry on state initiatives in the post-war period, as well as the above-mentioned changes in public esteem for their field of work and their own role as entrepreneurs. Inevitably their goals and their choice of ways to reach them have been influenced. A further part of the explanation lies in the educational and professional careers of this group, which in most cases differs significantly from their predecessors' (Table 1). With few exceptions, the Europreneurs entered their new leading roles in their forties or early fifties. Prior to that, in contrast to most of their predecessors, they had spent a large part of their professional careers in several different functions in their own companies or even outside those companies altogether.

And before that – again, unlike their predecessors, who had often had a technical education or a background in public administration – they had acquired a wide academic grounding in the sciences, law, philosophy or other liberal arts subjects. Long before they ever reached the top, they

Typical Europreneurs and their Predecessors

© McKinsey & Company, Inc.

Edzard Reuter, Daimler-Benz AG. CEO since 1987. Studied Mathematics, Physics and Law. Professional experience in media companies.

> Predecessor: **Werner Breitschwerdt**, electrical engineer. Entire career with Daimler-Benz

Percy Barnevik, ABB Asea Brown Boveri AG. President and CEO since 1988 (1980 – 7 CEO of Asea). Economist and MBA. Previous experience as economist and controller in industrial companies.

> Predecessor at Asea: **Torsten Lindström**, engineer. Previously an academic.

Didier Pineau-Valencienne, Schneider S.A. CEO since 1981. Economist. Previous experience with Banque Parisienne pour l'Industrie, CECA, Rhône-Poulenc.

> Predecessor: **René Engen**, engineer. Previous experience in Belgian and French industrial companies.

Sir Paul Girolami, Glaxo Holdings plc. Chairman since 1980. Economist. Previously worked as an accountant.

> Predecessor: **Sir Austin Bide**, chemist. Previously in Civil Service.

Marc Moret, Sandoz AG. President of Board of Directors since 1985. Economist. Before Sandoz worked for Swissair, Sulzer, Guigoz International and Nestlé.

> Predecessor: **Yves Dunant**, engineer and chemist. Entire career with Sandoz.   *Table 1*

had developed a truly international attitude. Many of them had spent long periods abroad, for professional or personal reasons: Strenger in Brazil, Reuter and Maljers in Turkey, Kaske in Japan, Herrhausen in the US.

As a result, they were excellently qualified for the new tasks facing the heads of the major European companies in the Eighties. For many years it had been common practice in some countries, Germany for instance, to treat the top man as only first among equals on the board of management. Some of the major department store groups – Karstadt, Kaufhof, Hertie and Horten – occasionally went as far as not even appointing a 'spokesman' for the executive board. There was a strong feeling that top-level collectives would manage companies better.

There were strong legal foundations for this attitude in the German law of 1965 on joint stock companies, according to which the chairman of a management board could not impose his will on the group as a whole. Such consensus had proved effective in times of predictable external developments and stable growth rates. In the thrills and spills of the Eighties, however, equality did not work nearly so well. No wonder. When competition becomes more and more a battle of outstanding ideas and of their rapid implementation in complex, unpredictable markets, then the traditional strengths of collective management are only moderately effective – particularly when aggressive competitors headed by strong leaders share the field. Besides, collectives rarely develop visions. They make it easier to neglect opportunities and harder to respond effectively to crises.

The supervisory boards that appointed the new breed of CEO had seen that the time was ripe for change. The public was waiting for it, as were corporate executives and employees, customers and suppliers. Much of traditional corporate management had developed into formal ritual.

What was needed was a catalyst, personal vision or leadership that could overcome bureaucracy in thought and deed,
cut down faceless administrative centres and trigger new
beginnings.

Even so, opting for a new style and orientation of leadership was not an easy decision. It required a fair amount of
determination to break with hidebound tradition and make
Alfred Herrhausen Deutsche Bank's sole spokesman. Or
to make Edzard Reuter, long-standing Financial Director
and a critical commentator on social developments, CEO
of Daimler-Benz. Or to appoint Jan Timmer head of Philips.
They all were people who would shake up many areas of
their companies and would speak out in public. Putting them
at the top was a risk. But it was perceived as a greater risk
to stick to the old, ingrained, bureaucratic ways. Without
a new management team and a new style at the top, it
would be impossible to cope with the multiple facets of
global businesses, with an environment marked by growing
interdependence that made it harder and harder to draw
clear dividing lines between formerly separate industries
and regions. Without such new men, it would be impossible
to provide the leadership, not of an administrator, but of a
corporate architect, a re-former and re-designer, a pioneer
of new strategies, or of a motivator who can inspire average
employees to above-average performance.

The new Europreneurs have faced up to these tasks.
In view of the increasing size and complexity of their
businesses, many of them collaborate particularly closely
with one or two outstanding colleagues in an inner circle
of management. These 'right-hand men' are part of the
extended top-management team, but are also singled out
by virtue of their specialist knowledge and, often, by shared
experiences with the CEO. In many cases, their special
skills make them the perfect foil to the top men, although the
attributes formerly ascribed to Edzard Reuter and Mercedes

boss Werner Niefer – 'head and hand', 'visionary and doer', 'proposer and disposer' – are certainly exaggerated. It is not unusual for the twosome or threesome to function by consensus as a kind of 'kitchen cabinet' outside the hierarchy, and it is not unusual for these close associates of a CEO to be the ones who will also give him constructive criticism on a personal level.

The rapid change initiated by the Europreneurs can be attributed to creative impatience. So many innovations to plan, so many issues to attack – and so little time left in which to do it all. In the Fifties and Sixties, the average period in office of a European CEO was twelve to fifteen years. A decade later the figure had dropped to ten to twelve years. Now it is more likely to be eight to ten years. As a result of the know-how explosion, particularly in electronics, the half-life of specialist knowledge has slumped to six or eight years. In many cases, CEOs no longer have a grasp of the know-how at the base of the pyramid – yet another reason to let young people take command faster and to provide stronger encouragement for broad-based management know-how.

Naturally there are exceptions – as demonstrated by the Allianz insurance group, which has only had five CEOs in its hundred-year history. But as a rule the men at the top have a maximum of ten years to implement their plans. Much of their planning, however, stretches far beyond this period – for example, the building of world-class skills in electronics or biotechnology or the design of a new aircraft. Like the CEOs of the post-war period, these men have initiated tasks that they cannot hope to see completed within their own period of office. It is, therefore, all the more important for them to have their succession well prepared, and they do seem to be putting this task up high on their priority lists. Some of the first Europreneurs have actually already handed over to their successors; for

others the change is not far ahead. In 1992 and in the first
half of 1993, Germany has witnessed the transition from
Strenger to Schneider at Bayer, from Karlheinz Kaske
to Heinrich von Pierer at Siemens, from Carl Hahn to
Ferdinand Piech at Volkswagen, and from Werner Niefer
to Helmut Werner at Mercedes-Benz. In Holland, Lo van
Wachem is being succeeded by Cornelius Herkströter at
Shell and Freddy Heineken by Gerard van Schaik. At
the top of Electrolux, Leif Johansson seems set to follow
Anders Scharp. In Great Britain, Mike Angus has handed
over to Mike Perry at Unilever. It would be easy to list
a dozen more examples of the 'changing of the guard' at
major European companies. In Germany alone, the leaders
of half the 100 largest companies will have retired on the
grounds of age by the mid-Nineties.

So far, this changing of the guard has revealed an interesting common pattern: a smooth transition from the 'old'
to the 'young' master, in which

☐ The successors have proved themselves in one or more
  'missions impossible' (von Pierer in the power-plant business in Iran; Werner in the turnaround of the commercial vehicles division; Schneider as the rescuer of
  Ruhrchemie).

☐ The successors have already been part of the top management team and have participated in the collective design
  of – and responsibility for – significant business decisions
  for several years.

☐ The outgoing CEOs remain available to their successors, or
  rather their companies, in the capacity of a supervisory
  board member or counsellor.

The new bosses taking the baton from outstanding Europreneurs have withstood many tests. As successors, they will be measured by their performance in satisfying the growing demands on the leadership role shaped by their predecessors. The fact that the new Europreneurs can count on growing cultural respect gives grounds for optimism. This impression was confirmed for Germany in an Allensbach survey of 1990: compared to a similar survey in 1983, more than twice as many participants (22 per cent compared to 10 per cent) said that the image of entrepreneurs had improved over the past years. The share of opinions given as 'improved' or 'stayed the same' increased in total from 54 to 69 per cent. Similarly, the Europeans came out relatively well in a world-wide overview in the context of the World Competitiveness Report in 1992, which surveyed how much 'public confidence' is placed in companies: eight out of the ten 'best' industrialized countries were European, including four of the top five (Diagram 10).

The difficult but expanding economic and political linkages among European nations has mollified public reaction to large corporations' cross-border ambitions. Furthermore, with public opinion less marked by spontaneous aversion to private enterprise – and unspecified mistrust of all it stands for – even bold corporate strokes are finding a more sympathetic audience. This is especially true when such entrepreneurs are emerging as the driving force behind efforts to help Eastern Europe and its peoples catch up with Western European levels of prosperity. With visible and growing success achieved by new private enterprise in Hungary or the Czech Republic, it will be more and more difficult to object on principle to the far more successful and longer-standing examples of such energy in the West.

Not that time-honoured leftist suspicions of economic power in private hands have disappeared. But melodramatic claims, such as that 'one hundred individuals at the heads

European Companies do relatively well in 'Confidence Competition'

Credibility index, 1992

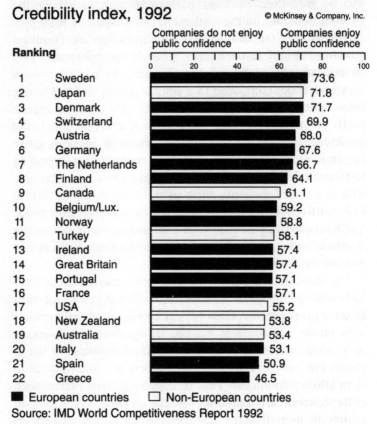

Diagram 10

of the biggest European companies actually determine the economic fate of millions', have lost a great deal of their force. At the same time, managerial mistakes, the misuse of power or criminal practices remain in the cross-fire of criticism. Which is a good thing, as is the fact that more – and more effective – checks and balances are now in place: media attention, public reporting requirements, annual general meetings with active participation by shareholders, and so on. All of this contributes to the high position that social responsibility, in the old European tradition of the founder generation, once more enjoys in modern managerial values.

An additional advantage of this basically positive climate seems particularly important to me: it makes it very much easier constructively to discuss and address remaining weaknesses and improvement opportunities. An attempt to locate the most important such danger spots soon produces a considerable list:

☐ Europeans have lost the lead in most high-tech areas (microelectronics, information technology, consumer electronics, etc.) to the US and Japan. Cost and speed have been neglected for the sake of quality.

☐ In light of the many demands made on companies by different stakeholders, their operating profits and cash-flow seem acceptable but not particularly ambitious compared to those of American companies. Europeans are still content with a relatively modest return on capital. And in boom periods many European companies, regrettably, have resigned themselves to wage demands by the trade unions not matched by productivity improvements.

☐ European companies rarely give up unattractive business units and continue to cross-subsidize unprofitable business areas, a form of patience that often keeps them from seizing opportunities in more attractive businesses.

☐ Europeans have not yet progressed very far in true globalization, despite their undisputed export leadership. As a rule, over 90 per cent of production and R and D activities are still based in their domestic markets; organizational structures are dominated by strong corporate centres back home; and top-management teams are mainly composed of home-country nationals. Well-known exceptions such as Nestlé, Shell, Unilever, Bosch and Siemens are much further along the road to globalization. But compared to IBM, Coca-Cola, Sony, Honda or Toyota, even they still have a long way to go.

☐ Europeans, overall the greatest inventors in industrial history, have dropped back substantially in today's innovation race. Europe does spend very respectable sums on R and D. There are an estimated 600,000 researchers and developers at work in the EC (in the US approx. 1 million; in Japan, 450,000), and public R and D spending alone comes to around 2 per cent of the gross domestic product (the US and Japan each spend 2.9 per cent). But completely new products rarely come from Europe. Most activities are incremental developments of existing product, process and system generations.

☐ A culture of 'friendly competition' makes it hard to break through established relationships. Public contracts – often sizeable – for the postal service, railways, utilities, government civil engineering and the armed forces are mostly placed with national suppliers. Considerations of supply security and compatibility with existing infrastructure play a role, as does local employment policy and an established old boys' network. In fact, many Europeans would be pleased to have their markets distributed *de facto* among established players. Even competitors that are themselves expanding abroad have little inclination to give up closed shop policies at home.

☐ Underlying attitudes and corporate growth have led to excessive internal hierarchies. Over-staffed levels of middle management often separate the top management from the base. Little has changed here in many companies in spite of the new competitive environment.

The legitimacy of business – and of management – has to be renewed on an ongoing basis. The Europreneurs will have to earn theirs, at least in part, by sustaining the momentum of the recent energy surge, and by effectively targeting it on the weaknesses sketched out above. It will take success in these areas for companies to satisfy the interests of their many constituencies. Among other things, that might well mean greater responsibility in future for closing gaps in social care increasingly left unfilled by public agencies in, say, education and health, or the integration of ethnic and religious minorities.

The management tasks of European industrialists thus appear more complex than those facing their counterparts in the US and Japan. In the absence of one overriding goal, such as shareholder value in the US or market share in Japan, European companies have to deal with more, and more varied, sets of objectives and constituencies. But there is more to it: in view of the legitimacy crisis of so many other institutions in society, the legitimate role of top management is being defined very broadly, and standards of judgement raised accordingly. No wonder managers are said to be overstrained.

Compared to fifteen or twenty years ago, the agenda and *modus operandi* of a top manager today have changed fundamentally. At that time, even the top people mainly worked at a single location; they led a controllably-sized organization; they were often familiar with even the most minor product variants, just as they were personally acquainted with their customers, suppliers and key employees. Today, practically every top manager spends at least half his time travelling. He maintains relationships with customers in Japan, the US and other European countries, and in addition works with industry associations and performs other public duties. Within the company, too, the task of management is more demanding: more independent and self-assured employees expect to be more sensitively guided, inspired and encouraged, instead of just being given orders.

The continuous need to strike a balance between internal demands and external expectations, between old, established products with familiar production processes and new, path-breaking product and production developments, between the needs of individual people management and corporation- or industry-related constraints, and between the interests of owners, employees and society, forces management to make extremely careful use of its authority and power. With such an agenda, the doubtful compliment that the corporations are apparently the only institutions in society that are still fully functional is not a great deal of help. On the contrary, the concern that managers might have too much on their plates cannot be dismissed.

I think, however, that many of the demands for greater social equality and farther-reaching solutions to environmental questions are bound to spread across the Triad. When that happens, European industrialists, with more practice in such issues, should have the edge. Although it may seem nonsensical on the face of it that they now spend around 20 per cent of their time on broadly-defined social commitments, this investment may eventually provide the institutions of business with surer foundations and more credible leadership in Europe than elsewhere.

IV

Management Culture

As role models for today's managers, the Europreneurs have set new standards, both internally and externally. Not only have they revitalized their sometimes highly bureaucratic companies and developed new fields of activity; they have also become involved in public debate and have shown themselves willing to accept social responsibility. As a result, they have raised the standard by which all entrepreneurial performance is measured. They and their successors, some of whom are about to take office, face an environment made more difficult by fierce global competition. They are also likely to be confronted with growing demands and expectations on the social front. And both these phenomena will only increase as overstrained government exchequers and overburdened public sources of expertise urgently seek escape routes. Recent public discussions of the necessary role for industry in social insurance, waste disposal, youth training and investment in Eastern Europe, may have pointed the way here. Indeed, social considerations in choosing production sites, ethical reservations regarding exports to trouble spots around the world, and – in Germany – the moral obligation to support reconstruction in East Germany are now irrevocably part of the management agenda. A critical public will pay ever closer attention to management actions through increased coverage of those actions in the media.

The standards of managerial achievement once defined by Alfred Herrhausen in his discussion of the social market economy apply now more than ever: 'Performance-based competition *and* social protection, individual freedom *and* responsibility, self-interest *and* market control.'[1] Herrhausen himself practised what he preached – witness his contributions to the Stiftung Deutsche Geschichte (German History Foundation), his role in the Circle of Friends of the private Witten-Herdecke University, his position as an adviser to the German Chancellor, his role in the revitalization of the Ruhr industrial area and his lectureship at the University of Cologne. The same commitment can be seen in many other European top managers – among them, BSN chief Antoine Riboud in France, Freddy Heineken in Holland, Stephan Schmidheiny and Ciba's Alex Krauer in Switzerland. In Great Britain, a select group of top managers – known as 'the great and the good' – went so far as to take three to five years out from their professional duties to undertake social tasks. (My former McKinsey colleague, Sir John Banham, was knighted for his contributions to the leadership of the Audit Commission and the Confederation of British Industry.)

To date, European companies and managers have carried the incontestable burdens of Eurocapitalism reasonably well. In some ways, they have even been able to transform

---

[1] A. Herrhausen, *Denken – Ordnen – Gestalten*, K. Weidemann, Berlin 1990.

them into advantages – for example, in the form of a relatively high social consensus or a well-qualified workforce. The supportive environment created by Eurocapitalist governments has undoubtedly helped. But certain facets of European management practice, comparatively little regarded, have also had a part to play. What the International Management Institute in Geneva once described as *the* factors for success in the Nineties – 'the art of management and the courage to lead' – are much in evidence among Europe's top executives.

Based on a strong tradition of economic and business teachings (consider the Swiss, Scandinavian, British and German professors), and enriched by recent US academic thinking and management tools, the Europeans have added an important qualitative dimension to management theory and practice. Consider, for example, the notable restructuring process undergone by many European companies in the Eighties. Supported by a relatively high standard of expertise in the workforce, they have succeeded in making the high labour-cost area of Central Europe into an area of high productivity with products of increasingly high value. An example of this is the textile industry in Germany, France and Great Britain, where half the manpower of ten years ago now creates considerably more value.

A long-term orientation, generally associated with superior product development, a results-oriented corporate strategy, stable customer and supplier relationships, as well as relatively modest demands for short-term profits, is a further European strength. So is the fact that European companies are often endowed from birth with a marked degree of internationalism. They have been exporting since they started to produce and, in the process, have learned more and more about integrating the wishes of foreign customers into product design and being on site to provide service to customers.

There are, however, five other facets of European management practice that are less well known as sources of entrepreneurial energy and performance: the 'team at the top', the 'long-leash' principle, a sound technology base, learning from politics, and the perfecting of what I call 'as-well-as' as opposed to 'either/or' management. Each deserves a closer look.

Team at the Top

Increasing corporate size and complexity have stimulated the development of an enlightened form of top management. For all the influence he may exercise by virtue of personality and office, the CEO (or equivalent) in Europe does not even come close to a presidential autocrat in the style of a Jack Welch at General Electric, Lou Gerstner at Nabisco and recently IBM, Lee Iacocca at Chrysler, or Bob Crandall at American Airlines. He is a member, first among equals, of a management team. American 'John-Wayne-ism' is foreign even to the most powerful European corporate leaders. Even an all-powerful PDG (Président Directeur Général) of the French variety increasingly acts as the captain of a team.

In spite of their countries' different legal structures, you will find that the teams around Edzard Reuter (Daimler-Benz), Hilmar Kopper (Deutsche Bank) and Karlheinz Kaske (Siemens) are led in a similar way to those around Didier Pineau-Valencienne (Schneider) and Antoine Riboud (BSN). And these, in turn, are similar to the teams headed by Paul Girolami (Glaxo), Floris Maljers (Unilever), Percy Barnevik (ABB) and Bo Bergen (Stora). As in soccer, not only the captains but the *teams* at such companies as these are thought of as outstanding in Europe.

In each case, overall responsibility for the company rests with a management board, usually consisting of six to ten members, or with a 'cabinet' of top managers, which meets once a week as a rule. The individual members of the team often have responsibility for specific areas in which none of the others – not even the CEO – can intervene. A similar structure, but with smaller teams of just three to four members, is generally repeated at the levels below the board – for example, in divisional management or on the boards of subsidiaries.

Board members often have a combination of product, functional and regional responsibilities, coupled with occasional special tasks. The Finance Director, for instance, can at the same time be responsible for a major US subsidiary. In many European companies (e.g. Schneider in France, BASF and Siemens in Germany), it is common for board members to oversee newly-acquired companies as an additional function. The long-standing tradition at Siemens, Philips and other companies of entrusting both an engineer and a commercial specialist with joint responsibility has more or less vanished at this and other managerial levels. This variety of the 'two-heads-are-better-than-one' principle turned out to be a two-headed monster with more disadvantages than advantages. The trend towards having boards that are largely free of individual functional responsibilities – as in the example of Siemens AG – is relatively new and still has to be put to the test. The trend towards smaller top management teams, on the other hand, found at Daimler-Benz, Siemens, Bayer, Volkswagen, Kingfisher, Generali, Schneider and British Airways, is already widespread.

This is possible, in part, because the majority of outstanding European companies rely – for reasons of motivation among other things – on teams that have been recruited and developed internally. There are occasional external additions (Schmitz at Deutsche Bank, Werner at Daimler-Benz), but internal career paths are the rule.

The road to full membership on the top team often passes through a kind of qualifying period of around two years. During this period and for some years afterwards, 'junior' team members are occasionally expected to take on special tasks such as the care of less important subsidiaries, or simply the organization of the board meetings. Those in waiting for the top team are well advised to keep their nerve and have patience. Premature departures driven by disappointments are not likely in most cases to be the most intelligent career steps.

It is extremely important for the team to be unanimous on new appointments and also, if possible, on the choice of Chairman, since management by teams is more dependent than other structures on good personal collaboration. This tight consensus has proved its worth in more than one crisis situation. For example, following the assassinations of Ernst Zimmermann of MTU, Karl Heinz Beckurts of Siemens, Alfred Herrhausen of Deutsche Bank and Detlev Rohwedder of the Treuhandanstalt, their respective successors Dinger, Danielmeyer, Kopper and Breuel were appointed very rapidly.

The extent to which the Chairman sets the tone of the team varies from company to company and from person to person. It is quite possible for a high-profile 'spokesman', who is seen externally by the public as the embodiment of a company, to work by and large on a collegial basis in-house in practical day-to-day operations. Management by sound argument and the power of persuasion usually achieves more than standing on the dignity of the CEO function, let alone ruling with an iron fist. This is all the more true when you consider that all these top managers head their own functions or business units more or less independently, living proof to the whole company of the principle of delegating operational responsibility. Enlightened CEOs are increasingly managing their companies with a team in which each individual knows his or her personal worth and in which, moreover, each individual knows that optimum contributions make the management team greater than the sum of its parts. Franz Beckenbauer formed Germany's 1990 World Cup-winning soccer team on this management principle.

Naturally, there is a down-side to cabinet-style management: there is a greater risk that conflicts of interest and differences of opinion may paralyse operating and decision-making capabilities than with the 'presidential' system which is the norm in US (and not unknown in many French and British) companies. To American managers, the unanimity required in the Deutsche Bank management board must seem clumsy, an obstacle to decision-making. A time-consuming search for compromise may occur, but is not likely to happen too often. These board-level people are normally personalities with strong willpower and strong powers of persuasion. Theirs is a kind of federal system with which Germany, Scandinavia and Switzerland have long been familiar – and which they have found to be a workable solution. Unavoidable tensions, like those occurring in any other type of government, are part of a well-established culture of conflict management and are relatively easy to control. And they are the price of a system with many tangible advantages, which would be hard to obtain by any other means.

On occasion, the team at the top does not consist only of the Vorstand – the management board or the top-management level – however defined. The nature of the team varies from country to country, and even within countries, as in Great Britain. In many cases, the Chairman of the Supervisory Board, while not a full-time member, is an important part of the management team. Examples include

Närger and before him Plettner at Siemens, Grünewald
and before him Hansen at Bayer, Angus at Unilever,
Giovanni Agnelli at Fiat and Peter Holmes at Shell Oil.
In much the same way, the extended management team
at the big German car-makers and at German and Swiss
chemical companies includes the head of the works council
as a senior workers' representative. In companies with a
high level of co-determination, such as Volkswagen and
Lufthansa, it also includes the presiding committee of the
Supervisory Board, which also has a trade union representative. Although these Supervisory Boards normally meet only
four times a year, they have many informal contacts with
members of the management team.

The full-time management team in Europe occasionally
includes members who do not belong to the formal top
management or executive board. These individuals are
often responsible for new businesses (like Peter Mihatsch
at Mannesmann, who is responsible for mobile phones),
for newly acquired companies (like Ernest H. Drew of
Celanese at Hoechst), or for important foreign subsidiaries
(like Rolf Eckrodt, head of MB do Brasil in Daimler-Benz's
Commercial Vehicles team). Or they have long-standing
personal relationships with the most senior executives
(as with Michel Staeb and PDG Pineau-Valencienne of
Schneider).

The composition of such a heterogeneous management
team changes in accordance with the tasks at hand and
the resulting corporate agenda. Occasions for intense collaboration may come with joint foreign trips, negotiations
with customers and suppliers or public appearances. It is
interesting to note that the members often co-opted *ad hoc*
do not lay claim to a permanent presence in the team. The
great strength of this approach lies in its flexibility – and in
the general wish to focus primarily on issues of substance
rather than personal ambition.

Although very few foreigners head European companies (Lindsay Owen Jones at L'Oreal, Helmut Maucher at Nestlé and Giuseppe Vita at Schering), some of the top teams are becoming increasingly international. Examples are Nestlé, Unilever, Shell and, more recently, Deutsche Bank and Volkswagen. These teams seem to fulfil the criteria for successful teamwork as defined by my colleagues Jon Katzenbach and Doug Smith in their recent book[1] – a small number of people with complementary skills who are committed to a common purpose, performance goals and approach, for which they hold themselves mutually accountable – but they fulfil them in a flexible, adaptable manner rather than in any rigid or dogmatic form.

Katzenbach and Smith found true 'teams at the top' to be very rare, particularly in the US environment due to the long-term challenges, the enormous workload of top managers and the natural individualism of top people. But this finding undoubtedly has to be amended for Europe's better-managed corporations. Despite the tendency to evaluate performance individually, the assessment of the team as a group still comes first in Europe. All in all, this is an extremely flexible system. Bertelsmann, for example, uses the team at the top model at home in Germany, but lets its American subsidiaries organize according to a strictly hierarchical CEO system in accordance with their culture. Much the same is true of Siemens, Hoechst, Schlumberger, Schneider, Unilever and Philips.

This system has its limitations, of course, especially in high-tech areas, where global markets are rapidly developing. In such environments, the time-consuming team-management style may be a serious obstacle. But there are plenty of counterexamples. It was probably not the

[1] Jon Katzenbach and Douglas Smith, *The Wisdom of Teams*, Boston, 1992.

least of Nixdorf's problems that owner Heinz Nixdorf had
pushed the company into concentrating too one-sidedly on
sales and marketing. His motto – 'Even *one* controller
is one too many' – led to a neglect of accounting and
finance, and after Nixdorf's death the company slid into
a major sales and liquidity crisis.

A factor inseparable from the team approach – perhaps its
most important aspect – is management's attitude towards
employees. Many of today's CEOs pride themselves on the
fact that they – in the tradition of the founder generation,
the Siemens, Boschs or Krupps, Leverhulmes, Philips,
Nobels and Thorns – feel personally involved with their
employees and see them more as partners in a long-term
relationship than as factors of production. It is still by no
means unusual for grandfather, father and son to work or
have worked for the same company.

This special esteem for the worker in Europe, and particularly Central Europe, is largely due to the European
tradition of education and training, which has resulted in
a considerable level of expertise in both blue-collar and
white-collar workers. Disparaging remarks, such as those
made recently by a representative of the Japanese government about the level of education and skills of American
workers, would be unlikely to occur to anyone in a discussion of European employees.

In Germany, Holland, France, Italy and Sweden, 90–95 per
cent of the adult population has completed school-leaving
qualifications. Over 70 per cent of employees have done
some sort of apprenticeship, in accordance with a European
tradition going back hundreds of years. The preponder-
ance of this dual education system means that more young
people go into vocational training than into an academic
education. It would be a pity if these proportions were to
be reversed, as appears to have been the case in Germany
since 1991. The skilled-craft tradition has produced the

specialist workers who have long been the mainstay of Central European economies.

Labour legislation – from Bismarck's social laws in 1883, via the delegation of the first workers' representatives into decision-making bodies in the Twenties, and through to the German co-determination laws of 1976 – has continuously increased employees' rights of co-determination at the corporate level. The leading members of the works councils, who often belong *de facto* to the inner circle of top management, see themselves as committed to the good of the company as a whole. Although they are usually trade union members themselves, they have on occasion opposed union demands on the grounds that they don't serve the interests of the company and its employees.

In a Europe of many variations, no country resembles the next in every detail. But in Western Europe they do share the basic pattern of *de facto* and *de jure* recognition of employees' interests, and of esteem for workers' contributions to corporate success. Indeed, many companies, not just in Germany, have pre-empted the demands of the workers' representatives over the years with voluntary social benefits. The role of workers' representatives at corporate management level, particularly in strategic decisions, is regarded in various ways in Europe, but co-determination at the workplace is universally accepted and also embedded in organization structures. The role of the trade unions, on the other hand, varies widely – from over 85 per cent worker organization in Sweden and 36 per cent in West Germany to 12 per cent in France. In general, the importance of trade unionism appears to be declining. In particular the once mighty unions of Great Britain appear – as a result of poor adaptability – to have lost for good their dominant role in society.

'Long-Leash' Management

The team approach has a direct effect on the organization structure and procedures of world-class European
companies. The process of decentralization, initiated more
than twenty-five years ago with the transition from functional to divisional organization, has made great progress
recently. With increasing globalization, product groups with
world-wide responsibility are growing in importance and
omnipotent country organizations declining. Clear examples of this can be seen at Nestlé, Unilever and Siemens.
The task of co-ordinating functional, regional and product
responsibilities lends itself to many different types of organizational solutions. But in each case, homogeneous and
self-managing business units have been formed, with largely
independent functional infrastructures and only a few activities, such as basic research and finance, remaining at
the corporate centre. These business-specific organization
units are normally relatively small, with, for example, an
average of 1,000 employees at ABB and AKZO and 3,000 to
5,000 at Siemens. So far these companies have mostly been
able to avoid building extra administrative overheads. An
absolutely classic case here is Bertelsmann, which now has
over 150 profit centres, and where headquarters expenses
amount to less than 3 per cent of sales.

Naturally, the European patchwork of, in some cases,
more than 100 subsidiaries and holdings, business units,
branches and country subsidiaries, reporting to their respective headquarters, grew historically in accordance with
different rules and priorities. However, the hybrid organization structures to which this gave rise are less random
or illogical than they might appear at first sight. One
common feature is that foreign subsidiaries are, as a rule,
miniature versions of the parent, even if – as in the case
of Glaxo, Unilever, Nestlé, Siemens and Hoechst, for

instance – operating units with world-wide overall product responsibilities are increasingly being put in place.

It is typical of these subsidiary-headquarters relationships that European top managers allow decentralized units significantly more room to manoeuvre than corporate centres in the USA or Japan normally do. In accordance with a deliberate policy of 'long-leash' management, there are relatively few written guidelines or performance targets, and reporting relationships are often not precisely defined. By contrast, many examples from my consulting experience suggest that most US managers abroad possess comprehensive policy handbooks, and that adherence to these policies is checked on a case-by-case basis by internal auditing departments. Similarly, Japanese expatriate managers often have to ask the corporate centre for approval of even quite minor details.

None the less, European companies do regularly pursue integrated strategies that require close-knit ties between parent and subsidiary. These include, for example, efforts to let individual subsidiaries grow into the role of world-class facilities for certain branches of production (as, say, with cable production at Siemens), to create group-wide Centres of Competence (such as the Belgian Johnson & Johnson subsidiary Janssen for pharmaceuticals or Johnson & Johnson Germany for tampons), or to establish world product centres (as Unilever has done for product groups such as Food, Detergents and Toiletries). In the task of designing and managing such a network – undoubtedly one of the most demanding management tasks in existence – the most successful European companies rely on a balancing act: integrating extensive local autonomy with a strong, shared corporate culture. Only an almost tangible, shared understanding of 'our way' – the widely anchored knowledge that 'that's the way we do things' – can ensure that diverse decentralized objectives and priorities combine to form a powerful whole without constant intervention based on formal rules. In companies like Daimler-Benz, Unilever, Glaxo, Schneider or Ciba-Geigy, expatriate managers of foreign subsidiaries are not handed a hard-and-fast copy of the company rules. They know the corporate culture and know how to move within it, even in a new environment.

The practice of long-leash management has, overall, been highly successful. Careful selection and development of key executives helps to generate world-wide consensus on basic issues and orientation. This attitude has less to do with detailed profit indicators than with mutually-held concepts of service, product quality, and concern for the well-being of the company as a whole. On this basis, little intervention by the corporate centre is required beyond strategic portfolio decisions. Should problems occur, it is up to the managers on site either to do the right thing, based on their own understanding of external and internal conditions, or to remember that they are, after all, at the end of some 'leash' – however long – and call for advice and support in good time. Glaxo's, Bayer's, Unilever's and Nestlé's foreign activities have certainly shown just as many deviations from business plans as those of their American and Japanese competitors, but local management had to see if it could sort the problems out independently first.

The development of these structures during the past ten years reflects a learning process. To avoid the conversion and transition problems that often occurred in the earlier introduction of divisional organizations, companies have chosen not to install new organizational structures in one fell swoop, as if unveiling a statue. Instead, the major reorganizations of the past few years – Siemens, Daimler-Benz, Hoechst, AKZO, Allianz, Nestlé, Philips and ABB – followed more of an evolutionary pattern: should further changes prove necessary because customers, suppliers or new technologies require it, then companies ought be able to make these changes without having to carry out fundamental structural reform every time. A system of 'shunting-cars' (to quote former Siemens CEO Kaske), which can be flexibly coupled and uncoupled, has replaced the previous system of rigid reorganization every ten years.

The focus of these new organizational approaches is also different. The main object was not to create new levels or boxes on an organization chart (although, of course, new structures did arise as units became smaller and self-managing). The principal aim has been to develop the framework needed for entrepreneurship: central and decentralized units were to take on the responsibility for which each was best suited, and decisions were to be made as autonomously as possible at all levels – and as closely as possible to the internal or external customer. The top priority, therefore, had to be finding the right managers, investing heavily in their development, defining jobs with a view to enhancing employees' satisfaction, and deepening long-term relationships with customers and suppliers. The enormous efforts being made in these areas by Daimler-Benz, Deutsche Bank, Shell, BSN, Grand Met and ICI are outstanding examples.

Most of the companies thus reorganized have been able to handle expansion without enlarging their senior management teams. As tasks were delegated away from the centre, the existing team at the top took on additional responsibility on administrative boards, supervisory boards, and similar bodies for newly acquired companies or restructured divisions. Following such a reorganization, Siemens no longer has six largely independent product divisions but fifteen, which all have more or less the same functional infrastructure. Two hierarchical levels have been removed. Hoechst, following a similar principle, has left the size of its management board practically unchanged, but every member is now responsible for a complete business unit and not, as was previously the case, for a limited product area, a function or a regional market. On occasion, the team at the top has even been reduced – as demonstrated by Kingfisher, Bayer and Daimler-Benz.

The 'triple responsibility' for functional, product-related and regional tasks which often developed at board level – particularly in banks – was not an accident, but a desired outcome. In combination with long-leash management at subordinate levels, this particular approach, in the opinion of Alfred Herrhausen, gave complex, large organizations the key to re-creating the classical conditions for entrepreneurial management. This approach works because the fundamentals are right: well-informed, highly qualified and well-motivated managers and employees enjoy much the same freedom of action in their own areas of responsibility as their superiors do in theirs. As a result, excessive formal supervision and detailed instructions become unnecessary.

A kind of 'management by balance sheet' has often emerged here as a control system – a skeleton framework of critical profit indicators and, perhaps, five to seven other performance indicators, such as market share, utilization, key customers, scrap rate, ingoing material prices and discount rates. The system appears superficial in comparison to the American style of auditing-based control, with its far greater variety of numbers and indicators. It is, indeed, a very different approach. Far fewer parameters are kept under observation, and even these are monitored in a fairly lax manner within established tolerance limits. The rest is left to the independent, entrepreneurial managers on site.

Embarrassing control-asserting meetings in the style of the legendary Harold Geneen at ITT – undoubtedly an extreme example even in the US – or the 'gotcha' budget and control meetings common in many other US companies are almost inconceivable in their European counterparts. Quite apart from the interpersonal problems they cause, such management 'on a short leash' has serious disadvantages. When initiative is undermined by a multitude of criteria tables and detailed control systems, it dies.

Control on a short leash demotivates people and – even if surface objectives are met – often achieves the opposite of the desired results. For example, years ago Siemens' domestic sales manager convinced his colleagues that, compared to all their competitors, they had the fewest bad customers. In actual fact, there were practically no defaulters. He believed that his performance was measured by that number, and he had achieved it – to great applause. The problem was that in the course of this 'optimization', access to new customers, and therefore growth, had fallen by the wayside. When Hermann Franz, Head Controller since 1988, took over corporate planning and development, he started immediately to get rid of the many excesses in the company's control toolkit. The result was above-average growth compared to competitors. Franz also set out to make fundamental changes in the traditional synergy-based concept of central distribution. A vertical distribution structure had not only allowed developers and production staff their own customer contacts; it took this sacrosanct Siemens dogma to absurd extremes. Today, every business unit concentrates on its own customer segments, using its own development and manufacturing resources.

Needless to say, European-type leaner control systems also have intrinsic weaknesses, felt strongly in the functional structures of old. In those days, sales knew exactly which deals to push; manufacturing optimized lot sizes, and logistics minimized inventories. It was easy to optimize functions in isolation; but it was also easy to damage the company as a whole in so doing. Integrating operations and information across all value-added stages – as, for example,

Hoechst, Sandoz and Glaxo have done – helps to remedy this.

'Balance sheet' control also has certain disadvantages as a tool for long-leash management. It offers only a periodic snapshot. Long-term investments, long-term alliances, pending warranty obligations – all these are neglected, as are the more or less unquantifiable factors, such as customer loyalty, staff qualifications, R and D potential and the advantages of proprietary distribution channels. Nevertheless, the advantages of this type of control are probably greater than its disadvantages because it promotes entrepreneurial decision-making at the site of the action. For example, the various industrial holdings of the Dutch conglomerate Begemann are basically controlled by a single indicator: monthly cash-flow. Bertelsmann, Glaxo, Air Liquide, Schneider, Nestlé, Unilever, Electrolux and Atlas-Copco also apply similar principles.

So, this 'balance sheet' approach is just like any other control system: the problems start when users forget its limitations. Such risks have increased with the advance of portfolio strategies in corporate planning, since the fixation on key products and markets inevitably lends more weight to the asset side of the balance sheet, i.e. the application of funds. The liabilities side of the balance sheet – availability of resources (and their potential) – gets easily neglected. What might R and D be able to contribute? What can a given sales channel do for us? These questions do not always get the attention they deserve.

But a rethinking process has started. Leading European companies are increasingly coming to realize that the actual bottleneck for strategic development is not capital or raw materials, but management potential. When it comes to finding the competence needed for building new businesses, for acquisitions or for developing new markets, attention is now being directed more strongly back to the right-hand side of the balance sheet (Diagram 11). The availability of resources tells you more about the feasibility of such projects than does an analysis of the application of funds side, however thorough. As GE Chairman Jack Welch has said: 'Strategy follows people.'

A few years ago, in response to a journalist's question, Hermann Franz of Siemens explained that the company had a number of interesting ideas for building its Japanese business, and had the requisite capital. From a strategic point of view, he also knew that Japan had to play a more important role in corporate policy. But the necessary management capacity simply was not available. The team was fully occupied with Europe and the US; Japan would

'Liabilities Side of the Balance Sheet': Availability and Potential of Resources

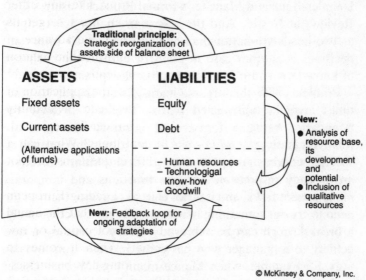

Traditional principle:
Strategic reorganization of assets side of balance sheet

ASSETS

Fixed assets

Current assets

(Alternative applications of funds)

LIABILITIES

Equity

Debt

– Human resources
– Technogigal know-how
– Goodwill

New:
● Analysis of resource base, its development and potential
● Inclusion of qualitative resources

New: Feedback loop for ongoing adaptation of strategies

© McKinsey & Company, Inc.

Diagram 11

have to wait for a few years. Meanwhile, priorities have changed. Following a major effort in the United States, Siemens has finally taken on the Japanese market.

A McKinsey analysis of the success patterns of thirty large European companies in 1991 pointed in the same direction. Wide-ranging competitive comparisons and calculation of every possible indicator and form of interdependence brought to light an unequivocal and hardly surprising result: the really decisive factor distinguishing outstandingly successful companies is good management. What matters is having good people at the right places, with the right kind of support, and with the determination and motivation to achieve above-average results. The key factor here is the successful combination of the hard and soft elements of management, and the soft ones seem to be particularly well developed in Europe. Bernhard Plettner's factory visits at Siemens are legendary. So are Reuter's budget meetings at Daimler-Benz and Maucher's formal Product Business Unit Reviews at Nestlé. And the way many major banks apply a 'two-heads-are-better-than-one' process in all important decisions is another case in point: it ensures the exchange of know-how and information across disciplines.

Problems with this organic management approach sometimes arise in unexpected places. Precisely because the boundaries between formal and informal structures are relatively fuzzy, the *ad hoc* use of interdisciplinary, project-specific working groups is often difficult. Many executives are already responsible for line functions and temporary management tasks, and it is not easy to convince them of the need to try out something fundamentally new. Occasionally, a breakthrough can be achieved only by entrusting a new activity to a manager who has come in fresh from outside – as, for example, when Mannesmann boss Werner Dieter undertook the diversification of the mobile telephone business in collaboration with Peter Mihatsch.

These problems, however, are never insuperable, and the benefits of temporary structures may be so high that the effort is definitely worth it. *Ad hoc* projects and special tasks – such as have been carried out by Daimler-Benz and Hoechst in the course of reorganization over the past few years – are important not least as an excellent learning ground for junior managers. To that end, the special assignments must go beyond the normal areas of accountability of the employee concerned. Examples are the review of planned deliveries to trouble spots for possibilities of misuse, or planning and directing the construction of a new plant.

Such special tasks do not free managers from normal day-to-day business: they are a temporary additional burden. Where they are performed with drive and motivation, they bring, as a rule, a great deal of official recognition. A temporary project manager will be invited to present his or her interim results at a board meeting, and the reports get circulated. Participation in special training sessions or unscheduled promotions can also be effective ways of saying that 'informal' tasks are important within a company. On the other hand, over-close supervision will aid neither progress nor motivation. Even if the project manager is based at headquarters, he should not have top management continually looking over his shoulder. There are many examples of superiors getting so much on the nerves of development project managers by continually asking about product introduction that a suboptimum product resulted. Here, too, long-leash management is a sign of trust and an encouragement to have self-confidence.

Most of the Europreneurs' generation know how to handle this informality. This is how Siemens came by its new multiplexing technique and how it built its Egyptian business, how Mercedes implemented its new production facility at Rastatt, and how AKZO reoriented its business structure. And it is how Ulrich Cartellieri of Deutsche Bank was able to establish his own IT systems solution for the Treasury Division without waiting for the company-wide IT architecture to be ready for introduction.

Only where such special projects and special paths are accepted and rewarded does the readiness to give commitment above the norm become widespread. Such a culture will not develop spontaneously in traditionally hierarchical European corporate structures, but it is all the more important that it does develop since most of these companies lack formal executive development. Exact ideas or plans for what Manager X or Y has to do to acquire the skills he or she will need in future positions usually do not exist.

To fill that gap, informal structures can be invaluable – for example, if an executive can broaden his or her experience as the manager of a foreign subsidiary or as a member of the supervisory board of a newly acquired domestic subsidiary. Such jobs are more likely to occur *ad hoc* than to be planned in any targeted manner. Naturally, they are more useful if they fit into individual development plans or when members of top management adopt the role of mentors to younger managers.

Implicit teaching by example, of course, goes on all the time. The way in which the personalities at the top allocate their time, which trips they make, and how they treat each other, influence the development of the upcoming generation. For example, when Mark Wössner of Bertelsmann recently spent a considerable part of his time with new acquisitions Bantam and Doubleday Dell in the US, he was giving a clear sign of how important it was to understand new markets, new customers and new competitors. Similarly, Alex Krauer of Ciba-Geigy also demonstrates clearly which issues are top priority when in divisional strategy meetings he constantly encourages his colleagues to raise the level of aspiration for a high-tech company.

More direct instructions are also occasionally available. Alfred Herrhausen repeatedly called for 'error-free thinking' – that is, calling on his people not to be always right, but to think through every aspect of an issue meticulously in a disciplined fashion. Edzard Reuter probably has the same thing in mind when he occasionally returns proposals or memoranda at Tuesday board meetings with the request to 'go back to the drawing board'. Exercises like this have a twofold purpose: solving the problem at hand better, and reinforcing the learning process in executive development.

Many of the best companies, such as British Airways, Schneider or Deutsche Bank, have put in place staff positions attached to the Chairman of the Board or other board members which offer excellent learning opportunities. Nowhere can an understanding of key corporate issues and of co-operation within the top team be better acquired than in collaboration on staff papers and participation in discussing them at board meetings. After a few years in such staff functions, the post-holders normally have the chance of moving on to attractive line positions.

A different, though related, aspect of the long-leash concept has to do with the arrangements for management succession. All the potential candidates have normally worked for a long time at senior levels, and have also gained wide-ranging line experience, often in at least one subsidiary. They have proved themselves in teamwork and know the advantages of collegial leadership compared to a hierarchical presidential style. In preparation for the next career step they are often assigned a particularly difficult special project at group level, be it the negotiation of an important alliance or the turnaround of a stubbornly loss-making division. And they are judged not least by how they prepare their own succession.

What the rising talents have to prove in all this – and what every participant in the long-leash concept internalizes –

is the pre-eminent importance of communication and, by extension, the futility of the old 'command and control' principle.

Technology as a Base

Many established European companies owe their origins to inventions by their founders. At Daimler-Benz the feeling still lingers that the invention of the car by Gottlieb Daimler and Carl Benz more than 100 years ago was the start of the company. The same applies to the electrical engineering inventions which started Bosch, Siemens, Philips, Nobel and Thorn, or the chemical and pharmaceutical inventions which fuelled the development of ICI, Solvay, Rhône-Poulenc, BASF and many European pharmaceutical companies. This technology base is expressed in many European companies by the anchoring of technological know-how in top management, in employee attitudes and in important management practices.

Up to a few years ago it would have been unthinkable for a non-chemist successfully to lead a chemical company or a non-engineer an electrical company. BASF, Bayer and Hoechst were no different in this respect from Solvay, Rhône-Poulenc or ICI. This situation has now changed. Characteristically, it only took one break with tradition at Bayer and BASF, for example, for non-chemists to be appointed CEO in the following generation as well (Strube after Albers at BASF; Schneider after Strenger at Bayer). Even so, technological know-how is usually embedded in the executive committee or management board in the form of high-ranking divisional and R and D managers. Moreover, even the 'non-techies' have acquired a great deal of basic technical and product-related knowledge over the years so that they can effectively represent the technology base of the company internally and externally.

In countries such as Great Britain and Sweden, there is a movement back toward giving the technology base key importance. After years in which generalists were on the march in Sweden and financial directors and controllers called the tune in the UK, companies like LM Ericsson, ABB and Atlas Copco are being praised for their engineering orientation in Sweden, and Racal, GKN and Lucas for a return to their 'technology base' in the UK.

In personnel management, technology orientation often means that selection, training and deployment of staff across all functional areas is oriented *primarily* to technical product and manufacturing requirements. The dual education system (school *and* a practical apprenticeship) practised in Germany, Austria and Switzerland has supported this orientation. It has also laid the groundwork for making technical competence a prime criterion for promotion. In France, the Netherlands, Belgium and Denmark, too, the relatively high share of GNP represented by the manufacturing sector is evidence of a technology dominance that goes back for generations. If you discuss these companies with a random sample of their employees, as a customer, a trade fair visitor, or even as a fellow passenger on flights or train journeys, you will repeatedly be amazed at how much emphasis is placed on the technical aspects of products and manufacturing processes. Everyone genuinely believes that better products, better-quality production and technically superior service, provide a competitive advantage that is hard to rival.

Liebherr Senior, at his company in Biberach with sales of DM4 billion, until shortly before his death, worked intensely with his design engineers on every detail of new truck cranes and refrigerators, and spent a considerable amount of time visiting production facilities and making suggestions for new configurations. His obsession with straight production flows, modern units and clean workshops (an original

Liebherr quotation: 'The way your workplace looks reflects the way the inside of your head looks') was representative of the attitude of many European industrialists.

In such an atmosphere it is no surprise that management practices such as the following are widespread:

☐ Virtually constant expenditure on research and development. Rates of 3–5 per cent of sales in the automotive industry, 6–8 per cent in electrical engineering and 7–10 per cent in chemicals lead the world. What is more, it is practically inconceivable for such R and D spending to expand and contract at the mercy of cyclical ups and downs in the economy (as was happening at Square D recently before its takeover by Schneider).

☐ Regular, relatively high depreciation on plant and equipment (approximately 5 per cent at manufacturers of capital goods). The thesis current at Siemens is that this depreciation has to be earned and that investments have to be made all over the world in order to remain competitive.

☐ Ongoing rationalization in production and closely related areas such as materials management and logistics. This is reflected in business plans as annual rationalization objectives of 2–3 per cent. Broad-based suggestion systems usually support these efforts towards continuous improvement on a day-to-day basis.

☐ New products/production techniques as an overriding corporate goal. Comments such as '60 per cent of products are less than five years old' (Siemens) or 'the production facilities of today have nothing in common with those of the Seventies' (BMW) reflect the importance of technical innovation in products and production processes. Top management attention is focused on new products and technologies, as is evident from the agendas of their meetings, visits, publications and high-profile actions.

This strong technology base has quite a few positive effects. For example:

☐ The possibility of expanding a business on the basis of leading-edge technologies. Examples include: Bertelsmann's printing technologies in the US, BOSS textile manufacturing in the US and Bayer's production of galenic products in the US.

☐ The opportunity to acquire companies with a weaker technology base. (Examples include: Siemens/Plessey, Daimler-Benz/Freightliner, Schneider/Square D and ABB/ Combustion Engineering.)

☐ Few product failures because new products are developed on the basis of proven in-house technological know-how.

☐ The primary attention of the whole organization focused on the actual source of its competitive advantage.

☐ A constant customer- or life cycle-orientation of the product or system offered.

At the same time, however, there are some negative effects:

☐ A hardware orientation is dominant and with it, frequently, a commitment to traditional technologies.

☐ 'Quality' predominates in development and manufacturing; 'time' and 'cost', which are equally important objectives, tend to be neglected.

☐ Radically new products are rarely developed, particularly in high-tech areas. Incrementalism rules.

Overall, however, building on a sound technology base is a remarkable strength of European companies. It keeps corporate awareness of their origins alive and thus, implicitly, an awareness of company-specific opportunities and limitations. Each company knows which business areas it masters and where it can contribute outstanding competence to new acquisitions. But it also knows that unrelated diversification does not make much sense.

Lessons from Politics

We live in the age of communication. What companies do – and don't do – is the subject of public interest, the more so as the corporation has increasingly become the last institution in modern society still undisputedly in working order. Internal and external communication has thus become a key top-management task. Behind this is not a growing vanity of the people at the top or the beginnings of a personality cult, but the imperative need to inform, convince and motivate a large number of stakeholders of widely varying origins. Management, especially in the major companies headed by Europreneurs, is happening less and less behind closed doors. As Helmut Maucher says, it is crucial to manage a company in such a way that 'everything you do could be published in the newspapers tomorrow'.

Management tasks are coming more and more to include politics as well. Accordingly, many of the tools and techniques of political decision-making and leadership can be very beneficially transferred to the management of large industrial companies. This applies to the need for in-house consensus-building as well as to that of generating public understanding and of securing the broadest possible information base for complex decisions.

In the Sixties, it was still possible for a Daimler-Benz R and D director to present a new car model to his colleagues as a *fait accompli*. A certain amount of information about customer wishes and competitors' developments might have gone into the design process, but design engineering was the province of the development department. That was where it was done. Ideas from 'outside' were neither desired nor, it was thought, useful or necessary. Now that has all changed – ecological, economic and marketing needs are integrated early into the design process. So are concerns about fuel consumption, environment friendliness, the recyclability of materials and the corresponding manufacturing processes and costs. As a result, the number of opinions and discussion partners to be consulted has grown. The head of Mercedes and his team spend around four to six weeks every year testing new variants themselves, discussing them with design engineers, analysing competing models and speaking to customers.

To prevent endless discussion and agreement processes from becoming a mechanism to prevent decision-making, managers have learned – from politics among other sources – to sound out opinions, anticipate expectations, and to form the internal and external coalitions necessary to expedite decisions. They have also learned from politics, which is the art of the possible, that a well-defined problem is half the solution, that it is possible to say no without slamming the door, that issues of content can be separated from people issues, and that commonalities have to be explored across functional or corporate borders. In addition, they have learned how to take advantage of a global network of branches and subsidiaries all over the world, which can be an invaluable source of information. Their importance to the corporate centre can certainly be compared to that of the embassies and consulates of sovereign states.

Properly integrated, these international networks ensure that problems and critical decisions are surfaced and effective counteraction initiated long before damage can occur. But to achieve this it is essential to maintain contact properly, to show understanding and a readiness to support local initiatives. It is also essential to be prepared when foreign outposts become 'lightning rods' for political aggression that is actually directed against the company's home government, as has happened, for example, to airlines and major banks.

Instruments from politics that have proved effective in management include task forces, committees and commissions. Relevant, too, is the ability to identify key stakeholders in good time and to win them over to one's own side. In-house factions -- and occasionally external interests -- have to be won over for important investment projects. Sometimes staff and line have to be played off against one another or opinions on critical issues tested in confidential discussions before they appear on the official agenda. Messages to the company's own organization can be usefully reinforced by public statements (Alfred Herrhausen was a master of this art). Politics has also taught the industrialists that in corporate decision-making it can be necessary to separate the ethics of personal opinion from those of professional responsibility. That detachment, along with a sense of proportion, are essential characteristics not only of professional politicians, but to a large extent of businessmen as well.

The fact that the techniques resemble each other so closely should be no surprise. In management, as in the world of politics, problems are not solved 'here and now' by sheer force. Solutions have to mature slowly, through discussion, trial and error, and gradual consensus building. I recently saw plans for an undoubtedly useful alliance between a German and an American company fail to materialize because the American partner demanded a decision too abruptly.

Naturally, using the political model also entails risks. The endless debates common in politics and the constant search for diluted compromises can paralyse corporate life. If, as often happens in politics, meetings, papers, working groups become an end in themselves and lose sight of implementation, it can mean creeping death for companies. Statements on political themes can also be a trap for the manager. Musings on social issues, publicly voiced by leaders of industry with supposedly an unlimited scope of action, are easily misunderstood as definitions of business policy. Hence Helmut Maucher, for example, warned against arousing impossible expectations by public discussions of business ethics.

Corporate leaders who expose themselves to the public with demands or critical comments can easily find themselves in a cross-fire of criticism. One only has to think of Jacques Calvet's call to protect the European automotive industry from Japanese competition, or Agnelli's and de Benedetti's comments on conditions in Italy. Such risks have to be dispassionately assessed. So, too, does the danger that an overly 'political' management style will turn into endless consensus-seeking or agreement on the lowest common denominator, leaving no scope for courageous, future-oriented decisions, and blocking urgently needed changes. A tendency to minimize risk instead of unlocking potential is inevitably coupled with political methods. And, finally, there is the problem of bureaucracy running riot, which is always latent in large companies, and will certainly not be reduced by borrowing from politics.

But these risks are manageable. Good top managers know how to avoid them and still adopt the most helpful methods from political practice – for instance, in strategic alliances between multinational companies, which are increasingly assuming the character of government treaties. Such agreements cover a much broader area than earlier patent and licence agreements or sales co-operations, as demonstrated for example by the 'treaties' between Siemens and Matsushita, Volvo and Renault, Swissair and SAS, Daimler-Benz and Mitsubishi. To the managers responsible for these alliances, one major aim is to stimulate competition between their internal functions, which often do not operate in the market.

The highly visible Daimler-Mitsubishi alliance, for instance, leaves a very great deal of scope for detailed development, but provides a basis for such varied common activities as the distribution of Mercedes cars in Japan, international purchasing of parts and components, the building of an administrative centre in Berlin, the design of Japanese diesel engines for German commercial vehicles, manufacturing, shared developments in factory automation and the mutual utilization of production plants.

Obviously, these alliances follow on from a European industrial tradition. Many companies, such as Siemens, have long had friendly links with other companies. These 'corporate friends' could be counted on when problems occurred. One of Siemens' long-standing friends is Daimler-Benz. Even since Daimler's takeover of direct competitor AEG, the management boards have still visited one another twice a year. The board of Lufthansa, too, meets once a year with that of Air France. In France, the connecting bond is membership of influential clubs such as 'Le Siècle', 'La Fondation Saint-Simon', or 'Echange et Projets'; in Great Britain it is the old boy network in the boards of the major companies.

The European tradition lies in institutional co-operation or at least co-existence, rather than in fierce competition of the kind typical in the American or Japanese domestic markets. In dealing with competitors, but also with suppliers, 'live and let live' has been more the rule than the exception. Stable long-term relationships traditionally have priority over short-term, one-sided advantage. Companies know that the competitor of today may be the potential partner of tomorrow, and that targeted mutual exchange of information ultimately benefits all concerned. The comment by former Volkswagen CEO Carl H. Hahn, that he would rather co-operate than compete with Japanese manufacturers in the huge Chinese market, illustrates this attitude. This is the only way Volkswagen can become the dominant supplier in the People's Republic of China by the year 2000.

But the new alliances do introduce a new quality of co-operation. They institutionalize partnership in their area of application, which as a rule is defined very broadly and unspecifically. At the same time, the partners are unrestricted competitors outside the joint project. For example, the co-operation between Bosch and Siemens in the area of household appliances does not alter the fact that they are direct competitors in car electrics and electronics. Saab-Scania co-operates with General Motors in the area of trucks, but is an intense competitor of GM's subsidiary Opel in the car business. Volvo and Renault, prior to their recent merger, had a history of co-operation in commercial vehicles but competition in cars.

The architects of these new alliances have learned a great deal from experience with earlier ones, but above all from the much older history of alliances between sovereign states. They know, for example, how much time and effort is required to make these partnerships grow and flourish. They know how much commitment they personally have to invest in the process. Trust between companies, as between states, does not happen overnight. And even defining the contents of a co-operative agreement relatively precisely is not necessarily helpful here. What visionary corporate

leaders decide is one thing, but what their functional departments make of it is often quite another. At subordinate
levels, the partners on the other side are often still regarded
– and treated – mainly as competition. An off-road vehicle
designer at Mercedes-Benz still thinks it is a nightmare to
use Japanese design engineering work. He is not alone.

The agreement between Daimler-Benz and General Electric to collaborate in aircraft engines encountered problems
in a different area. The co-operation only referred to a
small section of the areas of activity of the two companies.
In parallel, General Electric was free to sound out the
possibilities of co-operation with other manufacturers in
France and Great Britain. When it did so, Daimler–Benz
regarded the future of its own co-operation with GE as so
shaky that it decided to look around for another partner,
and eventually made a deal with United Technologies. If
the GE alliance had been more broadly defined from the
start, it might have ended differently.

In contrast, the more recent Daimler–Mitsubishi alliance
happily grants the Japanese partner the right to continue its
relationship with Chrysler and even to enter a new one with
Volvo. Daimler–Benz, in turn, is completely free to explore
the possibilities of a new relationship with United Technologies in the aerospace sector. The Daimler-Mitsubishi
alliance is unaffected by such actions, since it is very
long-term in focus and so broadly designed that the other
activities do not threaten its basic substance.

'As Well As' Management

Maintaining partnerships on many sides without offending
any of them is undoubtedly one of the major tasks of
today's top managers. And what applies to external relationships has its direct counterpart within a company.

Barely a single rule remains unchanged across the entire breadth of a business or for any length of time. The top managers of today have to understand that they are the parents of many gifted children, every one of which has its own needs – and that those needs are significantly different from what the top managers themselves experienced in their earlier fields of responsibility.

No newly-appointed CEO can expect the patterns of behaviour and success he could rely on during his own rise to power to remain valid in the new environment. During the first months of Mark Wössner's leadership of Bertelsmann AG, for example, there were fears that he would approach the management of publishers, book clubs, magazines and the music business in the same way that had worked so well for him in the printing industry. But it soon became evident that these fears were unfounded. After intensive analyses of the corporate culture of all of Bertelsmann's individual divisions, and after extensive customer contacts, Wössner soon surprised divisional experts with searching questions (*the* best top-management technique, in actual fact) about their businesses. The emphasis here is on the word 'soon'. Top managers learn fast that they have to differentiate. Different businesses require different approaches.

As little as ten or fifteen years ago, most large European companies had in-house rules for top-management decision-making. Everyone knew, for example, that 'we do not grow by acquisition' or that 'we develop a new model by following a specific sequence of steps'. It was clear to everyone that 'only internal careers lead to the top here', that 'we only accept contracts which give us a certain minimum margin', and that 'we sell only through our own distribution network'. Many of these kinds of rules have lost their universal validity over time. Increasingly, people have come to realize how much damage rigid adherence to dogmatic principles can do. There were, for example, huge

opportunity costs incurred by Siemens during the many
years it refused, out of habit and principle, to make acquisitions, until Karlheinz Kaske radically changed the rules.

Anyone preparing to occupy a top position in one of
these companies must have a well-developed instinct for
the specific differences between various divisions – and for
the management methods that best suit each particular environment. Being able to judge which rules and measures are
valid for the entire company and which are not is a critical
part of the learning process of a successful top manager.
Are there countries where we need to be present, or where
we absolutely should not be present? Are there products we
want nothing to do with? Are there potential allies we do
not want to do business with? Knowing the answers to
these questions is of crucial importance. And it is no less
important to know when the time has come to adjust any
one of those answers in the light of new conditions.

Corporate managers cannot remain immune to the changes
to which the world, as we all know, is now more than ever
subject. What is more, they must help to shape and drive
the changes if they want to do their jobs properly. Deutsche
Bank's entry into investment banking by its acquisition of
Morgan Grenfell did not accord with business tradition, but
is an important part of the bank's future activities. The
same applies to Daimler-Benz's diversification into traffic
systems, Siemens' decision to go into the leasing of local
area networks, AKZO's move to enter a co-operative agreement with Bayer, and LM Ericsson's decision to co-operate
with General Electric on mobile telephones. All these steps
would have appeared more or less inconceivable just ten
years ago.

The strategic pattern now emerging is that, largely because of increased fixed costs, alliances and other forms of
co-operation are increasingly being concluded in upstream
activities (research, product and production development),

while the same companies remain – quite visibly – competitors in downstream activities (sales, marketing, service).

For European top managers these changes can be reduced to a common denominator: 'as well as' has become significantly more important than 'either/or'. In the world of top management, categorical yes/no decisions – this is the way it is now and ever shall be – are not really possible. What is needed is the skill and the readiness to pursue a mixed bundle of solutions in parallel, depending on the situation. This new 'as well as' management practice – which also has a long tradition in political leadership – has a wide range of practical consequences. Companies used to have the choice of developing required technology in-house or outsourcing it. Today, the question is quite different. The technological spectrum has spread so widely that in-house development across the board cannot be financed. For example, Daimler-Benz employs over 9,000 people in car development, but the company also buys development services from Porsche's development centre in Weissach. One thing *as well as* the other.

In some R and D projects development work is sequential, in others a multi-pronged approach is adopted. Jürgen Schrempp, the head of DASA, has invented the ingenious technique of having 'red' and 'blue' teams competing in upstream development, and of having development work performed at Dornier *and* MBB. Siemens also acts on the 'as well as' principle: in the traditional area of electrical engineering, development is performed sequentially at one location, but development of new PABXs is being done in parallel in Florida and Munich until shortly before assembly.

The list of examples could be greatly expanded. Stand-alone solutions for task-specific data-processing systems exist side by side with the uniform corporate system at Deutsche Bank. Parts are made in-house but also sourced at Bosch. Part-time employees work extensively alongside full-timers at Siemens' Berlin dynamo plant. At Shell and BP, an efficient in-house logistics system does not exclude the possibility of using other transporters extensively. Greenfield internal expansion is on an equal footing with acquisition at Nestlé and Unilever. While pursuing a go-it-alone policy in some markets, Volkswagen and Nissan enter alliances in other fields. Products are made under a company's own name, but also for other companies, as with Bosch's car batteries.

Uninhibited discussion with competitors at trade fairs, in trade associations, at social functions is also typical for Europe. It should not be regarded – as Americans sometimes presume – as a subtle form of price fixing or of cartel-like behaviour. A salesman from BSHG would never dream of leaving a restaurant when a salesman from Electrolux arrives. But American practice would expect just that of a GE representative encountering a Westinghouse representative in a bar.

The tendency to work with, rather than against, one another is the typically European response to an increasingly complex environment. Today many of the old either/or boundaries – between business friends and competitors, for example – can no longer be so clearly drawn. What is needed is an integrated and flexible response, one that keeps open the entire treasure chest of possible solutions to the most varied problems and questions. Percy Barnevik sums up: 'At ABB we are dealing with three internal contradictions: We want to be global and local, large and small, decentralized and centralized at the same time.'[1]

'One right way' is neither a reasonable nor a realistic goal. Europreneurs accept that there are a number of legitimate courses to follow, each of which has advantages

[1] 'The Logic of Global Business', in *Harvard Business Review*, March–April 1991.

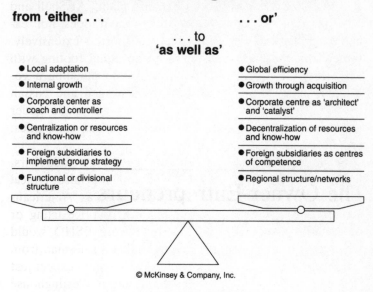

Change in top management task

from 'either . . .   **. . . or'**

**. . . to
'as well as'**

from 'either . . .	. . . or'
● Local adaptation	● Global efficiency
● Internal growth	● Growth through acquisition
● Corporate center as coach and controller	● Corporate centre as 'architect' and 'catalyst'
● Centralization or resources and know-how	● Decentralization of resources and know-how
● Foreign subsidiaries to implement group strategy	● Foreign subsidiaries as centres of competence
● Functional or divisional structure	● Regional structure/networks

© McKinsey & Company, Inc.

Diagram 12

under certain circumstances. 'As well as' management is a reservoir of options for action, a holistic framework within which corporate management moves (Diagram 12). Yes, juggling with such variety can be chaotic. But normally there is enough room to manoeuvre in companies to cope with the chaos. Particularly in times of rapid change, the European tradition of unity in variety – not in theory but in actual day-to-day practice – has a lot of advantages.

V

The Owner-Entrepreneurs

More than fifty Europreneurs, outstanding leaders at the top of big companies, are a considerable asset to Europe. The sales of Shell, Daimler-Benz and Nestlé alone totalled more than Denmark's GDP in 1992, and the capital expenditures of the largest fifty European companies outstrip the government spending of industrialized countries like Switzerland and Belgium. But the new momentum that these entrepreneurs have injected into Eurocapitalism since the mid-Eighties goes far beyond the importance-by-bulk of their companies. They serve as a role model for many others.

That is a good thing, for most of the economic landscape of Europe is made up of a huge, vaguely defined group of 'mid-sized' companies. They played a major part in the upturn during the second half of the Eighties. Big-company Europreneurs pointed the way for them and gave them encouragement. That may, in fact, have been their

Great Importance of Mid-Sized Companies in Europe

Economic structure of EC countries, 1986
per cent

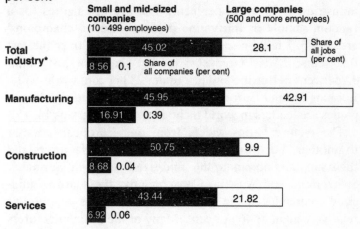

* Excluding primary sectors
Source: EC Directorate General XXIII, 1991

© McKinsey & Company, Inc.

Diagram 13

greatest contribution to overcoming Eurosclerosis.

In Western Germany, mid-sized companies – officially defined as companies employing between ten and 499 people – account for approximately 15 per cent of all employers and far more than half of all jobs. Eight out of ten new jobs created during the past few years have been in those companies. This picture seems to be the rule rather than the exception in Europe. Although EC statistics are still very scanty, they do show that in 1986 only one in a thousand firms was a 'large corporation' with 500 or more employees, and that almost half of all jobs were concentrated in the mid-sized firms, which accounted for just under 9 per cent of all companies (Diagram 13).

Better known, and even more impressive, are the figures on the somewhat larger companies that still count as mid-sized. As Professor Hermann Simon[1] found, the best of these in Germany have world market shares in their industries of 70 to 90 per cent. The average figures for a random sample of thirty-nine of these 'hidden champions' are: DM527 million sales; 16 per cent growth over the last five years; 2,904 employees; market shares of just under 32 per cent in Europe and just under 23 per cent world-wide. Looking around Europe, quite a number of mid-sized companies are leaders in world niche markets (Diagrams 14, 15).

The picture varies widely from one European country to another. For example, capital goods manufacturers and their suppliers dominate the 'mid-sized' sector in Germany, Switzerland and Austria. Consequently, the share of mid-sized companies in the secondary sector of the economy is relatively high, at 46 per cent. Many of these manufacturers are moving away from stand-alone products and towards systems and integrated solutions. As a rule, their R and D spending as a percentage of sales is as high as that of large companies.

In France, the mid-sized company culture is based on sound engineering know-how and the country's traditional strengths in consumer goods, particularly luxury goods. The French mid-sized companies also follow the example of the 'big guys': they do relatively little R and D and concentrate on consumer-related products. In Italy, the mid-sized companies have a strong grip on the textile industry, luxury goods, and the vast majority of retailing, catering and skilled trades. Despite the frequently voiced supposition that they have two sets of books, these companies have for years accounted for over 90 per cent of the corporate income taxes paid in the country.

[1] Hermann Simon, 'Hidden Champions – Speerspitze der deutschen Wirtschaft', in *Zeitschrift für Betriebswirtschaft*, 60th year, H.9/1990, 875–890.

International German Mid-Sized Companies, 1991

Companies	Products	Total sales DM mill.	Share of exports (%)
Andreas Stihl, Waiblingen	Motor saws	705	85
Trumpf, Ditzingen	Machine tools	555	53
Heidelberger Druckmaschinen, Heidelberg	Printing machinery	2,747	72
Körber*, Hamburg	Cigarette vending machines	578	86
Festo, Esslingen-Berkheim	Pneumatic products	≈ 1,000	55
Alfred Kärcher, Winnenden	Cleaning machinery	1,003	57
Meyer*, Papenburg	Dockyard	≈ 500	86
Weinig, Tauberbischoffsheim	Woodworking machinery	325	66
Sieper-Werke, Lüdenscheid/Müsen	Toy cars/mirrored wardrobes	200	35
Bizerba-Werke, Balingen	Electric scales	356	36
Westfalia Separator AG, Oelde	Separators	656	61
Hille & Müller, Düsseldorf	Battery cases	240	50

* 1990 figures

Source: Dafne, Creditreform, Textline, Hoppenstedt, Annual reports, McKinsey estimates

© McKinsey & Company, Inc.

Diagram 14

A Selection of International Mid-Sized Companies, 1991

Company (product)	Total sales DM mill.	Share of exports (%)
(F)		
BIC (Writing materials)	1,679	75
LVMH (Luxury goods)	6,500	80
Club Med (Vacation clubs)	2,327	76
Salomon (Sports gear)	766	93
Fabre (Pharmaceuticals)	530	10
(CH)		
Logitech (Computer moval)	243	94
Habasit (Converging systems)	230	74
Elco-Looser (Heating systems)	670	69
(I)		
Marzotto (Fashion/Textiles)	1,715	50
Fininvest [Berlusconi]* (Television/Media)	≈ 10,000	≈ 20
Benetton* (Clothes retailing)	≈ 2,700	≈ 90
Fochi (Engineering)	2,400	≈ 60
(GB)		
Body Shop (Natural cosmetics)	340	37
Carlton* (Television/Video)	2,199	30
Amstrad* (Electronics)	1,633	>50

Company (product)	Total sales DM mill.	Share of exports (%)
(NL)		
Heineken (Beer)	7,717	>90
Indivers* (Aircraft parts/maintenance)	148	>80
(A)		
Lenzing* (Chemicals [Cellulose])	834	74
Swarovski* (Glass/Optics)	865	84
(B)		
Saluc* (Billard balls)	22	97
Bekaert (Steel wire)	2,500	>40
(S)		
IKEA (Furniture)	≈ 7,000	≈ 80
(DK)		
Lego (Toys)	1,163	98
(SF)		
Kone (Elevators)	4,215	90
(N)		
Frank Mohn (Marine pumps)	≈ 200	≈ 80

* 1990 figures

Source: Dafne, Creditreform, Textline, Hoppenstedt, Annual reports, McKinsey estimates

Diagram 15

© McKinsey & Company, Inc.

In Britain, as in the US, the many successful start-ups in the service sector and consumer-goods production are impressive. By contrast, the classic privately owned industrial companies once numbering in their thousands (150 years ago, London boasted over 4,000 such companies, some with substantial manufacturing output), have largely been bought up or have vanished. The same applies in Sweden, where the once-powerful mid-sized, family-owned industrial companies have more or less disappeared.

Many of today's 'mid-sized' are actually quite large. Some such market leaders, as Liebherr in cranes – although long past the DM3 billion sales mark – prefer to describe themselves as mid-sized companies with a strong technology base. Freudenberg, one of the world's biggest suppliers of high-performance textiles and non-woven materials, regards itself as a 'federation of mid-sized companies'. Even Bosch, with sales of over DM30 billion, likes to think of itself as mid-sized because of its many mid-sized-type business units.

Germany has mid-sized companies to thank for much of its export surplus, and non-Europeans increasingly perceive European mid-sized companies as possible models for their own industry structures. Many of the traditional American mid-sized companies, which, like those in Europe, were family-owned for generations, have given up due to high inheritance taxes and the opportunities to go public and make a killing. Today, 12 per cent of the workplaces and 54 per cent of jobs in the US are in the mid-sized category. Most prominent are service businesses and high-tech start-ups like Microsoft, which now has one of the largest market capitalizations in all of US industry. The once characteristic feature of the Midwest – thousands of small and mid-sized family enterprises – has undergone quite a transformation. Today, large smokestack companies dominate the 'rust belt'.

The American magazine *Business Week* and management writer Tom Peters have argued that the German mid-sized company culture is a model from which America's underdeveloped export industry could learn more than from Japan's trading and industrial groups.

Japan has a particularly dynamic mid-sized company culture: 98 per cent of all companies are small or medium-sized and employ 58 per cent of the working population. There are around 180,000 new start-ups and 40,000 closures every year, on average. As suppliers, these companies play a key part in the impact of the famous global firms. They often hold dominant positions, particularly in the distribution system and as the source of high-performance

Personnel Cost of Automotive Manufacturers and Suppliers

Level of direct wage costs and agreed social benefits
(Index, 1990)

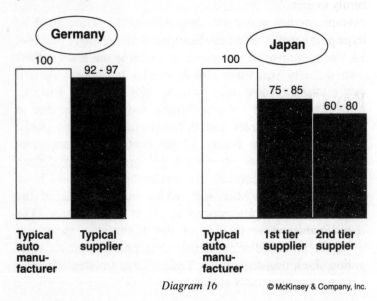

Diagram 16   © McKinsey & Company, Inc.

manufacturing technology. Stable relationships with customers (suppliers 'by appointment to' Toyota or Mitsubishi are rarely changed), coupled with regional tax advantages, afford these companies a certain amount of security. Compared to their European counterparts, they are much more dependent on key customers and they concentrate mainly on the Japanese domestic market.

The position of employees in these companies is relatively poor. Many smaller Japanese companies do not have trade unions. Some have working conditions which in Europe would bring the trade supervisory bodies down on their heads. Benefits such as holiday and training are virtually non-existent, which makes their strong work ethic particularly hard for Europeans to understand. Moreover, the typical mid-sized employer in the Western European industrialized countries offers (due, in part, to collective-bargaining structures) wages and social benefits similar to those of big business. In Japan, however, they are significantly lower. Workers at Japanese automotive suppliers, for example, receive wages that are only 60 to 85 per cent of the large companies' compensation levels (Diagram 16).

Key Characteristics

What are the typical characteristics of these mid-size European companies? The most conspicuous appear to be these:

1. *Family ownership*, mostly in the second or third generation, with the guiding corporate objective to *retain independence* – even in large companies like Boehringer Ingelheim or Diehl, with annual sales of over DM3 billion. Despite large family trees with many ramifications (e.g. Springer, Mohn, Bahlsen, Michelin, Boehringer

Ingelheim and Boehringer Mannheim), such companies' independence is rarely negotiable. Maximizing market value is usually not a management goal.

2. *Management by the owners* and/or by extremely competent general managers who have 'grown with' the company over the years. Owners play an important part in the running of a business, not by right of birth, but by demonstrated competence.

3. *A technology base* that secures competitive advantages for a product or a manufacturing process. In many cases, this technology base goes back to inventions by the founder of the firm. The strong role it plays in the corporate culture is illustrated by the heavy emphasis on technical competence in management and in the selection and training of employees. Normally, the 'transmission belt' between new developments and market introduction is very short.

4. *'Simple' organizational structures* ensuring high flexibility and competitive costs. Owner-managed companies rarely have more than four levels of management.

5. *International orientation* – usually through exports – which has frequently led to dominant positions in individual niches. As with larger firms, these Europeans are born exporters.

6. *Strong employee orientation* (skilled workers), guaranteeing high product quality. Employee loyalty derives not least from substantial investment in staff motivation and ongoing training. The companies' implicit contract across worker generations builds on solid apprentice training, and also integrates pensioners very actively into company life.

Bertelsmann of Gütersloh is a family firm which is a role model for many others. The visionary Reinhard Mohn was the third generation of his family to take it on, upon his return from captivity after the Second World War (1947). At that time, it was a fairly insignificant publishing house with its own printing operations. This particular case is an excellent example of how 'mid-sized companies' are transformed into major ones. Path-breaking ideas (setting up book clubs to distribute books, entering the magazine business), constant insistence on high product quality and unparalleled expansion initiated by young managers made Bertelsmann one of the largest media companies in the world within ten years of Mohn's taking the reins.

When the extremely self-disciplined Reinhard Mohn moved to the Chairmanship of the supervisory board upon reaching the age of 60, he had not only put his house in order, but had designed a specific Bertelsmann brand of business economics, rethought the role of an active supervisory board[1] (adopting elements from American board practice in the process), and published articles about the role of the corporation in society. Today, he still dedicates around 50 per cent of his time to his company; the rest is spent on social tasks such as the further development of Witten/Herdecke, Germany's first private university, Westphalian culture management, and the debate on changing conditions for the social market economy. His appointment to *Manager Magazin*'s new 'Business Hall of Fame' is a high-visibility acknowledgement of his unique entrepreneurial achievements.

His successor, Mark Wössner, joined Bertelsmann at the

---

[1] Reinhard Mohn, 'Die Führungspraxis in deutschen Aktiengesellschaften – Ansatzpunkte für eine Weiterentwicklung der dualen Führungsspitze', in Mohn/Henzler, *Zeitgemässe Gestaltung der Führungsspitze von Unternehmen*.

age of 27 and worked his way up via an assistantship and the management of the printing division, to become head of the company. Wössner has found his own identity and has come to be recognized as an industry leader in his own right. He steadily built up Bertelsmann's US commitment to the point where it now accounts for one fifth of sales, designed an attractive, balanced portfolio of new, high-growth areas and mature, established businesses, and created a competent, highly-motivated management crew. The fact that, in the process, Wössner had to become a highly-skilled expert in a wide variety of different media fields speaks for his mental agility. Today, the former mid-sized company has sales of DM17 billion, seven corporate divisions and more than 45,000 employees – and is considered in all quarters to be a truly excellent company.

The personalities – in most cases owners, sometimes the founders themselves – who built up the leading mid-sized companies, or are still at the helm, do not lag behind their colleagues from big industry in public regard or influence. Examples are Berthold Leibinger, the owner of Trumpf, Hans and Gad Rausing, who have made TetraPak into an enormously profitable packaging group of world importance, and J. J. van Oosterom of Holland, who has taken the dynamic software market leader Volmac to its present top position. These entrepreneurs are back in public esteem as businessmen who generate wealth and are committed to the common good in the long term. Their voices are heard far beyond the immediate concerns of their business. Their views on staff training and mobility, occupational diseases, new technologies, the social aspects of integrating foreigners into the community, and much else, are usually given serious attention by politicians. It is no wonder that these entrepreneurs are wooed by political parties across the spectrum from left to right.

In the last five years, European mid-sized companies

have been responsible for 60 per cent of new patent applications, despite receiving less than 10 per cent of total government research funds. Continual product innovation is typically the lifeblood of such companies, and it is not unusual for the owners to make it their top concern. Hans Schleussner, the head of the Frankfurt pharmaceutical and cosmetic manufacturer Biotest, is a case in point. He himself was the man behind several important inventions, from which he has built a company with a workforce of 1,000 and sales of DM260 million. To this day he spends around 40 per cent of his time on in-house development projects. The visionary Ernst Thomke developed the 'Swatch', thus creating together with Nicolaus Hayek the basis for a revival of the Swiss watch industry. After his separation from Hayek, the technology-obsessed Thomke turned to the aircraft industry, where he plans to achieve a turnaround within a few years with new models.

In Belgium, Dr Paul Janssen, until recently still the manager of the company he founded, put Janssen Pharmaceutica into the top five product developers in its industry. Now a subsidiary of Johnson & Johnson, the profitable billion-turnover company is consistently rated one of the most attractive employers in the whole of Europe.

This last feature in particular seems to be one of the most important secrets of success among the 'mid-size giants': their top managers spend an extraordinary amount of time and attention on attracting and retaining the best possible staff. Investments in personnel development and training, although often unquantifiable, are well above industry average, and many of the companies are champions of innovative profit-sharing models, with Bertelsmann an outstanding German example. These investments pay off in many ways – for example, Volmac has a turnover rate among employees of only 4 per cent versus 25 per cent for the industry.

The Vicissitudes of Success

On the way to their current position, European mid-sized companies have passed through a hard school of many ups and downs since the post-war reconstruction era. In the early days, when these companies became machines grinding out prosperity in a desolate, product-hungry world, their leaders had just the right skills: vast technical know-how, boundless energy, determination and stamina. At the beginning of the Fifties, two-thirds of the workers in France and Germany, three-quarters in Italy, and over 80 per cent in Switzerland, owed them their livelihoods. They embodied the overriding post-war hope: that the next generation would be better off.

In such a situation, it hardly mattered that their management style and organizational methods often lacked finesse. Or that, while getting on well with individual employees and usually with the works council, they had little time for trade unions, formal co-determination, or anything else that threatened to restrict their freedom of decision. Their will and ability to build something new, though no less impressive than that of the founder generation around the turn of the century, were significantly less visionary and rooted in grand social designs. Their horizons were often bounded by what they could or could not produce. And they were justified by the results: a blossoming economy and, in many cases, great personal wealth.

The change of climate in the Sixties and Seventies hit many of these entrepreneurs all the harder. In the face of slowing growth, and to the accompaniment of anti-business publications such as, in Germany, Bernd Engelmann's *Meine Freunde, die Millionäre* (My Friends the Millionaires) or the film *Wir Wunderkinder* (We *Wunderkinder*), the lustre of the reconstruction effort faded. In the eyes of large sectors of the public, the creators of the economic miracle were heartless, profit-hungry capitalists. Confronted by massive industrial and social criticism, they lacked the management skills and the flexibility to adapt to new requirements and expectations. For many of them, the worst part of all this was creeping self-doubt and embitterment about the thanklessness of a society – and, above all, an upcoming generation – for whom they had done so much.

Political pressures for a redistribution of wealth led to a growing inclination simply to throw in the towel. This was strengthened by the generation gap (suitable successors were rarely waiting in the wings) and by undercapitalization. In Germany, the traditionally low equity ratio of mid-sized companies declined further, in many cases by up to one half, in the Seventies. According to a report by Professor Horst Albach of the Institut für Mittelstandsforschung (Institute for Research into Mid-sized Companies) in Bonn, written in 1983[1], many of these companies had reached the limits of their growth. The constraint was not in technology, personnel or management capacity, but undercapitalization. 'The erosion of equity in many small and mid-sized companies has reached alarming proportions,' he noted. In actual fact, business closures and sell-outs of independent small and mid-sized companies reached a peak in the years after the first oil shock in 1973.

But the opposite was also to be observed. During the same period, leading mid-sized companies – associated in Germany with names like Töpfer, Körber, Nixdorf, Bertelsmann – developed a long-term perspective and built up progressive management systems and organizational structures. By setting up foundations to review broad

[1] Horst Albach, 'Die Bedeutung mittelständischer Unternehmen in der Marktwirtschaft', Institut für Mittelstandsforschung, Bonn, *IFM-Materialien* Nr. 4, 1983.

social developments, launching in-house staff development programmes and experimenting with advanced people-management approaches, they became pioneers of a changing entrepreneurial role. Reinhard Mohn, for example, built up a dynamic, extraordinarily young management team, to whom he offered attractive financial and career opportunities, complete with stock option schemes and development programmes.

If, today, the entrepreneur has regained a largely positive image in European public opinion, if management and industry are once more viewed as desirable career options for highly qualified young people, it is largely due to such mid-sized pioneers of entrepreneurship committed to social responsibility. Many of them achieved unprecedented, soaring growth. For example, Reinhold Würth, who expanded his trade in screws, dowels and connectors from the Stuttgart area into thirty-five countries, has established his proven business system and made himself a 'local insider' in all these countries. In the process, he has quadrupled his company's sales to DM2.5 billion within ten years. Würth manages this empire from a corporate centre more mobile than fixed (known as the 'Management Conference'). To discuss current business and agree on long-term objectives, around 200 Würth executives and their spouses convene in such out-of-the-way locations as Sardinia for annual managers' meetings.

Hans Peter Stihl, currently president of Germany's DIHT (Federation of Chambers of Industry and Commerce), is the owner of a company which is the technology leader in power-saw manufacturing. Since 1983 it has grown from sales of DM740 million to well over DM1 billion, and now has a world market share of 30 per cent. Production facilities in Switzerland and the US brought Stihl closer to his customers and, at the same time, made him less dependent on his high labour-cost home base.

In 1972, the Alfred Kärcher cleaning machinery company, in Winnenden near Stuttgart, achieved sales of approx. DM30 million with its high-pressure cleaners, as it was just one of many suppliers. Since then, Ms Irene Kärcher and Managing Director Roland Kamm have transformed the very foundations of the business. With new products and completely new areas of application (cleaning of containers, buildings), plus an international expansion drive (with subsidiaries now in over fifty countries), the company became a world market leader. With sales of over DM1 billion and an estimated equity ratio of over 40 per cent, Kärcher, under the third generation of family management, is now setting its sights on new growth objectives in Japan and the US.

Another particularly impressive example is the Württemberg company FESTO, owned by the Stoll brothers (Kurt and Wilfried, engineer and businessman respectively). It has developed over forty years into the biggest pneumatic equipment manufacturer in Europe and has achieved sales of over DM1 billion. The owners attribute the success of their product range of more than 6,000 pneumatic components in forty countries to a few cast-iron management principles: besides almost total rejection of outside shareholders, these include uncompromising product quality (last year they were the first supplier to be awarded ISO 9000, the international quality certificate), unmatched on-site service warranties and in-house management development. Nearly 8 per cent of staff are actively involved in vocational training. In addition, the company has an independent business unit offering a comprehensive, detailed programme of user training in their own and other companies' products.

Kurt and Wilfried Stoll frequently put their management philosophy up for debate in both internal and external meetings. Their many publications have provided food for thought on issues of integrated corporate management. They see further education as their contribution to society

– not to be achieved by political activity, but in and through the company. 'Basic and advanced training,' says Wilfried Stoll, 'is the issue of the future. Our survival depends on the quality of our staff.'

Another component of this philosophy is the principle of maximum scope for action within the open system of the company. In practice this means, first and foremost, accurate and rapid dissemination of information. It is part of the Stoll creed that 'nothing is worse for staff morale than poor information'. That is only a surface contradiction of the discretion with which confidential details of business development are treated. In accordance with a widespread tradition in European mid-sized companies, sales and profit information do not form part of external image-building.

Specific mid-sized industries often shape the character of entire regions. For example, in Germany there are around thirty manufacturers of fitted kitchens in the district of Herford, more than two dozen furniture manufacturers in the Bielefeld area and twenty-two lamp makers in the Neheim-Hüsten area. This grouping of manufacturers and suppliers, as well as support by local schools, vocational colleges and universities, is described by Michael Porter among others as one of Europe's outstanding regional advantages.

The structures sketched here are typically German, but the 'mid-sized company' phenemenon is broadly European. That is proved by statistics about company and workforce size, and it is demonstrated in concrete form by the many examples to be found in every Western European country. Consider Robertet, for example, one of the three leading French fragrance manufacturers. Since the mid-Eighties, its sales have grown by over 50 per cent to about $100 million – 70 per cent of which is earned abroad. Mid-sized world market leaders from France are Haemmerlin in wheelbarrows, SOMFY in automatic blinds and SUPERBA in knitting machines. Equally famous names from the United Kingdom include Clark (shoes), Carlton Communications, Amstrad (electronics), Littlewood (retailing) and Anita Roddick's Body Shop (natural cosmetics). Beer brewer Grolsch has long been popular far beyond the Netherlands, as demonstrated by, among other things, a share of exports of over 50 per cent and 12 per cent pre-tax profit.

In Italy, where mid-sized companies are widely regarded as the backbone of the economy – not just because of the high share of taxes they pay – we find the impressive case of machine-tool manufacturer Mandelli. This company has developed from a small, domestic family firm into one of the leading manufacturers of robotics systems in Italy, supplying big users all over Europe such as Rolls-Royce, Volvo, Daimler-Benz and Aerospatiale. With over 50 per cent of foreign sales and massive expenditure on the development of innovative systems solutions, entrepreneur Giancarlo Mandelli plans to be right in the forefront of the European single market.

From a base in Switzerland, dynamic inventor Borel with his company Logitech and its main product, the computer mouse, has penetrated the world market in the last ten years. The proofs of success are growth rates of between 20 and 100 per cent per annum, a world market share of 30 to 35 per cent, and around two-thirds of sales outside Europe. Similar Swiss examples are Moritz Suter with Crossair, Elco Looser with heating systems and Habasit with conveying systems.

Hans Widmer, until 1982 a director at McKinsey & Company, Zurich, is an unusual example of an owner-entrepreneur. After a brief but intense phase on the management board of Sandoz, he was ordered by his patron, board of directors President Marc Moret, to Berne as head of Wander. In a manner of speaking, he was being put in quarantine. Instead of returning to Basle after his success at Wander, Widmer bought a majority share in the textile machinery manufacturer Schweiter in 1986. With a completely new product generation, drastic rationalization of production, energizing of distribution, the acquisition of two competitors (Metzler AG and Samuel Vollenweider), and a merger with the textile machinery company Schärer to form SSM, he laid the foundations of a viable enterprise. A competent new management team then gave him plenty of spare time to turn around the high-tech company Tecan, where he took over as CEO in 1989. In 1991, he was appointed President of the board of directors of Oerlikon-Bührle and within a year took the company into profit, after years of losses amounting in total to over two and a half billion Swiss francs.

Outside their companies, owner-entrepreneurs in Germany, Italy, Holland, France and Great Britain show considerable commitment to social and public causes. It is no coincidence that one representative of the mid-sized companies followed another at the head of the BDI (Federation of German Industry). Tyll Necker, owner of cleaning-machinery manufacturer Hako-Werke, was succeeded by Heinrich Weiss, CEO and main shareholder of mechanical engineering company SMS AG – after whose departure his predecessor sprang once more into the breach. And it is equally typical for the Dutch entrepreneur B.W.M. Twaalfhoven to build up his aircraft parts company Indivers NV into an international aircraft maintenance network, and at the same time to be an active member of the European Foundation for Entrepreneurship Research.

New Conditions

As the role of the entrepreneur has changed over time, so has the profile of the people who choose this career path. This is particularly evident in the construction industry, where the many new start-ups tackling the reconstruction of Eastern Germany are sometimes reminiscent of the post-war boom. But a building magnate of the Fifties would hardly stand a chance here. More typical are the four young former McKinsey consultants who took over the Bau-GmbH in Ludwigslust near Schwerin at the beginning of 1991. They have translated sound knowledge of business economics and management concepts into practical turnaround work, discontinuing marginal businesses and strengthening the core business.

Another typical representative of the entrepreneurs of the last decade is Bernhard Schneider in Türkheim, who took on the Japanese in personal computers and is now – like every other European vendor – going through hard times. Or Wolfgang Ley, who rose from the position of cutter to become the manager of a textile company, and then the owner of Escada, one of the largest fashion manufacturers in the world, with current sales of DM1.3 billion. Or Richard Branson of the United Kingdom, who built a small record company into a mini-conglomerate including the successful airline Virgin Atlantic.

The task of the owner-entrepreneur has become harder. And it is not all that different these days from the job of running much bigger companies. But the present generation of entrepreneurs has a more differentiated educational background, is better versed in high-tech and societal trends, is more international in perspective and in its radius of action, and knows more about professional management than its predecessors. Many of the younger entrepreneurial leaders have taken an additional management degree on top of their technical training. Many have already found that going it alone is not always the best solution in business and have expanded their opportunities via equity stakes or co-operation agreements.

It seems probable that, by temperament and talent, many

of these people would have been entrepreneurs in past environments as well. But some of them, at least, would have been far more likely to seek a career in big business a generation ago. At any rate, today they all have to face up to very different challenges from their small-company predecessors. Competitors are bigger and more international, the public is more critical and more self-assured, environmental regulations are stricter and affect many more areas. True, there is still no substitute for an entrepreneurial and pioneering spirit – nothing will work without it. But more than ever, broad professional management skills are needed in addition.

It is a change of climate which also means that getting out of a business, and especially selling out, is no longer considered the personal defeat it was in the crisis years of the Seventies and early Eighties. Entrepreneurs like the Holy brothers, who sold the successful BOSS to Italian fashion designer Marzotto, regard such action much less emotionally, as one legitimate strategic option among several. Jochen and Uwe Holy made a deliberate decision to start again from small beginnings and to be hands-on entrepreneurs. Over DM400 million in revenue from the sale of BOSS supplied a welcome safety net.

The recent boom in company start-ups shows that this kind of challenge is being taken up on a broad front. In Germany alone, there were over 370,000 new start-ups in 1990; ten years previously the figure was just 178,000. Apart from the obvious reasons, such as the general economic upturn in the second half of the Eighties and the rise in public regard for entrepreneurial activity, the development was helped along by the growing importance of industries with markedly 'entrepreneurial' potential, such as software.

In technology-intensive areas – aerospace, for example, or nuclear power, or telecommunications – the midsized companies cannot, of course, compete independently against the strong players. But the European aerospace industry, according to DASA CEO Jürgen Schrempp, has many more mid-sized participants than, for example, the automotive industry. Mid-sized companies are sought-after subcontractors and suppliers, both for contract research and parts manufacturing. Indeed, the European aerospace industry works with over 10,000 small and mid-sized suppliers. The best mid-sized companies place great emphasis on investing in their own 'innovativeness' and in continual innovation. Machinery maker Trumpf, for instance, generates 60 per cent of its sales from products introduced within the last three years.

Classical capital-intensive industrial activities are less and less attractive to these new mid-sized companies. There are no such companies nowadays making automobiles, like Borgwand, or tape-recorders, like Uher. The decisive factors are opportunities for outsourcing part of the value added, and a focus on clearly defined niches which can be served at reasonable cost. This is the practice, for instance, of some suppliers of CIM (computer integrated manufacturing) solutions, and also the makers of new materials such as fibre-reinforced plastics or artificial diamonds.

In the high-tech sector, mid-sized activities in Germany and most other European countries fall far short of the magnitude of their counterparts in the US. Europe has no Bill Gates or Steve Jobs in the software field. Sooner or later, concentration is likely in the fragmented European software industry. CAP Gemini in France, headed by Serge Kampf, has sales of around DM345 million, and Volmac in the Netherlands, under Gabriel Dohmen, earns DM540 million, making them the European leaders. In Germany, Softlab leads the field with just under DM200 million. Under its dynamic, visionary founder Klaus Neugebauer, Softlab has shown how getting together with a strong partner (BMW) can strengthen a company's capital base and capability for expansion. Most new start-ups have sales in the region of DM10–20 million.

The European picture is dominated by start-ups based on proven manufacturing technology in established product areas. For example, the unassuming Müsener Kunstharzwerke has become an extremely dynamic enterprise in its third generation of owners, as Hartmut Sieper and his brother Volker successfully ventured into plastic furniture (Sieper brand mirrored wardrobes) and toy cars (Siku) on the basis of traditional injection mouldings (bathtubs, beer crates, etc.). And Roland Schafroth, a dynamic Munich businessman and long-standing supplier of fruit juice extracts to fast-food chains, seized an opportunity in the new Länder of Eastern Germany. He bought a factory for prefabricated parts in Suhl, and gave 250 employees new hope with his entrepreneurial vision.

Entrepreneurial energy is burgeoning primarily in areas not too dependent on technology – consumer goods, retailing, the hotel trade and other service areas. But this surge of energy is by no means limited to a small section of the economic landscape. It is encountered everywhere. More important still, it may well be more sustainable than comparable activities in the high-tech sector, where business is much more cyclical and financing needs are soaring from generation to generation.

The professionalism and expertise of the new owner-entrepreneurs have also changed their relationship with the top managers of established large companies. The days when CEOs saw mid-sized companies only as useful sources of supply are long gone; such companies are now also often regarded as models for big-industry practice. An MIT study around twelve years ago indicated that an employee in a large firm (over 10,000 employees) can 'survive' by using only 30 per cent or so of his or her capacity without being promoted and without being dismissed. This limit probably lies at something more like 70 per cent in mid-sized companies – one likely reason why many large companies are going to considerable lengths to introduce 'mid-sized structures'.

But large corporations use the small and mid-sized companies' store of experience and knowledge even more directly. Reinhold Würth, for example, an entrepreneur with a proven success record, is now on the supervisory board of Mercedes-Benz. Allgaier boss Dieter Hundt, chairman of the Baden-Württemberg iron and steel industry association and himself a successful machine-tool maker, has also accepted posts on various top supervisory bodies. Deutsche Bank has a firm belief in including excellent mid-sized company executives on the advisory bodies in its twenty German branches. Conversely, large companies have also been encouraging their own executives to go on the supervisory boards of successful mid-sized companies, and have in some cases taken equity holdings.

In short, their relationships are more multifarious and closer than ever before. Certainly, the smaller partner will always feel some tension between the roles of minor supplier and entrepreneur on an equal footing, with pride in his or her own – possibly superior – achievements. Overall, however, the trust-based relationship will prove to be a strength as the threshold (ie aggressive mid-size) companies find themselves more and more exposed to tough competition on a pan-European or even global scale. Up to now they have tended to flourish in areas dominated by companies of their own size and orientation. In Germany, that means companies with sales in the order of DM1 billion for the largest machine-tool and consumer-goods manufacturers, or around DM100 million for the leading software companies.

But the mid-sized companies also have other assets to

fall back on. Above all, there is the rise in public regard for entrepreneurial achievements, coupled with very strong customer loyalty secured by the leading manufacturers with a consistent policy of high product and service quality. Closeness to the customer is not least demonstrated by the fact that, wherever possible, systems solutions are offered instead of individual products. Examples are Kühne & Nagel's 'transportation solutions', Kärcher's complete-package 'cleaning solutions' or FESTO's 'intelligent control solutions'.

Both public esteem and customer loyalty profit from a strong corporate culture and 'no-frills' organization: these companies have very small corporate centres and minimum overhead from central functions. Almost every member of the workforce plays a direct role in the development, design, manufacturing or sale of their products. In addition, their workers are generally well qualified for their tasks, and are given further training as required. Relationships with customers and suppliers are very close. Sometimes the links go so far that companies follow their customers geographically. Examples are Bosch with its presence at Linköping's automobile test-track in Sweden, and the upcoming investment by automotive suppliers at new manufacturing locations in Eastern Germany, following Volkswagen to Zwickau, or Opel to Eisenach.

A research project conducted by some of my colleagues in collaboration with the Technical University in Darmstadt revealed further sources of operational strength.[1] For instance, for a certain volume of sales the best German machine-tool manufacturers only need one-fifth as many products as their less successful competitors. They can manufacture larger lots because, among other things, they push the 'freeze point' from which customer-specific

---

[1] Rommel et al., *Einfach überlegen*, Stuttgart 1992.

adaptation is needed as far downstream as possible in the manufacturing process. They have carved a place for themselves in the high-volume segments, and are doing their utmost, through constant product innovation, to hold their positions even against Asian competitors. They have fewer suppliers per part. They spend less on development, but they focus development activities better and thus achieve more. They have flatter organizations and react faster and more flexibly to market changes. All in all, their strength lies in simplicity, both of strategic objectives and operational execution. The pattern is plain. Hermann Simon sums it up as follows: 'Hidden Champions are successful competitors because they are outstandingly focused on customer needs. They possess strong competitive advantages in product quality, closeness to the customer, and service.'

Acknowledgement of the performance of the rising midsized companies and entrepreneurs does not begin and end with diffuse public recognition or an abatement of criticism. Professor Simon has proved that in a survey of 344 of his Masters degree students.[1] When he asked in 1991 whether they would like to start their own companies, 42 per cent said 'yes'. The year before, the figure was 34 per cent; ten years ago it had been no more than 5 per cent. I can mention concrete examples from *ad hoc* discussions with my own students. In 1991, three students set up the first software house in Latvia, another business student got together with an engineering graduate to produce a new material. Still others have sought an entrepreneurial outlet by setting up consultancies, systems houses and travel companies.

The fact that there is an increasing number of mid-sized companies up for sale does not necessarily contradict this

[1] Hermann Simon, *op.cit.*

trend. The upcoming change of generations has a part to play here. But the vitality of the companies concerned, the proven reservoir of potential entrepreneurs, and the broad interest of society in their role, remain sound foundations on which Eurocapitalism can build.

VI

The Challenges of the Future

Under the helmsmanship of the Europreneurs at the top of major companies and the dynamic bosses of mid-sized businesses, European industry made a good deal of headway in the second half of the Eighties. Restructuring measures and visionary entrepreneurial initiatives have significantly improved both productivity and competitiveness. In some industries, impressive progress was made in product development, manufacturing methods and technology management – all areas that have long been notorious weak spots in European industries. The growing market success of the Airbus is now well known, as is the modernization of European steel production (British Steel, Usinor-Sacilor, Thyssen), and the impressive developments in digital switch technology (Siemens, Alcatel), not to mention the renaissance of the European textile industry under the influence of product and marketing innovations from such companies as Benetton and the use of high-tech methods in design and production. What is more, the Europeans now also hold leading positions in environmental technology, energy conversion and distribution, public communications engineering, PBXs and laser research, as well as in several more future-oriented fields: photovoltaics, hydrogen-powered engines, sensor technology and traffic-guidance systems.

Given the turning-point at which Europe now finds itself, as described in the first chapter, there can be no doubt that a strong economy is more important than ever. Especially when instability in the former Eastern bloc gives way to warfare in Bosnia, when the slowing progress and rising cost of German unification tax the patience of the responsible middle class and fire the nationalist prejudice of the irresponsible social fringe, and when the road to a single market and a closer European union looks far more problematic than it did just a few heady years ago – especially in times like these the dangers of prolonged recession, retreat from fair and open trade, and industrial decay, are unusually serious. Only healthy economic growth can safely float all these European societies over the treacherous shoals of social and political realignment in a post-cold-war world. To repeat: a strong, entrepreneurially-driven economy is more important than ever.

This is true even though the one particularly serious potential development – an uncontrollable flow of immigration from the poorer regions of the east and south – cannot be directly influenced by entrepreneurial action. Political solutions to this problem must be found as a matter of urgency to prevent a fatal overburdening of Western European economies. Indeed, Europe – for generations a continent more accustomed to emigration than the reverse – is now turning into the largest net recipient of immigration in the Triad (Diagram 17).

It is essential, therefore, not to overlook the shadows in

Growing Immigration Pressure in Europe

Net immigration, in '000 persons

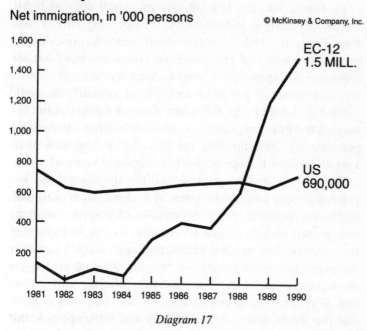

© McKinsey & Company, Inc.

EC-12
1.5 MILL.

US
690,000

Diagram 17

Europe's economic picture, as compared to the situation at the beginning of the Eighties. Today it is especially troubling to note that Europe is threatened with the loss of its technological and economic competitiveness in future-oriented industries, where it has not so far managed to catch up with the US and particularly Japan. We should not let ourselves be fooled by a decline of the US dollar or the fall of the Nikkei–Dow Index. In fact, American and Japanese suppliers – the Americans helped along by favourable exchange rates, the Japanese emerging even stronger from their liquidity squeeze – are further consolidating their positions. In other words, while the Europeans may well have made up some ground, they have by no means made up enough. The race is still going on, and it is likely to become even tougher.

To ensure that the key automotive, electrical and mechanical engineering industries in Europe stay in the running, politics and industry must restore and secure competitiveness and technological competence within the Europe–US–Japan Triad, where – depending on the industry – between 75 per cent and 90 per cent of the world market is located. At the same time, we must resist the understandable temptation to shy away from competitive pressure by concentrating on less demanding new markets in Eastern Europe and other threshold countries.

There is no need to go in detail into the many historical reasons for the Europeans' present backwardness. Europe's traditional position as the stronghold of science and technology had already begun to crumble by the beginning of this century. The gradual emancipation of the US from the dominant European model can be seen, for example, in the pioneering work of men like Edison, Westinghouse, Ford and DuPont. The repercussions of the two world wars, and the 'brain drain' of the Thirties and Fifties/Sixties only intensified and accelerated this development, as the list of Nobel prizewinners since the turn of the century clearly shows (Diagram 18). European developments had even less impact on the industrial rise of Japan before and after the Second World War. Particularly after the war, both in traditional sectors and important future-oriented industries Europe lost its technology lead. Although the criterion of size in itself may not tell us much, it is nevertheless remarkable that in such industries as electronics, automotive engineering and aerospace, the market leaders of today are all non-European companies.

In the key sector of 'mechatronics', the combination of sophisticated mechanical apparatus with electronics, whole industries have moved out of Europe. Between 1960 and

Lead in Pure Research lost to the USA

Number of Nobel prize winners for physics/chemistry/medicine as a percentage

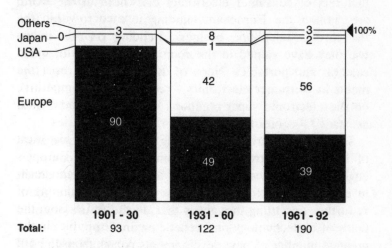

Source: Encyclopaedia Britannica

© McKinsey & Company, Inc.

Diagram 18

1988, for example, the share of world production held by European camera manufacturers dwindled from 22 per cent to 2 per cent. And there was an even more drastic drop for watch- and clockmakers: from 54 per cent to 3 per cent. According to American patent statistics, Europeans are still the leaders in mechanical engineering and are more or less level-pegging in electrical engineering. But they have been clearly overtaken by the Japanese in automotive engineering and even more noticeably in consumer electronics.

In consumer electronics, the competitiveness of manufacturing technology is critical. The virtual loss of storage technology activities in microelectronics means that Europe is not involved in a whole new wave of manufacturing technologies, such as second-generation surface-mounting techniques and manufacturing automation. By giving up consumer electronics, the Europeans now also lack strength in one of their core areas of operation. Indeed, the manufacturers of consumer electronics elsewhere in the world are, unlike the Europeans, finding it easy to step into the cordless-telephone business, building on the expertise they have gained in the compact electronics of video cameras and portables. None of the cutting-edge developments in consumer electronics – 'compu-TV', 'digital art', or the electronic super-notebook PDA ('personal digital assistant') – comes from Europe.

So, although Europe is still faring quite well in some areas of high-tech electronics – telecommunications, computer engineering, medical technologies and PABXs – the deficit in consumer electronics will be very hard to make good. A further unsettling thought is that, in the future-oriented fields of biotechnology and genetic engineering, by far the greatest number of new developments comes from the US (Diagram 19).

Europe even seems to be losing position in the traditionally European, and particularly German, field of pharmaceuticals. In a ten-year comparison, the US slightly increased its market share in new preparations during the second half of the Eighties and the Japanese were able to more than double theirs, while the German, French and Italian figures were substantially down. Exceptions like Glaxo's noteworthy role in new preparations for the central nervous system have not been able to reverse Europe's weakening position. The European aerospace industry, which never regained its former autonomy and system leadership after the Second World War, tells a similar story.

This competitive weakness is particularly worrying because the gap in innovation and technology is accompanied by a clear deficit in productivity. On all three critical

USA Clear Leader in Technologies of the Future

Percentage of discoveries* in biotechnology and genetic engineering according to countries of origin, 1985-88

100% = 11,222

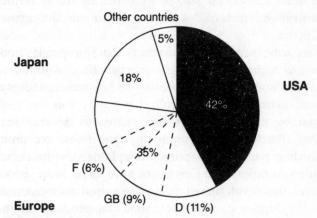

Other countries

Japan

USA

Europe

F (6%)

GB (9%)   D (11%)

* Applications for patents in a minimum of 2 countries

Source: IFO 28/90   © McKinsey & Company, Inc.

Diagram 19

dimensions – cost, time and quality – Europe lags way behind the world's best.

Differences in *manufacturing costs* have become increasingly evident in recent years, and the trend is for the gap to widen. Japanese manufacturers currently produce conventional electrical goods 25 per cent more cheaply and passenger and commercial vehicles around 30 per cent more cheaply than their European competitors. Their cost advantage in electronic products is as high as 50 per cent. Only part of this cost advantage, around 30 per cent, can be attributed to lower factor costs (personnel and materials). Half the remaining advantage – 35 per cent – is accounted for by cost-optimized work organization and less vertical integration; the other half comes from better, more production-friendly and more cost-effective design. The disconcerting thing about these comparisons is that only five years ago the cost differences for electronic products and motor vehicles were each approximately ten percentage points smaller, and that Japanese companies expect further rationalization effects of 2–4 per cent per annum throughout the Nineties.

As regards *speed of development*, the Europeans' poor showing is significant for high-tech products, whether in electronics, automotive engineering or medical technology. Japanese manufacturers typically need only half the time required by their European competitors to develop new products. Particularly in commodity-type electronic products, such as personal computers, telephones, fax machines and video-recorders, the Europeans have so far been unable to create the development culture required to introduce, as do the Japanese, new generations of products in the market every twelve to eighteen months. European car manufacturers are faced with the same problem. McKinsey studies repeatedly confirm that the Japanese take around three years to bring a new automobile generation to the point of production; the Europeans, around six to seven.

Japanese companies work with an innovation philosophy of small steps. This contrasts sharply with the 'big hit' principle of most European competitors. Taking small steps allows for rapid correction and adjustment; a 'big hit' approach involves high risks from miscalculations, incorrect product design and unfavourable manufacturing-cost structures. The Japanese way of continuously testing products on the market and quite happily accepting initial new product failure rates of between 70 and 80 per cent is hard for European perfectionism to grasp.

To date, Europe has been unable to get anywhere near Japan's excellent achievements in minimizing *defect rates* in the manufacturing process or in reducing warranty costs. In electronics manufacturing, for example, reject rates in Europe are between four to five times as high as in Japan. As Friedrich Baur, former head of the Siemens AG's components division and a great technology visionary, assesses the situation, 'Not even in ten years could we close the gap with the Japanese; their lead is the product of a zero-error working culture amongst employees, which has developed over the generations.' Indeed, in many European industrial companies the ratio of employees in manufacturing to employees in quality control is at least one to one. The reason: a persistent need to run expensive product checks or audits on complex products before they are delivered to customers.

Given these competitive failings, European companies could well be tempted to switch their focus to the new markets of Eastern Europe and avoid competition in the Triad. Geographical proximity and historical links in this area should make it relatively easy for them – especially with financial support from the state – to open up new markets. A breathing space of this nature would, however, further increase the gap between Europe and true world-class players. In the longer term, it would also put a question mark against Europe's position in its domestic markets as well as in the threshold countries.

If we are to avoid an industry-by-industry retreat into a defensive and ultimately protectionist 'Fortress Europe', if we are to create the wealth needed to keep Eurocapitalism in working order, European industry will have to face up aggressively to competition against the best in the world. In this context I can see four essential challenges that must be met: internationalization, environmental protection, innovation management and information technology. The degree to which European companies today are equipped to tackle them varies.

The Challenge of Internationalization: Three Directions

Probably the greatest benefit of the 'Europe 92' initiative was that Europeans stopped regarding their neighbouring countries in Europe as foreign markets and started to see them as core 'domestic' markets within the broader international market of the Triad. Today, this experience is being repeated on a wider scale. For the Western industrial nations, the opening up of Eastern Europe and the rise of a number of newly industrializing and threshold countries are extending the relevant economic area of the Triad: North America (plus Mexico), Western Europe (plus Eastern Europe) and Japan (plus the Pacific area).

Nothing does more to improve the performance of individual companies and whole industries than the battle for the three core markets – the US, Western Europe and Japan – with their sophisticated customers and world-class suppliers. From here, additional regions, both in the extended Triad and in newly industrialized (threshold) countries, can be developed sequentially. The danger, of course, is that this geopolitical economic development will turn into a battle between regional trading blocs. For European companies, the challenge of internationalization is threefold: globalization, making the Single Market a practical reality in Europe, and developing the markets of Eastern Europe.

Globalization

For more than ten years now, the volume of world trade has grown annually at nearly twice the rate of the world's

real gross domestic product. Today, just under 20 per cent
of the goods produced world-wide are exported. The reality
of international networking, however, goes much further
than the cross-frontier flows of goods. The penetration of
foreign markets often happens well beyond the reach of
trade statistics in the multifarious activities of companies
in the latter stages of globalization, which regard all regions
of the Triad as their 'home market'. As insiders they have
laboratories, manufacturing facilities and sales networks
in each of these regions; they employ local workers at
all stages of the value-added process, and they foster relationships with local suppliers, banks and customers.

The driving forces behind both the export boom and
globalization are, to some extent, identical. World trade
thrives on the stimulation of demand, most notably through
convergence of purchasing power in developed countries,
and the world-wide availability of information which is making buyer preferences more homogeneous around the globe.
The shopping lists of Europeans, Japanese and Americans
have increasingly become more alike. In addition to such
demand pull, there is a powerful push from the supply
side: rapidly-growing development and manufacturing costs
must pay back over ever shorter product life-cycles, which
means that a sufficient sales volume can be achieved only
by serving the whole Triad market. The traditional view that
national markets plus incremental exports will suffice to
amortize these costs no longer holds. For many companies,
the full Triad market, with over 700 million consumers, has
become the only meaningful yardstick for new products and
new manufacturing operations.

Ten years ago European manufacturers could still produce
a new automobile generation for around DM800 million in
development costs and manufacturing investment. Today,
they have to reckon with three to four times this amount. In
the case of semiconductors, development costs increase by

roughly 50 per cent for each new product generation, and the costs of a new manufacturing plant by 100 per cent. In communications engineering, an electromechanical telephone-switching system was developed at the beginning of the Seventies in Europe for the equivalent of $100–150 million and operated for twenty years with negligible maintenance costs. Today, research and development costs for state-of-the-art digital switching systems come to between $1 and 2 billion, and have a projected economic life of little more than ten years – in spite of continuous and expensive revisions of their operating software.

These developments have triggered a process of globalization that will decisively change the structure of the world economy by the end of this decade. In the year 2000, global products will account for an estimated 30 per cent of the gross national product of the industrialized countries (in 1990, the comparable figure was 20 per cent). By the standards of their American and Japanese competitors, however, the vast majority of European companies – with the exception of a few like Nestlé, Unilever, Royal Dutch/Shell and BP – have been rather hesitant in their approach to the future-oriented task of globalization.

Empirical studies show that there are basically six stages of globalization, each associated with a different set of entrepreneurial risks:

☐ *Stage 1:* A company in stage 1 covers its foreign markets with exports. It has a sales branch and, where applicable, a service organization in each target country. The entrepreneurial risk of an export strategy of this kind lies in market uncertainty and in defaults on receivables. It is, however, usually possible to reduce this risk substantially through careful day-to-day management.

☐ *Stage 2:* A company in stage 2 maintains isolated foreign holdings in the form of assembly plants. It assembles 'on site' to get closer to the market or to overcome trade barriers. Thus, for this model to work, there must be a continuous flow of semi-finished products from the home base. The risks involved at this stage, which relate to transaction costs and the level of exposure of assets in foreign markets, are considerably higher than in stage 1.

☐ *Stage 3:* A company now has complete foreign manufacturing bases, and its purchasing increasingly relies on local sources. Suppliers from the home market follow the globalizing company with their own foreign subsidiaries. With the exception of minor adjustments in local markets, product ranges generally correspond to that of the home base. The entrepreneurial risk is higher than in both earlier stages. This is because it is more difficult to compensate for fluctuations in capacity utilization, and control from the head office becomes increasingly complicated and costly.

☐ *Stage 4:* In addition to complete manufacturing, the foreign commitment now extends to development and product design. Goods are produced for local markets but also for international markets, and the foreign base is closely integrated into the parent company's international network. At the same time, the foreign base operates largely independently in the local market: the local development of the industry essentially determines the development of the business. The entrepreneurial risk tends to decrease here, in spite of higher capital investment, as the result of better adjustment to local market conditions and a better integration in the company's international division of labour.

☐ *Stage 5:* By stage 5 a company has fully developed into an insider in the national markets it serves. At this level, research also takes place in the foreign subsidiaries, which participate both in the scientific community of the host country and in the supra-regional co-operation and exchange of personnel within the company. A complete value-added chain produces goods for domestic sale and for export. Risk containment is even better than in stage 4, as 'fair' competitive conditions in relation to local suppliers are coupled with the advantages of the company's international network.

☐ *Stage 6:* Here, in the ultimate form of globalization, the full value-added process in the local markets of the Triad is part of the company's overall concept. The global company is present in all important markets with a share of sales corresponding to their true market potential. In each country it has tailored its business system optimally to the conditions of the national market and competitive scene. In research, the corporate world is divided into centres of competence, which employ the world's top experts irrespective of national origin. Local development teams perform global development work, often in collaboration with development and design teams in other countries, sometimes using satellite links to make the most of time-zone advantages. Manufacturing utilizes modern international link-up facilities with suppliers and customers at all stages of production, and sales and marketing secure optimal interaction of global product and local customer orientation. Such a polycentric organization can develop its strengths to the full by the international staffing of management teams.

While entrepreneurial risk starts to decline from stage 4 on, transnational business approaches cannot be optimally utilized until stage 6. At this stage a company gains access to the best human resources, the least expensive sources of finance, and the most secure and least expensive long-term supply of raw materials. Companies that have reached stage 6 are less vulnerable to dips in the economy – being an insider acts as a shield against exchange-rate fluctuations, and market opportunities in the various Triad markets can be recognized and exploited quickly.

The most successful proponents of globalization – companies like IBM, Coca-Cola, Honda and Sony (company motto: 'Think global, act local') – today have the presence of domestic companies ('global local citizens') in labour, capital, supply and sales markets across the Triad. Sales volume and employment are distributed geographically to allow for most regional fluctuations to be offset elsewhere. For example, IBM has been able to compensate for cyclical weaknesses in the US over the last several years with good earnings in Japan and to some extent also in Europe. In contrast, Honda, probably the most technologically advanced car maker in the world today, has been using a 'hold' strategy in Japan to sustain its expansion strategy in Europe.

With its telephone factory in Singapore, AT&T has proved that it is not only possible to produce goods in the Far East but also to learn some important lessons in design-to-cost. Experience gained in Singapore has been imported to its US factories. Today, the company manufactures telephones in Singapore, China, the US and Mexico. In the future, it will also produce in Thailand. The Singapore factory, a specialist in low-cost design, is responsible for several of the designs manufactured. The globally operating company has now introduced a system of internal competition: the six international locations are asked to name their price for manufacturing each new product. The best bid wins the order. According to AT&T, the lessons learned in Singapore now make it possible to produce cordless telephones in

Shreveport, USA, at the same costs as in Singapore.

European companies – whose international standing is primarily determined by their strong position at home – still have a long way to go before reaching such global market and competitive positions. This is especially true for German companies, which otherwise often play a pioneering role within the EC. Direct presence abroad with foreign manufacturing bases was the exception for a long time among German companies. And where it existed, it was focused on the traditionally German-friendly countries of Latin America, Asia and the Near East.

Since the collapse of the Bretton Woods system of fixed exchange rates in 1973, German companies have increased their foreign investment far more sharply than their exports: from 1973 to 1991, direct investments rose by an average of 12.3 per cent per annum; exports by 7.6 per cent. But this investment growth falls short of globalization in the geographical sense discussed above. German development of markets via foreign manufacturing facilities has been aimed at the major European industrialized countries and the US. Particularly where manufacturing facilities acquired in the US are concerned, however, failures so far outnumber the success stories.

In Japan, German companies have significant market positions only in certain niches, and even here preference is given to export strategies. Even alliances are still mainly in their initial stages. In line with this, around 55 per cent of total direct investments held by German companies abroad in 1990 were in other parts of Europe, 23 per cent in the US, and less than 2 per cent in Japan. The prevailing model, according to which 95–100 per cent of development, 85–95 per cent of manufacturing, and 60–70 per cent of sales take place on home ground, is changing – but slowly. The international positions of other European companies – in Norway (Norsk Hydro, Statoil), Sweden (Atlas Copco,

LM Ericsson, Electrolux, TetraPak), Switzerland (Nestlé, ABB, Sandoz, Ciba-Geigy, Hoffmann La Roche, Crédit Suisse) or the Netherlands (Shell, Akzo, Unilever, Philips) – are far stronger.

On the six-stage path to globalization, most European companies are probably in stages 1 to 3. In automotive engineering and information technology, Europe trails well behind Japanese and American manufacturers. The situation looks somewhat different in telecommunications. Here, European manufacturers (in particular Alcatel and Siemens) are at the forefront and, in some cases, have also set up development units in the US and in Third World countries. The big chemical companies are furthest along the path to globalization: Bayer, BASF, Hoechst, Rhône-Poulenc, ICI and Solvay have probably already reached stage 3, in some cases even stage 4. In certain product areas, companies such as Siemens, ABB, Bosch, GKN, CGE and Schneider can legitimately make the same claim.

As noted previously, French, German and Swiss mid-sized companies play a special role. On the basis of traditionally cautious export strategies, some of them have moved into extremely strong positions in the world market and, in certain cases, have become world market leaders in the markets they serve. Many successful medium-sized businesses now have the product basis and 'critical sales mass' needed for extensive globalization, as the success of companies such as Dürr, FESTO, Kärcher, Bizerba, Mahle, Westphalia Separator, Hille & Müller, Stihl and Trumpf confirms. When Ludwigsburg-based Meissner & Wurst celebrated the twenty-fifth anniversary of its clean-room division in 1992 (80 years after the founding of the company as a manufacturer of ventilation equipment), 400 international customers, many from the Far East, were present. As the world's most sought-after clean-room manufacturer for the semiconductor industry, the company today is supplier to new semiconductor foundries in Taiwan and Korea as well as to its customers in Europe. The company has its own development and applications laboratories in several countries.

French company LVMH, owner of the luxury brands Louis Vuitton and Moët-Hennessy, currently earns 80 per cent of its sales on the world market. Similarly, it took Martin Hilti of Liechtenstein only a generation to reach world class with his mounting technology company founded after the war. Today the company, headed by a largely non-family management team, operates on a global scale with a sales volume of over 2 billion Swiss francs.

The success of these mid-sized companies is not normally based predominantly on global integration of production and R and D activities. It is more common for development and production to be predominantly national (usually 100 per cent and over 95 per cent, respectively), with sales and marketing strategies to cover the world market (exports of over 70 per cent are not unusual), and a strong local service strategy. Today, in the early Nineties, internationalization concepts previously followed by German and the majority of other European companies no longer fill the bill. Dramatic changes in market and competitive conditions, the economic restructuring of Eastern Europe, and the shift of world economic growth from the industrialized countries to the dynamic developing economies in Asia and Latin America, call for a new understanding of globalization.

It is very difficult to anticipate the pace of globalization in individual markets and product areas, but it is more likely to pick up than to slacken. And it is becoming increasingly rare for a single company to be able to swim against this tide. For global companies, it is now essential to have insider positions in Western Europe *and* the US *and* Japan – that is, access to the best human and physical resources and the most attractive customer segments in the world. From the European perspective this involves requirements such as these:

1. *Utilization of the many options for creating a presence in core markets.* Establishing 'greenfield' foreign bases – a long-time preference of European and especially German companies – soon reaches the limits of management capacity and frequently takes too long. Resorting to acquisitions takes care of part of the time problem but carries more risks than, say, strategic alliances. French companies have tended to be particularly strong on cross-border mergers and acquisitions, which is one of the key forces behind the recent expansion of their international presence.

   Strategic partnerships may prove to have an ambivalent effect on a company's movement towards globalization: on the one hand, access to a partner's resources reduces the pressure to push forward with one's own globalization; on the other, initial market experiences within an alliance can provide the information and motivation necessary for such independent action.

2. *Strict adherence to the 'nine commandments' of globalization.* These rules for success (Table 2) are, to a certain extent, directly in conflict with traditional European beliefs and behaviour. Most companies, for example, still have to make the switch from a distinctively domestic-market orientation to a focus on international core markets right from the product development stage. With the exception of the Scandinavian countries, Switzerland and the Netherlands, product specifications generally reflect the needs of customers in the domestic market; it is the domestic market where pilot installations get tested, and the marketing concept is tailored to the home country

The Nine Commandments for Successful Globalization

and not . . .

1. **Concentration on the US, Europe and Japan**

   Creating and servicing a world-wide 'patchwork' ('UN model')

2. **International orientation of product design**

   Concentration on national features followed by step-by-step 'internationalization'

3. **Advance market investment**

   Waiting for the necessary sales revenue to finance expansion into new markets

4. **International organization of supporting functions and services**

   Occasionally 'helping out' if need arises or bottlenecks occur

5. **International planning of manufacturing programmes and delivery logistics**

   'Offloading' quantities of goods not absorbed by the domestic market

6. **Top management influence on product responsibility of country units**

   Uncoordinated action by fully autonomous country units

7. **Joint development of product/market strategies by head office and country units**

   Central projects delegated to decentral 'henchmen'

8. **Tailoring of control systems to allow realistic assessment of startup losses from an entrepreneurial point of view**

   Indiscriminate application of standardized success criteria

9. **Creation of a position as a fully integrated insider in the foreign market through own subsidiaries or alliances**

   Guest role as exporter or 'hit-and-run' activities

© McKinsey & Company, Inc.

Table 2

and includes, at best, traditional European export markets. In a global business, however, the product has to be oriented to the needs of the international market while still on the drawing board.

New product introduction has to make the transition from the 'waterfall' to the 'sprinkler' model. The traditional sequence – introduction at home first to test the water, followed by entry into other familiar European countries, then countries in which the company is traditionally strong, then European countries with a difficult competitive structure, and finally overseas – may save resources, but can also take between five and seven years to complete. This gradualist approach no longer satisfies the demands of global competition. This is particularly true of high-tech products, whose life cycle is often shorter than the procedure outlined above.

In terms of funding, massive initial investment has to replace the step-by-step accumulation of resources and the cautious building of foreign presence in parallel with the gradual expansion of the business. The manufacturing activities of global companies are organized from the outset with world volume in mind, and market tests sound out customer wishes in the US and Japan as thoroughly as in Europe. Global companies ensure that sufficient distribution capacity and advertising support are available, and that each country subsidiary can offer product documentation and other information in the local language in good time.

Finally, establishing adequate presence in the key markets of the US and Japan is more important than tracking down new 'blank spots' in which to acquire market positions.

European Single Market

Despite recent uncertainties along the road to Maastricht, and despite growing doubts about the effectiveness of the ERM, let alone the likelihood of a true European Monetary Union, the development of a single market will inevitably proceed. With 340 million consumers and a 41 per cent share of world trade, such a market will substantially improve the competitive fortunes of the companies on which Europe's future most directly depends. Up to now, even the best of these companies have been at a disadvantage *vis-à-vis* their American and Japanese counterparts because of their smaller and more fragmented domestic markets. But as deregulation permits access to new markets and segments, they will be able to achieve substantial economies of scale.

At the individual company level, the complete orientation of management structures and systems to the conditions of the single market, which is five times the size of the German domestic market and twenty times that of the Netherlands, will be essential for success. The work of 'orientation' will include:

☐ *Optimizing plant configuration.* The possibility of serving all European markets from the home market and/or from logistically favourable neighbouring markets will permit consolidation of previously fragmented locations. For this reason, leading European companies such as Unilever, Johnson & Johnson, Henkel and Nestlé have begun to concentrate their production capacity in a few logistically well-positioned locations. This, in turn, allows significantly larger production volumes, better capacity utilization and higher productivity. Unilever, for example, which in the mid-Seventies had thirteen factories in thirteen European countries, had concentrated manufacturing into four factories in four countries by

1989. A European chemical company has decided to concentrate its manufacturing activities even more drastically by reducing its sixty production sites to only fourteen. The cost savings that such concentration is likely to bring are estimated at between 20 and 40 per cent of logistics costs or 3 to 8 per cent of total costs. This trend also extends to the reorganization of electrical engineering plants, which are often far too small and were originally established mainly on account of local content regulations. Under single-market conditions it makes more sense to handle all power engineering and installation technology at the main national headquarters of Siemens (Erlangen), ABB (Baden and Mannheim), CGE (Paris) and GEC.

☐ *Exploiting economies of scale in logistics.* As restrictions such as waiting times at borders and the regulation of cabotage and of haulage rates in Europe disappear, transport costs will be reduced considerably. In high-price countries such as the Federal Republic of Germany there may be an additional squeeze on the price of transport services due to the entry in local markets of highly efficient Western European transport companies and cheap Southern European players.

As a result, the profitability radius – the distance over which goods are transported without the transport costs eating up all the profits – will increase considerably for all industries, particularly where cross-border transactions are concerned. According to some estimates, this will lead to an increase in logistics flows of an average of 50 to 60 per cent by the year 2000, accompanied by a drastic alteration in the logistics for production, storage and distribution of commodities and consumer goods. It will be possible to reduce inventories radically, shift to just-in-time delivery, and enhance logistics and transportation performance. Manufacturers who can pass on

the advantage of favourable logistics costs to their customers will be able to gain market share. At the same
time, there will be opportunities for high-end, value-
oriented Europe-wide suppliers of logistics and transportation services such as Kühne & Nagel, which achieved
above-average sales revenues in Germany, Greece and
the Netherlands in 1992, and is set for further expansion
through co-operation agreements.

☐ *Internationalization of sourcing.* When manufacturers face
increasing competition among suppliers from neighbouring European states, the bargaining power of customers
improves. On public contracts from the railways, post
office, energy and other utilities, as well as construction tenders and military procurement projects, the involvement of foreign suppliers may allow more effective
cost control and efficient use of taxpayers' money. A
rough estimate indicates that this alone could enhance
the efficiency of public sourcing budgets – now some
$400 billion in total – by at least 10 per cent.

In the private sector, breaking up the constraints of
predominantly national supplier relationships and greater
reliance on outsourcing should open up an even larger
savings potential. The successful transition to a Europe-
wide sourcing strategy at GM Europe after 1987 bears
witness to the reserves of effectiveness and efficiency
which can be released in this way.

Development of Markets in Eastern Europe

Until the outbreak of the First World War, tsarist Russia was one of Western and Central Europe's most important trading partners. Supplies of grain from White Russia, the Ukraine and Poland ensured the supply of food in the German empire. The rise of many Central European towns such as Baden-Baden would have been unthinkable without the constant influx of Russian visitors to their health spas in the nineteenth century. Similarly, the growth of the Krupp armaments concern would have been impossible without the support of – and know-how transfer from – tsarist artillery experts. Before that, history shows that Prussian support (von Clausewitz/von Stein) was indispensable to Russia. Even earlier, Tsar Peter the Great brought a great number of Western experts into his country to help it catch up with the West.

Two world wars and the Russian Revolution put an end to the ties and trade relations that had long been of vital importance to Prussian Germany. The Soviet economic reforms of the Twenties and Thirties then transformed Russia into a largely autarchical and autonomous centrally-controlled economy. Its guiding principle was the extensive utilization of the traditional mercantilist success factors of size, population and mineral resources. Today, in terms of Western performance measures, the economies of the current CIS states (real per capita income in 1992: $1,850) and the other former Comecon states of Eastern Europe ($3,500) are comparable with those of threshold countries ($3,300).

At first glance Western Europeans might seem well advised to concentrate predominantly on supplies to the East because of its huge pent-up demand in all areas of the economy. The former Comecon countries are currently in a much worse situation than were Western European countries after the Second World War. In the West 'only' around 20 to 25 per cent of the industrial base had been destroyed, and the business climate was marked by considerable entrepreneurial energy, a motivated workforce and sophisticated consumers. In the East, the current industrial base is only 20 to 25 per cent of that in the West, an entrepreneur class is practically non-existent, workers are disillusioned by the radical changes and layoffs, and consumers have never experienced even the simplest mechanisms of supply and demand.

Faced with the progressive decline in their economies's assets, these governments not only have to ensure political stability and a sufficient supply of food, they must also build

Stock of Automobiles in Eastern Europe: Small and Outdated

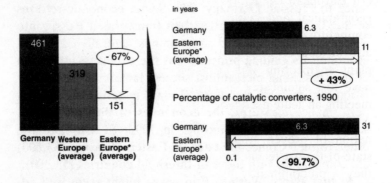

Automobiles per 1,000 inhabitants, 1988

Average age of automobile stock, 1991

in years

Germany 6.3
Eastern Europe* (average) 11 + 43%

Percentage of catalytic converters, 1990

Germany 6.3 31
Eastern Europe* (average) 0.1 - 99.7%

461 319 - 67% 151

Germany   Western Europe* (average)   Eastern Europe* (average)

* Incl. Soviet Union/CIS

Source: Economic Intelligence Unit, VDA

Diagram 20   © McKinsey & Company, Inc.

up an efficient infrastructure for trade and industry, transfer urgently needed basic technologies from the West, introduce modern management and administrative techniques and encourage private enterprise.

All Eastern European markets are marked by an extreme undersupply of high-quality consumer goods, consumer durables and all types of high-tech products. For example, the number of television sets in Eastern Europe, including the CIS states, is estimated at 90 per cent of Western European levels (i.e. approximately 290 sets per 1,000 inhabitants). But these are predominantly black and white sets and generally of low technical quality. Telephone lines and subscriber extensions are only about a quarter of the Western European average, and personal computers are only 5 per cent as common as in Western Europe. The automobiles registered, at only half the Western European level, are virtually all due for replacement (Diagram 20).

With a total of over 400 million consumers and pent-up demand which is virtually impossible to satisfy even in the medium term, this market can be developed by Western European companies with relative ease. Besides their geographical and cultural competitive advantages versus competitors from other parts of the Triad, Europeans will also be able to benefit from their traditional strengths in plant engineering and infrastructure development, which have lost significance in high-technology markets but are meeting an acute need here. In the enormous environmental protection market, Europeans can offer a unique combination of proven system solutions and newly developed state-of-the-art technologies. In nuclear power technology, they – predominantly the French (CGE, Framatom) and German (ABB, Siemens) companies – also have a clear lead. This should stand them in good stead for the forthcoming

overhaul and modernization of the dilapidated nuclear re-
actors in the former Communist bloc countries.

Even at their current levels of productivity, Western
Europeans have a considerable edge in Eastern Europe. For
example, in the steel or automotive industries production
per employee is two to five times higher than in Eastern
European companies. And the lead is even more marked
in the consumer-durables and consumer-goods industries,
where higher productivity is accompanied by more up-to-
date products.

When converting all these considerations into hard business policy, two factors must be taken into account. On the
one hand, really good sales opportunities in Eastern Europe
may well exist only in the very long term; low purchasing
power will balance out the vastness of the Eastern markets
for years to come. In terms of gross national product and financial resources, Eastern Europe's potential for absorbing
Western goods is comparable to that of threshold countries.
It would, therefore, be a fatal error to concentrate too much
on the Eastern European arena. Even large European companies, some of which have made substantial investments in
Eastern Europe, are cautious in their assessment of capital
return and amortization. Volkswagen (Czech Republic),
ABB (Poland), Siemens (Czech Republic) and Air Liquide
(Russia) reckon in generations when they discuss the de-
velopment of their Eastern commitments.

On the other hand, categorizing these countries simply
as threshold countries does not do justice to their cultural
development, nor to the unusually high level of education
and training amongst broad sections of their populations,
nor to their world-class achievements in selected areas
of industry and science. For this reason, it would be a
mistake blindly to transfer to Eastern Europe solutions
tailored to developing countries, or to attempt a repeat
of the Western European economic miracle of the Fifties.
Instead, it will be necessary to target the specific strengths
of each individual economy (valuable mineral resources,

high-tech potential) and to develop long-term models for co-operation in these areas.

The following tasks would seem to be of particular importance in this context:

1. *Preserving the valuable part of the technology basis in Eastern Europe and the CIS.* Much will depend upon whether the traditional strengths of these countries in research and aerospace technology can be utilized. The ailing aerospace organizations in the former Soviet Union are looking for partners. Capacity for rocket and satellite launches, scarce in Western Europe and America, is available in abundance there. Kourou in Guinea, the launchpad for European rockets, is a minor spaceport compared to Baikonur, the world's largest space launchpad – and one that is under-utilized. Furthermore, the countries of the former Soviet Union have a wealth of theoretical and methodological knowledge in many technological areas that is on a par with that of leading Western research institutions. The number of academics employed in ministries, universities, archives, museums and the Academy of Sciences of the former USSR is estimated at 1.3 million, 80 per cent of whom are scientists and engineers.

2. *Supplying the emerging markets primarily with advanced technologies.* Obviously, it would be very tempting to exploit the unexpected potential in Eastern Europe for selling 'old', mature technologies. In the longer term, however, this might do more harm than good, both to Western suppliers, who choose the easy way out, and to Eastern customers, who would still be condemned to the life of the laggard. Western Europeans should, therefore, adhere to high industrial and technical standards when

opening upmarkets in the East: they should consistently focus on tasks that strengthen their international competitiveness, not on amortizing their weaknesses.

The chance of a completely new start invites freer use of new technologies. It is no coincidence that Saudi Arabia at the beginning of the Eighties had a more modern telephone network than the Federal Republic of Germany, or that some of the most highly automated Japanese manufacturing plants are based in Singapore. For many of the semi-industrialized markets, new transport systems will become important in the coming years. Building an infrastructure provides a good opportunity for high-tech solutions.

In Eastern Europe and the new states of the Federal Republic of Germany, as well as in the industrial nations, the environment is one of the most important areas throwing up new technological challenges. Eliminating environmental damage and creating less environmentally harmful technologies are major markets of the future.

Where development is not restricted by a rigid framework of all-pervading regulations, major high-tech projects may be conceivable – which brings to mind ideas like a magnetic levitation railway line connecting Berlin, Warsaw and Moscow, new airport infrastructures or progressive solutions in power engineering. Particularly in this context, companies may have attractive opportunities to build up sustainable leadership positions, above and beyond merely supplying plant and equipment, by bringing to bear superior know-how as systems operators.

3. *Exploiting opportunities for global world-class co-operation.* The re-industrialization of Eastern Europe, and particularly of the former Soviet Union, calls for new approaches. Car-making and other high-tech manufacturing plants in the east of Russia, built in co-operation with

Western Europe, could also be of interest to the Japanese market. This will be a case for high-tech rather than low-tech. Nor will Japan and Korea leave the future markets in eastern Europe untouched in the long term. Joint projects with interesting world-class partners could reduce the risk for European companies and provide valuable learning experience. Examples could be joint ventures between Western European and Japanese companies for the development of the infrastructure in Siberia, for the utilization of space facilities, or for such major projects as advanced-technology rail networks.

If priority one in the move toward globalization is to create insider positions in the core markets of Western Europe, the US and Japan, priority two is to secure a technology-driven place in the budding markets of Eastern Europe and other threshold countries. Insider positions in the US and Japan make it possible for European companies to gain additional business volume, flexibility and learning experience in low-cost/high-performance manufacturing. Presence in the markets of Eastern Europe, Latin America and the Pacific can give the Europeans a share in the economic growth of these regions and help safeguard them against possible – and, to a certain extent, demographically predictable – growth risks.

Furthermore, the transfer of jobs and prosperity to the emerging markets of Eastern Europe may also help to stabilize the fledgling democracies and stem the threatening tide of immigration. It is obvious that, in view of the gigantic projects and the amount of ground to be covered, individual companies cannot tackle this task single-handed. But the model of constructive partnership between government and industry, tried and tested in the past, should come into its own here.

The Environmental Challenge: New Problems, New Opportunities

The 'Club of Rome' and its startling theses, the Green parties in Central Europe, the adoption of green concerns by all political parties, the discussions regarding the basic right to unspoiled nature, the serious environmental damage in the former Communist countries of Eastern Europe – all these are evidence that among the concerns of society environmental protection now has high priority. Of course, the urgency of the problem is being veiled by the insidiousness of spreading soil, air and water pollution – and by the often subconscious attitude that the current generation will be OK and that their descendants will just have to look out for themselves. But even so, the development of ideas on environmental protection in Europe has taken on a heartening dynamism.

Environmental protection, which for many years was viewed as the responsibility of social policy, is increasingly becoming an issue for modern corporate management. In step with the massive, cumulative industrialization during the last forty years, the ecological balance between pollution and regeneration has been tipped. The last generation is responsible for nearly 90 per cent of the environmental damage now evident. A problem comparable in proportion to the social question at the end of the early capitalist era, today's environmental issue proffers a two fold challenge: first, to handle the burdens imposed on companies by the obligation to behave in an environmentally-conscious way and by their liability for environmental damage; second, to make the most of the opportunities provided by a huge, newly emerging market for environmental technology and services.

In Europe, environmental costs are comparatively high. European companies estimate that 2.1 per cent of sales is spent on environmental protection. Chemical group BASF alone reported DM1.45 billion expenditures on the environment (capital investments and operating costs) in its 1991 accounts. However, the threat to sales may present a greater problem than the cost burden in the future, since more stringent legal requirements and changing demand trends are to be expected. Major grocery chains such as Ahold in the Netherlands, Migros in Switzerland and Tengelmann in Germany, are pointing the way by increasingly banning products that are harmful to the environment or difficult to dispose of. In Germany, a well-known example is the personal commitment of Tengelmann owner Erivan Haub, who no longer permits detergents containing phosphate, CFC sprays, mercury batteries or chocolate products containing artificial colourings in his stores. Manufacturers failing to find suitable substitutes in time could be hard hit.

Among suppliers of environmental technology, European companies are the world leaders. For example, Schlumberger has developed drilling machines with extremely low oil and lubricating-grease consumption, and has patented highly-advanced methods of analysis for processing complex chemical waste. Sandoz founded its subsidiary MBT Environmental Engineering in order to utilize the experience gained from the environmental catastrophe in Basle. The subsidiary offers services for decontaminating soil and water, analysis of environmental risks that may pose a threat to health and engineering services for clean-up and recycling projects. Metallgesellschaft – once a fairly dull mining, metallurgy and mechanical engineering group – now generates around one-third of its sales in environmental protection activities. Its value-added chain has been structured and extended to form an overall 'mini-circular flow economy' – with activities ranging from primary industry through plant engineering and environmental technology to environmental services. The group's services include, for instance, restoration of contaminated soil, waste disposal, recycling and sale of waste from steel and aluminium production, disposal of old cars and manufacturing chemical filters.

Erdal Rex, well-known producer of traditional household cleaning agents, currently holds a market share of 20 per cent with its environmentally-friendly 'Frosch' product line. Practically all consumer-goods manufacturers now offer products with a similar positioning on 'environmental friendliness' as their implied value to the customer. The list of suppliers of – in the broadest sense – environmentally friendly products includes many thousands of companies in Germany alone. The number of suppliers of environmental technology is estimated at around 7,300.

A 1991 McKinsey study confirms that the general issue of the environment is relatively high on the management agenda of European companies. This puts European entrepreneurs among the pioneers of environmentally-aware management. They are more convinced than their counterparts in the US and Japan that they will be able to raise the standards of environmental protection substantially by the year 2000, and that they will be able to pass on the costs of more environment-friendly products and manufacturing processes to environment-conscious customers. A majority of top managers surveyed reported not only that they were prepared to implement environmental measures in response to legislation, but that they would also make a proactive contribution. The heads of European industry maintain that they would be able to cope even with a 50 per cent reduction in legal pollution levels, on the condition that market rules are standardized to prevent distortions in competition. If this condition is met, European entrepreneurs find national or EC-wide rulings equally acceptable as voluntary commitments. Speaking for the whole of the chemical industry, Bayer CEO Manfred Schneider comments, 'Given equal ecological requirements, we do not fear for our competitiveness.'

Receptiveness in industry to environmental initiatives reflects the level of ecological awareness among a European public that expresses its expectations of trade and industry much less tolerantly than people in many areas of the US or Japan. In the densely populated countries of Western Europe, a series of dangerous incidents, from the chemical contamination of the Rhine to the nuclear accident at Chernobyl, along with the high level of pollution caused by toxic emissions and waste problems in the highly industrialized areas of Central Europe, has created a special awareness of the environment. In recent years, Europe has witnessed more clearly than the US or Japan that environmental damage does not respect national borders.

Government institutions and private companies have frequently worked together to develop innovative solutions to environmental problems. Some notable successes are the exemplary monitoring systems for the operation of nuclear power plants, or the environmental information system set up in Baden-Württemberg, which provides on-line information on water and air quality and constantly monitors soil quality.

Some leading companies go far beyond legal obligations to invest in researching more environment-friendly products and manufacturing methods. Among the more conspicuous moves are the experiments at Opel and Mercedes-Benz with water-soluble paints, the introduction of phosphate-free detergents by Henkel, BMW's car-recycling plant, Schmidheiny's abandonment of asbestos products, or VW's commitment to take back cars at the end of their useful life, followed by similar pledges from Renault and Peugeot-Talbot. Volvo's pioneering work has not only stimulated progress in the development of the catalytic converter, but has also heightened public awareness with its training programmes and environmental audits.

IBM Germany has anchored responsibility for the environment very firmly in line management and is determined to better the legal requirements by a clear margin. In product design, IBM is making increased efforts to take recycling into account right from the design stage ('design to recycle'). The company recently brought a 'green PC' on to the market. In 1991 alone, 2,200 tonnes of old units were recycled, and the volume of special waste has been reduced within five years to a quarter of its former amount. As a supplier to the environmental market, the company offers an expert system for testing whether products are environmentally harmless.

These achievements, and the general willingness of companies to make an active commitment to environmental policy, cannot blind us to one fundamental problem: a basic inequality in starting conditions. General environmental legislation and the system of control to ensure that this legislation is observed are more acute in Europe than in Japan or the US – with corresponding differences in costs. As global competition grows, this will no doubt become an increasingly important factor. And even within Europe the rules of the game are anything but uniform. As detailed analysis of McKinsey's management survey on the environment shows, there are three different approaches to environmental issues in Europe, which correspond to three different geographical groupings:

Northern and Central Europeans play a leadership role. Especially in Northern Europe, companies have begun to look beyond their everyday business and turn their attention towards anticipating environmental questions. These pioneering activities have been stimulated by progressive environmental policy in Denmark, Germany and the Netherlands, as well as in the EFTA states of Finland, Norway, Austria, Sweden and Switzerland. Beyond up-to-the-minute issues regarding the avoidance or disposal of waste (particularly hazardous waste), corporate interest in this area primarily focuses on product life-cycle concepts. These concepts aim for an integrated view of the value-added process, from product development through manufacturing and distribution to the taking back, disposal and recycling of old products. Devised in the majority of cases as a response to government pressure, they are altering the orientation, value-added chains and success factors of whole industries. The newly adopted responsibility of manufacturers for what happens to their products after they have been sold demands entirely new forms of co-operation among suppliers, manufacturers, customers and competitors.

As a result, the environmental issue is becoming a major driving force behind economic progress. For example, Europe is currently toying with the idea of testing market-oriented environmental regulations similar to the tradeable 'pollution credits' introduced under the Clean Air Act in the US. In Germany, a joint initiative of the packaging and consumer-goods industries and wholesalers/retailers in response to government pressure is also breaking new ground – though not without its fair share of teething troubles. The 'Grüner Punkt' (green dot) is designed to ensure the fullest possible return and recycling of packaging materials.

Ecological balance sheets also bear witness to Northern Europe's role as leader. Originally devised in Switzerland, they have been adopted by a growing number of German companies to determine the environmental effects – resources use, emissions, waste – of all goods and services sourced, manufactured and distributed. In addition to their contribution to the corporate image, these balance sheets also effectively supplement corporate accounting and – when used as a control tool – offer a way of curbing costs, particularly overhead.

Countries such as Belgium, France and Britain are 'followers'. Companies in these countries do have a similar awareness of the problems and, to a certain extent, share the priorities of the 'leader' countries. Yet where the leaders forge ahead with constructive and occasionally ground-breaking action, these countries tend to hold back and wait. That said, once the need for a given measure is actually recognized, it will generally be implemented with imagination and commitment.

In an industry comparison, virtually all the process industries would be in this group of followers. As a result of the specifics of their production, all these industries have been increasingly subjected to regulatory initiatives in the last twenty years. Power companies, which especially in the Southern European countries still tend to be environmental laggards, have now joined the 'follower' group in the more environmentally-aware countries. In general, legal limits, particularly for air pollution, are now largely observed. Some companies are also diversifying into the environmental business, chiefly in the areas of waste disposal and water supply, where they can address their traditional customer base in local government, private households, trade and industry. In the use of new technologies or the reduction of CO_2 emissions, however, these countries still seem to have the brakes on.

The Southern Europeans are the 'laggards'. Companies in Italy, Spain and Portugal are still primarily concerned with noise and odour pollution, acid rain and air pollution – issues that are no longer of top priority for their northern neighbours. Observing regulations is the major objective in the south, with the majority of companies responding to regulatory intervention and incentives such as subsidies and tax benefits. Very rarely do companies make proactive use of environmental protection as a field for new business activities.

Among industries, those that are relatively distant from their markets or their end users are typically the ones that lag behind. These include primary industry, which in countries with a poor environmental policy and an underdeveloped environmental administration, is one of the largest polluters and consumers of natural resources. Paradoxically, agriculture is also one of the laggards in almost every country. Politicians' vision of agriculture as a guardian of the countryside has so far worked only in exceptional cases, such as the mountain farmers of South Tyrol.

These differences in the stringency of environmental regulations create serious distortions in competition within Europe. Many top managers from the leader nations are, therefore, calling for harmonization, primarily at the EC level. Among them is Bayer CEO Manfred Schneider, a committed advocate of environmentally-harmless products and production methods. Take the example of dilute acid processing. As a proponent of the strict German environmental regulations regarding titanium dioxide, Schneider is no longer willing to accept that competitors in the titanium dioxide market that manufacture their products in France and Britain gain competitive advantages from being allowed to discharge the dilute acid created during the production process into estuaries and coastal waters. He finds it unacceptable that Bayer 'produces' losses despite full-capacity utilization simply because the processing of dilute acid adds 15–20 per cent to production cost. However, relief through standardization of regulations is not in sight.

From the different behaviour patterns outlined above, we can expect the EC countries to continue to share similar environmental policy objectives in the future, but to

apply different degrees of reforming zeal and implementation speed. However, while the EC guidelines adopted
in the past were chiefly oriented to the preferences of the
'follower' group, we can expect a shift towards the preferences of the 'leader' group as newly joining EFTA countries
create new majorities in the Council of Ministers.

Even then, uniform EC-wide solutions to problems such
as the emission of carbon dioxide and life-cycle responsibility are unlikely. The current positions of leaders, followers
and laggards are still too far apart. For example, Germany
intends to reduce emissions of CO_2 by up to 25 per cent
against their 1988 level by the year 2005. Hot on the
heels of Germany's high standards is Denmark, with the
Netherlands following a little further behind. Italy, France
and Britain have agreed to aim for stabilization by the
year 2000 or 2005. But no other EC country has announced official reduction targets.

However, it is by no means certain whether progress on
the environment front will actually be determined by the
stringency of regulations or whether the market will, in fact,
set its own pace. Examples of such developments are the
initiatives in the retail trade mentioned above, as well as
the increasing ecological awareness of consumers. Further
examples are the experiments in the Netherlands with 'contracts' or 'voluntary agreements' between industry and the
government on, for example, reducing power consumption
in the steel and chemical industries. 'Voluntary agreements'
seem to be coming up with particularly good results. Industry knows that constructive co-operation is preferable to
the body of regulations that would otherwise be imposed
by the government. Last but not least, the rules of the
game are being changed by the environmental awareness of
Central European consumers. On a world-wide scale, these
consumers can safely be said to be the most acutely aware
of environmental hazards. The excess packaging found in

the hotel cleaning services or the retail trade in the US, or totally polluted areas like Fujiyama in Japan, are practically inconceivable in Central Europe today.

It is unlikely that industry leaders in particular will be content to wait for new legal regulations in the future. They will, instead, take the initiative themselves. Followers and especially laggards could run the risk of missing a change in the market because of their delaying tactics and, as a result, ultimately place themselves at a massive competitive disadvantage. At Bayer, Manfred Schneider has turned the adoption of new environmental initiatives into ongoing practice. It is worth noting that companies that have experienced an environmental accident of some kind (Sandoz, Union Carbide) have almost always become leaders on the environmental scene.

Management of the environment is a central issue for top management. This will call for:

☐ *Pre-emptive situational analysis*. The fact that environmental conditions and approaches are not the same in the various regions means that it is useful to know exactly what effect potential political decisions will have on individual companies. Many top managers consider this kind of pre-emptive assessment of future policy to be virtually impossible. In the McKinsey survey they frequently argued that governmental environmental policy was notoriously inconsistent and therefore unpredictable. Our experience, however, is that an environmental policy assessment is, in reality, much easier than forecasts on issues like the movements of the dollar, oil prices, or political developments in Eastern Europe. With the aid of information on environmental policy, regional and industry specifics, it is usually possible to predict reliably enough the basic shape of the decisions that will be taken within five to seven years at the EC or national level.

No company that operates on an international scale can today afford to ignore the potential effects of national or international environmental policy. If the impact is minimal, for example because the industry is predominantly made up of followers or laggards – as is the case with the utilities in many parts of the industrialized world – it may be enough to estimate the costs incurred in complying with present and future regulations. If, however, the effects on the population are more serious (as in the chemical industry) or if strong leaders determine the pace of developments in the industry (as in the grocery trade), a more complex evaluation is necessary – a wide range of economic policy instruments and voluntary measures have to be taken into account.

☐ *Strategic positioning.* Whether anticipated developments should be accommodated in advance or reactively must be determined by conditions within the industry, among other factors. But any decision should be based on detailed analysis and be made deliberately. Pursuing a strategy as a leader can be a very costly and risky business if it goes against industry trends – for example, in an industry where followers and laggards are in the majority. By their very nature, pioneers operate in unexplored territory. Thus cars with catalytic converters were ahead of their time in the markets of Southern Europe until just a few years ago – local industry had not yet reached this level, and customers were not asking for them. The story was no different in traffic safety, an area related to environmental protection. The pioneering development of airbags and anti-lock braking system (both by Mercedes-Benz with Bosch) took a long time to become the generally accepted standard.

Conversely, the same level of risk may be involved in being a follower in an area where strong leaders develop new procedures that are readily accepted by customers and end users, thereby pushing established products and services out of the market. A sure-fire recipe for failure is a 'laggard' approach in an international industry with strong leaders or in a very progressive country. This has been one of the main reasons behind the sales difficulties experienced by US car makers, who were slow to respond to the demand for fuel-saving models. In the chemical industry, any company stepping into the fray against Bayer, Dow and DuPont – all renowned in their product areas as environmental leaders – must march to the beat of these companies' drums.

Taking all this into account, it is clear that there can be no catch-all 'green is good for you' strategic thrust that is right for all companies. The words of Wolfgang Roth of the German Social Democratic Party (SPD), who says that environmental protection could be a real money-spinner if only companies would realize it, apply to some cases, but certainly not all.

☐ *Co-operation to make the most of opportunities for action.* Even big industrial companies are unable to undertake major environmental projects single-handed. In the automotive industry, for example, recycling projects, no less than the long-term changeover to alternative fuels, new traffic systems, or new product concepts, all require industry-wide co-operation. This includes partnerships with competitors, the restructuring of relationships with suppliers and customers, and increased co-operation with unions, ecological interest groups and policymakers. As co-operation of this kind becomes more and more significant, an important competitive advantage can be had by being at the negotiating table when the political agenda gets drawn up.

Environmental protection does not take the form of an old-fashioned, union-style, organized representation of interests. Instead, across all political parties, among an increasingly critical public, and in far-sighted companies, an increasingly important 'green' movement is emerging. For example, our survey revealed that immediate actions to counteract the greenhouse effect met with widespread approval by companies. Even a 10 per cent price increase for fossil fuels or a 50 per cent energy tax were said to be acceptable under certain conditions. Similarly, I remember how over 90 per cent of the 120 students in my lecture class voted for an immediate ban – with no period of grace – on CFCs.

Given this scenario, a little more courage would do public opinion leaders and decision-makers no harm. Perhaps all they need is the sober perspective which a look over the fence into the world of business accounting could provide: there, depreciation of 3–5 per cent is deducted from the value of factories and plants every year. In a highly developed country, a comparable sum ought to be set aside for environmental protection. In other words, to maintain the value of the environment, 'standard' depreciation could be regularly taken in the same way as for production equipment. The cost of eliminating environmental damage in Western Germany (1990) is estimated at up to DM140 billion per year. This represents a good 5 per cent of the gross national product – or a standard tax depreciation burden for plant and machinery. Today, only one-quarter of that amount, or DM35.7 billion, is spent on environmental protection measures in Germany.

In short, neither the arguments nor the possibilities for action have been exhausted so far. It is important to reach social consensus on objectively justified causes for concern, and then to act consistently on them. There is no doubt that environmental protection is going to be a core challenge for companies in the industrialized countries, and that it will have much to do with their long-term success or failure.

The Challenge of Innovation: Technology Management for the Market

Since the start of the industrial age, a constant flow of innovations has been the lifeblood of European economies. The high standing of the sciences ensured substantial R and D budgets and close ties between companies and scientific colleges. Sound engineering know-how contributed both to the continuous development of manufacturing technology and to the combination of individual products into 'systems' custom-designed for individual buyers. As long as the competitive game was played by the customary rules, European capital- and consumer-goods manufacturers continued to chalk up successes.

Such successes were built on the consciousness of a sound scientific foundation (nowhere else in the world can boast as many institutes, scientists, technical publications or patents), and trust in a confident, albeit often expensive, R and D base. The development departments of many car makers, for example, enjoyed an almost legendary reputation as a result of never producing an out-and-out flop. Continuous rationalization of the manufacturing process, it was felt, was bound to create the most modern production plants. And state-of-the-art plants were management's absolute pride, and were shown off to customers, business colleagues and politicians alike.

Little wonder that modern techniques of innovation management seldom met with ready approval amongst company
executives. R and D departments were often corporate
hallowed ground and were protected as such. Everyone
knew that there was no place for an analytical input/output
mentality here. The order to 'sit down and invent' was
as ineffectual as the question, 'Why can't you be
creative?' The idea of relating input, as measured by R and
D man-years, to output, as measured by relevant technical
parameters, was unfamiliar. The phenomena of the technology S-curve diagnosed by my colleague Dick Foster[1]
were only reluctantly taken on board and accepted as a
way of monitoring a company's position. Salvation was
generally seen to be in *more* R and D spending, not in
concentrating on selected issues. This is not surprising
when we consider that, up until a few years ago, some R and
D managers still denied the controllability of development
activities. ('It all comes down to chance,' they'd say. 'Read
Monod.')

Drawing up a technology portfolio of R and D projects
listed according to technical targets (with probabilities
of achieving the targets) was taken by development
departments to be a doomed attempt to control the uncontrollable. Moreover, combining such a technology portfolio
with a strategic business portfolio appeared to scientists
and technicians to be an unreasonable attempt to meet
an unattainable quantitative demand. One R and D head
is reported to have said, 'We can't let today's R and D
investment turn into medium-term business plans.'

As a result, useful approaches and techniques – dividing
approved development projects into upstream and downstream phases, establishing a systems architecture, employing strong project managers, and using constant 'milestone

---

[1] Richard Foster, *Innovation – The Attacker's Advantage*, New York
1986.

checks' on the progress of a project – looked like un-welcome instruments from the management consultancy toolbox. Conventional wisdom was adamant about their lack of practicality.

☐ Divisions between 'upstream' (idea-driven) and 'down-stream' (schedule-driven) phases were not possible because the development of ideas was an ongoing process.

☐ Systems architecture could not be defined ex-ante because it changed constantly, and therefore no systems architect could have an overall perspective.

☐ Strong project managers were not useful because the real development work took place only in the (functional) departments.

☐ Project control by technical and financial milestones was not possible because advances in development occur spontaneously and intermittently.

Things have changed since then. Many European companies have introduced modern management tools into their product and process development. Like other regions with few natural resources, Europe is proving that the 'hard' mercantilistic factors of size, population and sources of raw materials and energy, no longer determine the health of a national economy. 'Soft' factors – the quality of human resources, technology know-how, and (entre-preneurial) innovative power – are now more important. These factors form the basis for economic and technical innovation. Companies with innovative products and/or manufacturing technologies create new growth and em-ployment, not only in high-tech growth industries but also in 'mature' ones, as the example of Thyssen recently showed.

Today, 35 per cent of Thyssen's products, although derived from mature technologies, are less than five years old.

The central issue for many European companies, nevertheless, appears to be rapid and smooth accomplishment of the structural change from mature to new technologies. The advance of modern data-processing and communication technology into a wide variety of industries and corporate functions has resulted in microelectronics, information technology and telecommunications becoming key industries in the high-tech competition of the Triad. It is no coincidence that the *Cebit* electronics fair was separated from the capital-goods core of the Hanover Fair a few years ago; as an independent area, information and communication technology now has a trade fair of its own.

Microelectronic products with IT-related applications in a multitude of industries now generate world-wide sales revenue of around $317 billion, which was about 2 per cent of the gross national product of the Triad in 1991. A further increase to around $600 billion is expected by the year 2000. At the corporate level, investments in information technology in the US have increased from around 2.1 per cent (1960) of total investment to more than ten times that figure (25–28 per cent in 1990). IT now represents 40 per cent of R and D costs in the electrical industry and 24 per cent of logistics costs for purchasing and distribution in the retail trade.

Given the importance and the extraordinarily high growth potential of microelectronic applications, the Europeans' deficit as suppliers of microelectronic products is worrying. Nevertheless, it would be wrong to talk about a general European creative and innovative deficit in this technology or in its likely successor, optoelectronics. Jacques Maisonrouge, the former head of IBM Europe, said the Europeans are no less innovative than the Americans or the Japanese. On the contrary, their experience base and large stock of high-calibre scientists had actually given them a lead in terms of inventions. The problem was, he said, that Europeans had for decades had problems with transferring their development ideas to the marketplace – an area in which the Americans and especially the Japanese were far more adept.

European companies have indeed regularly come up with excellent technical achievements – from the Siemens Modell 2002, the first transistorized computer (1954), through the liquid crystals of E. Merck, the Bull workstation (1987) launched on the market at the same time as the first of the Sun-Microsystems models, to Hell's fax machine – which have then failed to make a big breakthrough in the market. So there must be other reasons for the relative backwardness of the Europeans in this area.

What Europe is lacking most, it seems, is the fertile 'climate' which has proved so productive in the electronics sectors of Silicon Valley, Japan and Taiwan: the exchange of know-how between a multitude of players, the high educational standard of developers and production staff, numerous suppliers and customers who pass on new ideas to the manufacturers or whose demands stimulate new approaches. Even the high personnel turnover of over 20 per cent in Silicon Valley and along Route 128 contributes to know-how transfer and structural change.

Many European manufacturers are also hampered by their lack of customer orientation. In many cases companies are too obsessed with technological finesse – with all its effects on costs – to pay close attention to real customer preferences. Recent examples, which in many respects are typical and therefore not without importance for other sectors, are the experiences of two German computer start-ups, Supremum and Parsytec.

The press announcement at the beginning of 1991 was brief and, after the withdrawal of state funding, came as no surprise to the initiated: 'Bonn Supremum GmbH scales back.' Supremum, the co-ordinating company of the ambitious, first purely German supercomputer project – intended to perform five billion computing operations per second ('gigaflops') on some 256 parallel processors – was now to concentrate its activities on maintenance work and marketing smaller-sized computers. After five years in development and a cost of more than DM200 million, at least DM160 million of which was injected by Bonn, the joint venture of public and private investors unveiled its first-generation product, the most powerful version of which could carry out 890 million computations per second ('megaflops') on sixty-four processors. In 1991, Supremum managed to sell just five of these models, including one to its main shareholder. Neither industry nor public research institutes saw much of a chance in the market for the Supremum computer, which used primarily US standard components for lack of suitable European alternatives. The eighteen to twenty planned software packages just never happened.

The counter-example also comes from Germany. The small Aachen-based company Parsytec has shown that modern parallel computers of the Supremum category can be developed much faster, more cost-effectively, and with great commercial success, even in Europe. With low public funding – a grant of DM800,000 in the start-up phase – and in spite of the supposedly overwhelming competition by Supremum, Parsytec was able to develop a whole product family of parallel computers, including mainframes with 256 and 400 microprocessors. In 1991 the company, which had regularly notched up a growth rate of 50 to 100 per cent per year, generated annual sales of DM25 million with a workforce of 150. It markets its products in nineteen countries and has subsidiaries in the US and Britain. Two hundred computer systems of different sizes have been installed world-wide – in multinationals such as Shell, Daimler-Benz, Matsushita, British Aerospace, Matra and Volkswagen, as well as in universities and research institutes. To break through to a computing capability which goes beyond the standards of current supercomputing, and to facilitate applications in modern climate and chaos research, Parsytec plans to introduce a new family of products with large systems of over 16,000 processors and a capacity of 400 gigaflops.

While the main goal at Supremum was to produce a national technical and scientific achievement, Parsytec was more interested in customer-oriented solutions. The software on offer is limited to application-specific solutions for computing-intensive tasks and real-time industrial applications. Technology, purchasing and distribution are consistently European – a deliberate policy. As Parsytec CEO Falk D. Kübler comments, 'We have demonstrated faster and more cheaply that parallel computers have a great future. And our achievement is a European one through and through.'

If we analyse the reasons for the failure of the Supremum project and other European high-tech projects, five sources come to light:

The S-curve dynamics are poorly understood. Plotting technical performance against the input of development man-years result in an S-curve, which can be used as a fair approximation of technological progress in product and process development. In the initial stages of a new technology, high development spending (capital, personnel, expert reports, materials and equipment, tests, etc.) tends to bring a disproportionately low level of technical progress. But as soon as a breakthrough has been made, there is an explosive expansion in performance. Technological performance now grows much faster than effort expended until it approaches the physical limits of the technology. Thereafter, even with a further increase in effort and expenditure it becomes more and more difficult to make technical progress.

A classic example of the S-curve phenomenon is the substitution of various materials in the production of tyre cords. The first synthetic fibre to replace the original cotton was rayon. It was superior to cotton in critical parameters such as strength, thermal resistance, road-holding and material fatigue. Over several years manufacturers invested more than $100 million in further improving rayon. The first $60 million of this investment produced a performance gain of 800 per cent over the starting point; the next $15 million a further 25 per cent; but the final $25 million only a 5 per cent improvement. Rayon technology had reached its limits. In actual fact, the manufacturers could have saved the final $40 million.

Nylon manufacturer DuPont soon had a similar experience in the bid to find a successor to rayon as the material for tyre cords. Not realizing that nylon was already near the top of its technological S-curve, the company invested a further $75 million but was able to gain only a slight edge in performance over rayon. The 'victor' was Celanese with its still young polyester technology. Performance improvement was two and a half times that of DuPont with nylon, for only half the investment.

The only way out of the growing dilemma of excessive expenditure on familiar technologies for insufficient results is a (naturally risky) quantum leap to the new S-curve of the next technology, initially at a lower performance level. Europeans traditionally find it hard to let go of proven technologies at the right time, as is widely known. What seems to be less well known is that European companies are also prone to spectacular mistakes at the start of S-curves.

The list of errors of judgement is long, and the costs gigantic. The first Wankel engine, the first facsimile machines, the first 'fast-breeder' reactor, the first workstations, the first gallium arsenide chips, a technically superior video system – the lack of market understanding shows up again and again. Often, pioneering European companies attempt to patent their know-how, keep it to themselves and move the market alone. However, if user behaviours need to be changed, or if as many industry players as possible are to be convinced to adopt standardized formats and components, or if social consensus is required, this path almost always leads to disaster. Europeans must exploit innovations more quickly by seeking alliances, granting licences, and winning others over to the same technical standards and letting them share the rewards.

The value to the customer of the new product was not defined precisely enough. Innovative products from European manufacturers often fail although technically brilliant, forward-looking solutions have been found. The problem: the value to the customer has not been defined precisely enough. The customer often receives technical answers to questions he never even asked. This results in the launch of over-complicated, over-expensive and over-delicate innovations, which are let loose on the unsuspecting customers – often late – as 'technical solutions' to the problems of tomorrow. Today, however, many of their features prove superfluous. The German videotext system ('btx') is a case in point: an idea that was right in principle – to give the private individual access to data banks – but was realized badly. The system that came on to the market was too expensive, its operation immature, its user interface technically inadequate, and, above all, its customers completely unprepared.

In addition, even in consumer goods Europeans tend to exhaust lucrative niches in high-end customer segments first, preferably in their national home markets, before developing volume segments with simplified versions of their products. This means that market opportunities are not fully or systematically exploited, and cost advantages from economies of scale are left untapped.

One of the main reasons why value to the customer is so poorly defined in Europe, and, by association, market potential so poorly identified, is the deep split in corporate culture between R and D and sales/marketing. Despite declared interest in cross-functional co-operation, they are still very separate worlds for many companies. The consequence of this split is that large R and D budgets are not checked regularly and rigorously enough from the market point of view. Too many resources get poured into marginal, unfocused product optimization or unspecific basic research. In the chemical and electrical industries, for example, only 10–20 per cent of R and D funds are usually available for real innovations aimed at market leadership.

European developers must get closer to the customer, pay attention to user behaviour and to the sources of user value. Second-hand information from sales and service colleagues is no substitute for first-hand customer analysis. This is particularly true if the introduction of a product will require the user to change his or her behaviour – for example, if managers are to switch to electronic file management or to use electronic mail instead of paper. Comprehensive use of laptops by the sales team of an automobile company saved time and costs in the tens of millions. However, this was made possible by intensive user tests conducted by the manufacturer during the design and implementation phases. One of the reasons for the rigorous 'verticalization' of the new Siemens organization was Hermann Franz's conviction that it was high time to part with the company's time-honoured principle of not letting a developer or production expert loose on a customer.

Well-informed developers must also be more closely involved in business policy decisions on innovations, and they must gain a better understanding of general business issues. Portfolio techniques, joint visits by developers and salespeople to the US and Japan, as well as regular, company-wide strategy meetings, can be of help.

Suppliers are fragmented. Although Europe now has quite a number of multinational companies, only a few European companies can boast a world market position similar to that of General Motors, Ford, Exxon, Mitsubishi, Matsushita, Hitachi and the like. This can be partly explained by post-war developments, with every European country supporting its own high-tech champions in the hope of becoming technologically autonomous. The unintended result: a large number of suppliers with relatively small markets, virtually all protected and highly priced.

If we look at the market shares of leading European suppliers by country, it appears that their relatively strong market positions are often the result of a dominant position in their own home markets. Market shares in other important industrialized countries – still often regarded as 'foreign' and treated accordingly – tend to be marginal. As a result, many companies do not have the critical mass or the necessary staying power to establish convincing new product concepts right across the board, including in the high-volume segments. This applies – with exceptions such as the cigarette industry and advertising – to virtually all industries and businesses in Europe.

Such fragmentation is particularly noticeable in the German software and services market. Around 2,500 small and tiny suppliers vie for position in a market that is of crucial importance to technological development. Only a very few, among them Software AG and SAP, have international standing. The majority are companies with an annual sales volume of a few million DM that supply non-standardized software and services to largely local customers. (The American company EDS, with more than

47,000 employees, French Cap Gemini with almost 17,000 employees and Dutch Volmac with over 3,000 employees are many times larger than their largest German competitors.) It seems likely that few of the players in this 'cottage industry' will survive the arrival of powerful foreign competitors under the auspices of the single European market.

In the future, we can expect a multitude of mergers or other forms of co-operation in Europe to allow companies to grow to international scale. This is particularly necessary in industries such as telecommunications, where development investment cannot be amortized in the smaller European markets. Many Europeans will also be facing the question of which stages of the value-added chain should remain in-house. Concentrating on fewer value-added stages could provide the critical mass companies require if they can link up with other manufacturers to compensate for their weaker areas.

The product range is not sufficiently oriented to strategic core businesses. A very wide range of different products and services is characteristic of all leading European technology-based companies. European electrical companies traditionally see themselves as full-line producers of electrical and electronic products, consumer durables and capital goods alike. This universal, Euro-typical business goal is becoming untenable as a result of the high number of country-specific variants. It can also be found in the European chemical and pharmaceutical companies, plastics-processing and mechanical-engineering companies, and even the major banks and insurance companies.

All too often, what are actually very impressive corporate R and D resources are spread over too many areas and so can only be used to defend the status quo. Similarly, top-management attention has to be spread over too many different areas, which undercuts a company's ability to respond to market needs. It does not have to be this way. The development of business policy at Siemens AG, for instance, shows that the company is aiming for critical mass in priority fields through targeted acquisitions (Rolm, Nixdorf and Bendix) and alliances (Matsushita). Similar results may perhaps be expected in the future from the reorganization of business activities at Philips AG under their dynamic CEO Jan Timmer – and from the restructuring, in response to gentle pressure from the government, at Thomson and Alcatel.

Research and development are too dependent on government grants. National and EC-wide research programmes, such as Esprit, play a major role in the development of Europe's technology base. As in the United States, industrial research policy in Europe is a recognized area of government responsibility. In 1988, a total of 41.3 per cent of R and D costs were financed by the state in Europe (Japan 19.9 per cent, US 48.9 per cent). But this support is also too spread out. The existence of more than 1,300 scientific institutes in Germany alone implies subcritical mass, a situation in which resources are frequently distributed according to a kind of pro-rata basis.

The generally positive co-operation between government and industry suffers from two fundamental ills: a large proportion of state aid – in the form of joint-project financing or non-repayable subsidies for individual companies – flows into predominantly science/technology-oriented basic research, where too little attention is paid to transforming the results into marketable products. Because subsidized research is profitable even without customer contact, there is an increasing tendency to develop new technologies or products purely for in-house reasons – as the example of Supremum shows – instead of going straight to the needs of the customer from day one. Again and again, highly innovative research lies dormant for years as a high-tech

artefact because it has no relevance to the market or because
the related technologies needed for implementation were
not developed at the same time. In optoelectronics, for
example, the excellent achievements of European laser
research may well come to nothing because, so far, only
the Japanese have the manufacturing technologies needed
for commercialization.

There is an equally worrying, subsidy-fed tendency for
companies to abandon innovative technologies and product concepts as soon as public funds run out or public
orders fail to materialize. Siemens, SEL and AEG all decided not to commercialize their optoelectronic know-how,
gained at the beginning of the Eighties, because at that
time the Federal Post Office was not yet interested in a
rapid development of glass-fibre technology. The experience of the Porsyt joint project on the development of
CASE (computer-aided software engineering) tools is also
typical. The technological aim of the project – catching
up with the US software industry's performance standards – was achieved. Several years after completion,
however, the results had still not been turned into commercial reality.

Against this background, the conditions of the single
European market call for the following tasks to be addressed
both EC-wide and on the national level:

1. *Reaching consensus on the importance of promoting high-
   tech industries.* Instead of subsidizing mature industries
   such as coal and steel, governments should invest in
   the future by supporting high-tech sectors such as electronics, aerospace, information, communications technology. The objective here should not be to build up
   individual industries in isolation but to create an organic network: alongside such end-user industries as
   consumer electronics or HDTV, it will be necessary

to develop efficient component manufacture, process engineering plant engineering, and advanced materials. At the moment, European manufacturers seem to be very much fragmenting their energies.

A major driving force behind innovation must be provided by the liberalization and deregulation of markets. Experience shows that finalizing standards too hastily can block cost and performance optimization. Conversely, nothing has a more beneficial effect on the competitive search for optimal solutions that stimulation of demand by open-minded users at the earliest-possible stage. In telecommunications especially, standardization policy has become a key factor: premature standardization can produce flops, such as German videotext, while late standardization can deter users from experimenting. In Europe today we are a long way behind in data communication because standardization restricted this field at a very early stage. For instance, regulators have banned or refused to approve certain types of modems. Uninformed users, who have been unable to experiment their way into the new age, now represent a major impediment to emerging European suppliers intent on developing this market.

2. *Developing effective incentives to implement state-subsidized technology and product concepts.* In view of growing pressure from rationalization in mature industries, targeted support for innovative products and industries is needed to unlock the employment potential of these areas. Tax benefits could be granted to truly pioneering companies. Or they could be guaranteed exclusive rights for a period of five to seven years, similar to those of the orphan drug-related procedures of the FDA in the US. Directly promoting the use of new technologies is another possibility focused on, say,

the use of CAD (computer-aided design) or new corporate data networks. State procurement in defence,
aeronautics, rail networks and telecoms could also be
directed towards giving preference to innovative technologies and quickly establishing internationally competitive
innovation standards.

These incentives might be accompanied by a graduated
system of 'penalities', such as granting interested third
parties access to new technologies and product concepts
that have remained unused, or leaving 'offenders' out of
future funded projects. Or governments might require
the repayment of subsidies on a graduated scale. In
addition, the conditions for awarding non-repayable subsidies should be reviewed, making grants non-repayable
only if a patent is registered or if a product or technology
is introduced to the market. All major projects anywhere
in Europe should be awarded at the EC level and be
open to all European companies. Lead countries with
special expertise could act as a kind of sponsor for
certain industries or projects.

3. *Ensuring strict design-to-cost/quality/service via simultaneous engineering and lean manufacturing.* In the long
   run, international competitiveness will depend on a successful turnaround from high-cost/high performance to
   low-cost/high performance. Today, European design-to-
   cost is most advanced among volume producers of components supplying machinery and automotive companies.
   Standard diesel engines, for example, are designed to
   similar standards of efficiency in Japan, England, the
   US and Germany. Cost differences, if any, amount to no
   more than 5–10 per cent. Europeans lag in areas like automotive production, telecommunications and electronics.
   Here, around one-third of the European manufacturers'
   cost disadvantage of some 25–50 per cent against the

Japanese can be attributed to deficiencies in design-to-cost.

Optimization must extend to both product range and manufacturing process. We need a change in mentality brought about, for instance, by introducing manufacturability indices, development-related costing and many short internal feedback loops from manufacturing to development. The boundaries between development and manufacturing must become less rigid – for example, by shifting test planning, possibly even production planning, testing and quality control to the development function. But a whole range of other routes to integration must also be sought. These include having developers and production staff report to the same operations manager, introducing regular job rotation, employing manufacturing people as development heads, giving developers and manufacturing staff similar compensation, setting up integrated product planning groups, and so on.

4. *Using alliances and strategic partnerships to proliferate innovations.* A number of international examples spring to mind here. Xerox was able to establish its Ethernet technology for local area networks as the industry standard by offering a licence to all competitors and semiconductor manufacturers for $1,000 (practically a gift). The benefit to Xerox was that – in contrast to the IBM concept – the majority of the intelligence in Ethernet is shifted to the terminals linked up in the network. Xerox's particular strengths in man/machine interfaces and the associated software therefore promised to lend the company a major advantage in this field. A little later, the man/machine interface solutions from the Xerox Star found their way into Apple products Macintosh and Lisa, and they are also at the core of the Windows user interface, now an industry standard.

Similarly, Matsushita had a clear advantage over Sony in video technology from the outset: the company issued licences for its VHS technology to many other manufacturers and quickly concluded marketing agreements with major retail channels and department-store chains in the US and Japan. Meanwhile Sony missed the opportunity of spreading its own distinctive 'Beta' technology through alliances with competitors. It failed. So did Philips. Even by undercutting prices, Sony made no headway in the market. Later Sony put the lesson it had learned to good use when it introduced its data diskettes: by staging a large-scale attack with many licenceholders, it created a new industry standard.

The Challenge of Information Technology: Revolution in Products, Markets, Processes

In 1960, banks and insurance companies spent less than 2 per cent of their total investment on computer technology. Thirty years later, in 1990, the figure was around 20 per cent and rising. Large industrial companies today spend almost as much on computer support as on research and development, namely 3–4 per cent of their sales revenue. Like R and D expenditure, spending on information technology has a crucial influence on safeguarding the future of these companies. The fact that in Germany, for example, the number of specialists like DP operators, systems analysts and programmers has quadrupled to nearly 400,000 in the last fifteen years confirms the trend: information technology is penetrating all areas of business (and of everyday life) more and more completely and quickly.

Through far-sighted exploitation of this development, innovative companies have secured prominent competitive positions in sometimes difficult, overcrowded markets. The Italian clothes manufacturer Benetton, for instance, was able to increase its market share massively around the world primarily because intelligent, computerized processing of point-of-sale data allowed unprecedentedly rapid reactions to market requirements. Thanks to a highly sophisticated logistics system, the Quelle mail-order company can now guarantee delivery of goods to customers within 48 hours. Heidelberger Druckmaschinen (printing machines), too, became a world market leader not least as a result of its substantial investment in flexible, computer-aided manufacturing systems, which competitors so far have been unable to match.

In the future, the combination of increasingly powerful hardware and software with the additional capabilities provided by networking and interactive systems will further boost this kind of opportunity for differentiation. All the greater will be the risk for companies that miss the boat. The great areas of application are basically already marked out, from the computer technologies in development and manufacturing right up to 'intelligent' systems support for management tasks in the broadest sense.

After some dashed hopes and some unexpected successes, computer-integrated manufacturing (CIM), the buzzword of the manufacturing industry since the beginning of the Seventies, can now be judged from a more sober perspective. The idea of a prefabricated patent recipe has given way to that of a concept which must be largely tailor-made to the needs of each company and implemented as a major project. Its place on the future management agenda is ensured, since its essential feature, the integration of computer systems with one another and with a company's business processes, will be one of the key issues of the coming decade.

An important building block of CIM applications – and the central focus of future development – are CAD (computer-aided design) systems. Higher computing capacity and more advanced software will increasingly enable simulation exercises to find out how materials and products will behave both in the manufacturing process and in actual use. More advanced simulation techniques open up further applications – for example, by having customers select furniture in a three-dimensional 'Cyberspace' showroom. Computer-aided production (CAP), which links order-processing with manufacturing, will use robots and driverless transport systems to bring the vision of an unmanned or 'lights-off' factory closer to reality.

Transportation of the products manufactured in this way will continue to rely mainly on rail or road haulage in Europe for some time to come. However, computer-aided logistics systems will also bring previously unattainable advances – for example, by drastically reducing the amount of money (around DM40 billion) wasted every year in the EC on empty return journeys. In the future, systems developers envisage freight companies being able to determine, via a European-wide information network, where loads are waiting to be collected and where their trucks are. That way, the trucks will be able to collect loads near their drop-off points before they return to base. The same satellite links that make such information networks possible will also be used to maintain the flow of traffic on Europe's increasingly congested roads. Computers will calculate preselected routes, taking into consideration roadworks, traffic jams and other obstacles, and will display this in map format on board each vehicle. European leaders in this field, all with developments well advanced, are Philips, Bosch and Daimler-Benz.

At the same time, more and more powerful management information systems are being developed for the tasks of corporate management. These systems give managers an overview of important developments within their companies and their environment by offering up-to-the-minute access to aggregated data. In addition, links with networks make it possible to access more detailed internal and external data banks, for instance to track down the causes of deviations from plan. These constantly available data, processed with the assistance of expert systems, allow future developments and probabilities to be calculated more effectively and efficiently, giving rise to company-specific decision-support systems.

The implications of this IT 'revolution' will confront European managers with several major changes in their strategic environment:

1. From stand-alone products to system solutions. Co-operation between companies will become more important than ever before. Obvious examples are the developments in the automotive industry and mobile phone installations. If, as looks increasingly likely, the car can retain its appeal as a means of transport only if traffic-guidance systems keep the traffic on the streets moving, the logical consequence is mutual co-operation among a wide variety of industries and companies. Car makers will have to co-operate with the electrical and plant engineering industries, which manufacture sensors, videocameras, and other products for the capture of important information such as the volume of traffic and road conditions. Planning offices and road-construction companies will have to ensure the necessary induction loops, signal towers and similar installations. The computer industry has to provide data storage and evaluation software. The telecommunications industry must ensure transmission of information to control centres and individual drivers, relying on the aerospace industry to provide sufficient satellite capacity. Finally, automotive suppliers will take care of the receiving and display technology inside the vehicle and, in so doing, will depend on computers with cartographic software.

The story will be similar for mobile phone installations such as the 'D' network in Germany. Network operators must work together with manufacturers of telephone exchanges and subscriber equipment on the actual technical processes of telecommunication. Next, the commercial processing of bills will require registration, identification and calculation of every connection made, by distance, duration and applicable rate. Hundreds of thousands of users, due to their mobility, will be making use of exchanges and computers not their own – for example, a call from Rome to London by a user registered in Frankfurt. For Europe-wide – and possibly even world-wide – usage, the technological complexity and the high cost of these linkages can be mastered only by co-operation that spans companies and industries.

European companies can contribute to and play a role in these developments mainly in three areas:

☐ *Design and development of software.* European companies have a relatively good starting position in the increasingly important software business. In contrast to their presence in the hardware market, Japanese and other Asian suppliers have hardly put in an appearance in this area so far, perhaps because binary coding does not fit easily into their culture, mentality or way of thinking. It will be interesting to see whether this will change with the advent of object-oriented programming, whose symbols probably bear more resemblance to the oriental alphabets. American manufacturers concentrate mainly on operating-system software, tools for software development and a comprehensive range of PC software. By contrast, European companies have repeatedly proven their competence in the promising field of applications software. The best current example is the spectacular growth of the German software company SAP. Offering software modules for all commercial and administrative tasks within a company, SAP has created such a level of demand on the user side that even the major hardware manufacturers are making an effort to offer the latest versions of this software on their computers.

☐ *Systems integration.* The interaction of different technologies in a large system demands complex integration work, particularly for interface management and communication. Apart from in-depth technical components know-how, the basis for success in this market is an understanding of systems integration coupled with substantial resources for timely project completion. These conditions are in place in Europe, as demonstrated by several high-growth service companies which have either passed the half-a-billion DM sales mark or are well on their way towards doing so: Cap Gemini, Sema Group and Sligos in France, FINSIEL in Italy, Logica in Britain, and Volmac and Programmator (Cap Gemini's recent acquisitions) in Holland and Sweden. German systems integrators such as PSI and the Cap-debis subsidiaries, GEI and SCS, are currently much smaller but seem to be on the right track.

There is no noticeable predominance of American suppliers in the field of systems integration, in spite of strong companies such as EDS, Computer Science Corporation, Computer Associates and Andersen Consulting, because the US computer manufacturers have so far been slow to commit themselves to this market. Of the Japanese competitors, only CSK and Intec are in the same league as the Europeans, but they have to date chosen to restrict their activities almost exclusively to the Asian market.

☐ *Project management.* Handling major projects, for example in plant engineering, is traditionally one of the strengths of European, and particularly German, companies. These skills can also be brought to bear in major information-technology projects. A significant market presence can be achieved through co-operation with highly qualified partners, even with limited in-house effort. Mannesmann Mobilfunk's D2 cellular phone network, which has just recently gone into operation, is a good example. So is the consortium currently being formed on the initiative of BMW, with the participation of MAN and RWE, to develop the E-network planned for the mid-Nineties. Quite apart from its importance for the operation of the system in question, the know-how gained in this way offers a headstart in experience for similar systems likely to be built in the future in Europe and around the world.

2. *New opportunities in new markets.* In addition to existing products and businesses, which should be upgraded through information technology, more thought than before should now be given to new and unfamiliar areas of activity. For example:

☐ The progress of networking – via terrestrial links, satellite links or radio-link systems – offers a variety of opportunities for improved or new information services to commercial and private users. Even though these 'value-added services', as they are known, are not yet widely accepted or widespread in Europe, they may prove to be a future market of extraordinarily high potential. Environmental protection is one of the reasons. In 1991, around 40 per cent of paper and board consumption in Germany went into printed matter – a per capita volume of 80kg, which could be reduced substantially using electronic media. In view of the almost exponential growth in the volume of knowledge and information, it is impossible to overestimate either the possibilities of constant updating of electronic data, or the practically unlimited recording and processing capacity coupled with video and audio technologies.

Numerous alliances, particularly between American and Japanese computer manufacturers, suppliers of consumer electronics and well-known media groups, have already formed in this emerging multimedia market. With the exception of Philips and to some extent Bertelsmann, European companies have not yet made an appearance on a global scale in this multi-billion DM business of the future. But it is the grouping of know-how and resources across the three industries that makes it possible to discover and service new markets.

□ Increased networking also opens up a further market in quite a different area, which has similar potential and is so far largely uncharted: security and data protection. Realistic figures on the – as yet little publicized – damage caused by computer crime and computer crashes in Europe are not yet available, but insiders say that they are growing all the time. Whether such damage is caused by unauthorized bank transfers, research and development espionage, unauthorized interference in manufacturing control systems, or a bolt of lightning, neither computer manufacturers, software developers nor the operators are in a position to guarantee the safety of information. For good system integrators, this offers a wide field, especially since over one billion DM of computer budgets are already being invested every year in information security in Germany alone.

3. New degrees of freedom for internal organization. For the internal organization of a company, information technology may be comparable in importance to the introduction of industrial manufacturing in its day. Managed with consistency – and good sense – the effects will be felt in all functions. For example, traditional patterns of behaviour and procedures will alter if, as a matter of principle, information is collected only once for multiple uses. Also, with broadly accessible information, the conventional model of 'information from the bottom-up, orders from the top-down' will become obsolete.

Information technology will also help to resolve traditional, and to some extent outdated, industrial manufacturing processes. It offers, for example, the freedom to work at home and to define 'bite-sized chunk' work packages. Above all, through decentralized information access and networking IT can now, for the first time ever, create the basis on which decentralization can proceed while maintaining organizational integration and unity.

Used in this way information technology is, however, also becoming a unit of output in its own right (the information is the product) and a considerable cost factor. It is, therefore, all the more important to create the necessary organizational conditions to boost its performance. In some areas, this demands deviating considerably from traditional structures and attitudes. It also demands the consistent attention of top management.

☐ The data processing department is responsible for providing the ever-expanding IT infrastructure for all other departments. In this role it essentially represents the nerve-centre of performance for the entire organization. In some cases, competitiveness can stand or fall by competent advice on applications-related questions. The chief IT manager must therefore be highly knowledgeable about the relevant technologies, but must also have good judgement on questions of efficiency. If not himself a member of the management board, the information manager must at least be closely linked to the board – where he must find competent and receptive discussion partners and decision-makers.

☐ Employees must be prepared for the changes that modern information technology will make in small but constant steps. Communication in this area commonly leaves room for a great deal of improvement, and general as well as specialized training should be afforded the highest priority. The aim is for all managers, and in the longer run for all employees, to hold a 'driving licence' for IT.

☐ An IT strategy should be developed in conjunction with corporate strategy, clearly defining the key tasks of the information processing function. Experts estimate the cost of, say, a comprehensive CIM system solution in an international company at several billion DM in capital expenditure, presenting even major industrial companies with financial and capacity problems. Concentration of such support on the business' core processes is therefore essential. Out of considerations like these, one top-flight bank, operating in the international foreign exchange market, restricts its internal software development to a trading programme; whatever else it needs is sourced outside. Hard choices have to be made.

We nevertheless hear with increasing frequency of huge systems being built to deal with all conceivable

aspects of customer needs and internal performance parameters. Often, however, these gigantic systems take
several years to develop, and their completion date is
somewhere in the distant future – a disturbing thought in
view of our rapidly changing environmental conditions,
if nothing else.

To prevent resources being wasted, contracting out
standard services is a wise policy. If economies of scale
have been achieved in the company itself, and the key
skills exist to serve external demand, the possibility of
establishing an independent business unit and offering
proprietary IT services to the market is worth serious
consideration.

There is no doubt that Europe is still having problems with
these and other conditions for exploiting IT's enormous potential. Manufacturers are not technically or economically
competitive, and users have not yet sufficiently renounced
familiar habits such as handwritten notes or manual order
forms. We do not need to look too far for the reasons. A
little regarded fact is that Europe's linguistic fragmentation
has, apart from anything else, severely restricted the sales
of hardware and software abroad. The translation of documentation and user manuals alone has generally proved a
very tricky hurdle. In addition, the powerful monopoly of
the post and telecommunications services in most European
countries, in contrast to the US, has barred the way to the
competition that generates innovation.

When the IT revolution started, most managers belonged
to a generation which, in the run-up to retirement, wanted
nothing to do with modern information processing. With
successive generations of new managers, however, the tide
will change.

Last but not least, the pressure to adapt was probably
just not strong enough in the past. European companies

were able to maintain their competitive edge for a long time with their superior product and manufacturing quality. With the growing significance of the time factor even this is changing, and the conventional sequential working methods of European specialists will increasingly make way for computer-aided group work. BMW's head of development, Wolfgang Reitzle, reveals a vision: 'There is no reason why a car shouldn't be developed Triad-wide. Technically, it is feasible for a German development team to send the results of a day's work over to its Californian colleagues by satellite. They would work on it for eight hours and then send it over to their Japanese colleagues, who, in turn, would send it back to the Germans at the end of their day. The result would be a drastic reduction in development time.'

VII

Consequences for Industries and Companies

Internationalization, environmental protection, innovation, information technology – the pressure for change and the need for action implicit in these 'challenges of the future' add up to a very full agenda for European top management (Table 3).

Picking out these four areas for special top-level attention may seem somewhat arbitrary in view of the multitude of other issues on the agenda. What, for example, of the fast pace of developments in South-East Asia, the intensifying north-south conflict between industrialized and developing countries, the turmoil in the international financial system, the rise in the number of political troublespots and the widespread value change in society? All these issues will demand the attention of corporate managers and will influence the type and extent of the action they will, and can, take. That said, it seems to me that the direct challenge for management is nowhere as great as in the four tasks of

Four Major Challenges for European Companies

	Impact → *and management responsibilities*
I. International-ization	
● Globalization	● Tougher world-wide competition → *Adapting the product range to global business/niche strategy or market withdrawal*
● Europe '92	● Capacity pressure ● Reorganization of logistics → *'European scale' of factories and logistics* → *Europe-wide purchasing (especially by public enterprise)* → *Entering previously closed markets/ defending customer relationships*
● Eastern Europe	● Enormous pent-up demand in consumer goods, consumer durables, infrastructure → *Selecting countries, technologies and approaches*
II. Environmental protection	● Cost of recycling, bans on certain products ● Emergence of markets for environmental protection → *Securing the product base* → *Developing products/systems for active utilization of market opportunities*

Four Major Challenges for European Companies (cont.)

	Impact → *and management responsibilities*
III. Innovation management	● Ongoing changes in input/output due to technological progress → *Determining position on the technology S-curve* → *Setting priorities for optimal success in R&D* → *New cost-effective products/systems* → *Shorter time to market*
IV. Information technology	
● for users:	● Fundamental change in all elements of the value-added chain → *Optimal use of IT/S in all functional areas* → *IT/S as potential competitive advantage*
● for suppliers:	● Technology-driven change in products → *Appropriate product/market strategy* → *Strategic alliances*

Table 3

Source: International Trade, McKinsey analysis

internationalization, environmental protection, innovation
and the use of information technology. Performance here
will determine a company's ability to master the other
tasks.

If we try to assess how well European industry is equipped
to meet these challenges and to internalize them – that
is, to respond to them in an entrepreneurial spirit – the
picture is one of general strength, though marred by some
serious weaknesses, especially in high technology (Table 4).
What this will mean in practice may be illustrated by a
brief look at three key sectors – the automotive, chemical and electrical industries – and at the likely shape of
the 'company of tomorrow'.

The Automotive Industry

The automotive industry has had a huge, formative impact,
both direct and indirect, on technical progress and economic
development in the Triad countries of North America,
Western Europe and Japan. Few industries have been the
object of so much written comment or public debate as the
automotive industry, whose products were first designed
and built in Germany, mass-produced after the First World
War on Henry Ford's and Alfred Sloan's assembly lines and,
since the 1960s, have increasingly become the centrepiece
of Japan's success as an exporter on the world market. As
the largest car market in the world, Europe, particularly
the EC countries, has become the new 'battlefield' of this
increasingly globalizing industry.

With a total output in 1991 of 14.5 million units, the automotive industry is probably Europe's largest employer if
both direct and indirect employment are taken into account.

Position of European Companies

Future challenges	Strengths	Weaknesses	Overall assessment
Internationalization			
• Globalization	– International experience	– Few insider positions outside home market	–
• Europe '92	– Experience of Common Market	– Adjustment difficulties within the deregulation and restructuring process	+
• Eastern Europe	– Traditional historical and cultural ties	– Bottleneck in financing gigantic demand	+
Environmental protection	– Broadest base of experience in active and passive environmental management	– Diverging guidelines/ implementation in individual European countries	+
Innovation management	– High R&D expenditure – Large number of scientists – Longest practical experience (patents etc.)	– Neglect of time and cost – Little 'design-to-cost'	+
Information technology	– Broad basis of applications	– Lack of acceptance of technology – Slow commercialization – Neglect of time and costs	–

Table 4

In the European Community alone, one million employees of supplier companies and 7.8 million 'indirect' employees in transport services, petrol stations, the police and similar sectors can be added to the 1.5 million employed by car manufacturers themselves. What this actually means is that, on average, every tenth job in Europe is dependent on the automotive industry.

The forecasts of the mid-Sixties that this market would be shared world-wide by five auto manufacturers within thirty years have not come true. None the less, corporate takeovers of companies such as Alfa Romeo by Fiat, Seat by VW, Saab by GM and Jaguar by Ford show that, at least in Europe in the current competitive environment, a process of consolidation is under way in which only the best players will be able to survive with autonomy. The end of the longest automobile boom in post-war history (1982 to 1990), the realization of the European single market, and the increased presence of non-European, particularly Japanese, companies offering superior quality and price-performance ratios, have added momentum to this development. As a consequence, the supplier industry in particular will undergo further extensive restructuring on a Europe-wide scale, with sharp reductions in the number of market participants and employees.

The consequences for the remaining European high-volume OEMs (Original Equipment Manufacturers) such as VW, Fiat, PSA and Renault/Volvo, as well as the luxury car makers such as Daimler-Benz and BMW, will extend to all elements of the value-added chain. In comparison with Toyota or Honda, for instance, and depending to a greater or lesser extent on the manufacturer, location and model class, all of these OEMs are currently facing considerable performance gaps. To improve or restore competitiveness, drastic changes will have to be made in all areas: product development (design-to-cost, reduction of development times, simultaneous engineering), purchasing and production (eliminating cost disadvantages, reducing throughput times, upgrading quality and flexibility), and distribution and service (customer satisfaction, quality of service, effectiveness and efficiency of marketing and distribution channels).

For German auto makers, which have focused largely on producing in Germany and have organized and managed their companies accordingly, the crux of the competitive challenge lies in compensating for their 30–45 per cent cost disadvantage. This contrasts with the situation of French OEMs. Their cost problems are less pressing as a result of extensive restructuring measures in the early Eighties and relatively favourable location-specific costs, but they are at a disadvantage on the product side (although the tide may be about to turn in this respect, particularly at Renault). Fiat, concentrating mainly on the low end and its domestic market in Italy, is struggling with cost, product and market-positioning problems. Sweden's car makers have substantial cost and model problems. British manufacturers are currently taking lessons from Japanese transplants. The European offshoots of GM and Ford are likely to count among the more successful members of their respective corporate groups.

An inkling of what is at stake in Europe can be gleaned from a brief look at the US. On the home turf of America's 'Big Three', Japanese manufacturers' share of the market in 1992 amounted to approximately 30 per cent, achieved through exports to the US and local production. If this experience is not to recur as Western Europe deregulates and integrates, and if European OEMs wish to exploit fully the market opportunities emerging in Eastern Europe, they must close – or at least substantially reduce – their current productivity and cost gaps compared with the Japanese. At the same time, through faster development of market-oriented innovations that deliver superior value to the customer, they must ensure that whatever performance and technology-related lead they still hold remains intact.

In terms of the four major challenges noted above this need for action varies in extent and urgency:

Internationalization. Direct exports alone will not bring success in the globalizing automotive industry of the future; manufacturers will also need to have development and production facilities in key markets. In spite of international sales success and relatively early investment (particularly in the case of VW in the US and Latin America), the Europeans are still at a disadvantage against their competitors in the Triad. The American manufacturers Ford and General Motors have been operating components and assembly plants in Western Europe, Asia and Latin America for decades; in Europe they have come to be regarded as 'insiders' and key market players. Following the lead of Toyota, Nissan and Honda, Japanese car manufacturers initially began to develop crucial overseas markets with direct exports of affordable, mass-produced but good-quality vehicles. More recently, the Japanese have expanded their operations by introducing an increasingly varied range of cars, including luxury models (Toyota Lexus, Nissan Infiniti), and by setting up a network of international 'transplants'. In contrast, the Europeans have concentrated primarily on national manufacturing operations and have no factories outside Europe (with the single exception of VW/Autolatina in Latin America). It seems likely that, with but a few exceptions (e.g. the BMW plant in the US and VW's joint-venture assembly plant in China), they will remain rooted in European soil for the foreseeable future.

Luxury car makers such as Daimler-Benz and BMW, with a naturally limited volume of production, have so far gained success in the markets of the Triad with a global export strategy under the slogan 'Made in Germany'. However, fluctuations in exchange rates, disadvantages in factor costs and productivity, and above all an increasing competitive squeeze in the luxury-end segments may mean that maintaining a world-wide presence will take on new dimensions in the future.

For the volume-segment manufacturers, VW, Fiat, Renault and PSA, absence from the other Triad markets of North America and Japan is probably irreversible by now. These manufacturers will, therefore, have to devote all their energies to defending their positions in the nascent single European market. (Despite the voluntary restraint agreement, current estimates suggest that the share of Japanese manufacturers in the EC could rise from today's 10 per cent to over 20 per cent by the time the agreement expires in 1999.) These manufacturers should also take advantage of their favourable geographical and cultural position to build a presence in the markets of Eastern Europe. With its acquisition of Skoda, VW has led the way.

Beyond these measures, a concerted effort to penetrate attractive overseas markets outside the Triad, like Mexico, Argentina and South-East Asia, either independently or with suitable partners, could expand and secure their sales base. However, time may be running out for the Europeans, as such opportunities may dwindle in the next few years as a result both of the development of national automobile industries in countries like Korea, Taiwan, India and China, and of the expected expansionary efforts of global players such as GM, Ford, Toyota and Nissan.

Environmental protection. This should present the perfect arena for the Europeans to prove themselves, as they have the longest and most varied experience in this area. Yet they have recently encountered considerable difficulties in satisfying the American Clean Air Act or matching the level of technology and costs offered by Japanese environmental protection packages.

The environmental damage caused by a vehicle can be divided into three phases – during production, during its useful life and when it is scrapped – and the extent to which industry action is required varies from phase to phase. Considerable progress has already been made in car production, examples being the Wolfsburg water-treatment system, or the reduced toxicity of modern water-soluble paints. In addition to the automotive industry itself, the production processes of suppliers also need to be designed with the environment in mind, and there is still a lot of work to be done.

During the useful life of a vehicle, an average of nine to ten years' running time, harmful emissions can still be considerably reduced by, for example, using alternative drive systems such as hybrid motors, which will not, however, substantially reduce total primary energy consumption. In fact, the real leverage in effectively reducing fuel consumption lies in reducing overall private transport.

At the scrapping stage, as much as 75 per cent of vehicles are recycled today. This number may be set to increase to between 90 and 95 per cent in the next ten to fifteen years, following the development of 'disposal-friendly' vehicles currently in progress. But the additional expense and the environmental damage involved in the recycling processes are currently still too high for further recycling to make sense.

Innovation/productivity/quality. In the past, the Europeans were able to compensate for their cost disadvantages with price premiums, thanks to superior quality, road performance, design and image in comparison with overseas rivals. To survive in the future, however, they must now move quickly to overcome these disadvantages permanently. They have no choice but to attain the objective of 'simplicity' in all operational and strategic areas. New, even revolutionary approaches to product design, manufacturing and division of labour, will be among the main items on this agenda.

The dominant role played by automotive engineering and product development has so far been one of the major sources of success for the European manufacturers, some of whom still build the most technologically sophisticated vehicles on the market. Nevertheless, the increasing superiority of Japanese innovation could soon eliminate this advantage, particularly if the Europeans fail to overcome their quality and service problems. In the US, for example, a survey of motor vehicles based on J. D. Power's ratings of customer satisfaction puts Japanese models well ahead of their European rivals, some of which have even been overtaken by a few US models.

When discussing quality, a distinction must be made between the performance features of a vehicle and the reliability with which it lives up to those features. The Japanese recognized the latter as a key success factor – and have developed it to perfection based on concepts originally developed in the West, such as TQM (total quality management) and QFD (quality function deployment). The Europeans will be able to offer quality, reliability and consistency in their products and services at world-class level only if attitudes and practices in development and production are changed sufficiently to put such widely recognized concepts into operation at all levels. For example, in order to avoid costly quality control and reworking, product quality must be an integral task as early as the design and production stages. This is the only way the Europeans can close their competitive gap in 'defects per vehicle', which is often accompanied by a patchy quality of service in dealer networks.

The European car manufacturers' and suppliers' technology leadership, with their innovations in engines, chassis and in comfort and safety (fuel injection, ABS, low noise levels, crash safety), has in part given way to Japanese innovations (active suspension systems, four-wheel drive,

and the like). In the future, the principal challenge facing
the innovative capabilities of the European automotive
industry, and the industry's greatest chance to differentiate itself from the Japanese and Americans, may well
lie elsewhere: in redefining the role of the car against
the backdrop of increasingly congested roads, growing
environmental awareness and changed societal values.
The twentieth century, as the age of the car and private
transport, is almost at an end. New ground rules are certain
to apply in the twenty-first century, even if ideas about what
form these will take are still vague.

There is a close connection between these considerations and the environmental issue. The alarming findings
on the increasing scarcity of resources in the Club of
Rome's report, 'The Limits to Growth', have raised public
awareness, particularly in Europe. This awareness may
well motivate European manufacturers to introduce these
prominent issues into the arena of world-wide competition. By setting the pace here and developing superior,
environment-friendly concepts in car design and transport systems, accompanied by greater individualization of
model packages, the Europeans could secure an important
basis for the industry's future well beyond the borders
of its European home market.

Information technology. Despite having adopted CIM/
CAD applications at an early stage, the European automotive industry is by no means world-class in its level of
IT/S usage. The problem does not appear to be a lack of
technology, as countless visits to Japanese manufacturing
plants confirm. The common verdict: 'They don't have any
production equipment, manufacturing methods or CIM applications that we don't already have.' Instead, the decisive
factors are the optimal integration of hardware and software
in Japanese manufacturing, the continuous improvement
of control and inspection processes, the uncompromising

commitment to quality (assembly problems or installation faults bring the production line to a standstill), and the close co-operation and involvement of OEMs with suppliers.

Even the most comprehensive collection of experiences and thoughts on internationalization, environmental protection, innovation and information technology is unable to produce a 100 per cent reliable scenario for the future. Yet it seems fair to assume that Europe will not see a repeat of what happened in the US, where the EC's share of the import market for passenger vehicles fell by one-third between 1986 and 1989, and where domestic manufacturers lost well over one-third of their production volume within six years. True, European high-volume suppliers such as Renault, VW, Fiat, Opel and Ford are likely to lose sales in their home markets. At the high end, Mercedes-Benz, BMW and Audi may only be able at best to defend their current market shares against the Japanese advance. None the less, the European automotive industry appears to be better armed now than the American industry was in the mid-1980s.

Where a transfer of leadership took place recently in the European automobile industry (e.g. Hahn to Piech at VW, Niefer to Werner at Mercedes, Hughes to Herman at Opel), the new generation has an automotive background and has already had dealings with the Japanese industry in one way or another. Moreover, the Europeans will likely continue – as in the most recent trade agreement with Japan, which was spearheaded by the French and Italian automotive industry and runs until 1999 – to protect their markets from too drastic a loss of jobs.

More than anything, however, the automotive industry must now be aware that the world scenario is changing. The competitive advantage of Japanese manufacturers in Japan will decline. For one thing, Japan is becoming an increasingly expensive location for production. In addition, the signs are multiplying that in certain areas of car production the Japanese are operating virtually at 'core cost'. In the last few years, US companies have considerably improved their product development and production, and the emerging NAFTA free-trade zone will no doubt be one of the most attractive locations in the coming decade. Another factor in changing world competition will be the rapid development of the automotive industry in the countries of South-East Asia; this will be spurred by the drastic upsurge in domestic demand and massive technical support from Japanese manufacturers, who are increasingly looking to these countries for relief from bottlenecks at home. Ultimately, too, Eastern Europe will develop, if very slowly, as an attractive potential market and an inexpensive production base.

It is this complex terrain that the European automotive industry must have in mind when taking its bearings following the inevitable massive scaling down of unit costs: instead of single-mindedly staring at Japanese export and transplant strategies, European car makers should think ahead to the post-Japan period! The level of state support, their technology base and the new production and market potential in Eastern Europe – all these factors will stand the European car manufacturers in very good stead and should help them maintain their position in international competition.

The Chemical Industry

The chemical industry is one of the strongest sectors of the European economy. With sales totalling around DM600 billion, almost two million employees in the EC, and such household names as ICI, Rhône-Poulenc, Solvay, Bayer, Hoechst, BASF, Sandoz, Hoffmann La Roche or Ciba-Geigy, the industry has attained world status in the course of the last two generations. For all the heterogeneous nature of these companies, it can still be said that the European chemical industry as a whole holds top rank in the world. This can be partly attributed to the long tradition of an exemplary standard of university education, at least in the classical areas of the industry. The combination of highly qualified staff and a highly developed practice of job rotation between R and D-related and other corporate functions has given the industry an impressive mixture of specialist and generalist management competence. The fact that some chemical companies require their staff to prove themselves in foreign posts enhances the industry's ability to hold its own in increasingly international competition.

The industry also owes part of its strength to a technical infrastructure that has developed over many decades, operates efficiently and is largely paid up. Close connections within the industry also help – along the Rhine from Basle to Rotterdam, the chemical industry is its own best customer. Finally, the overwhelming majority of chemical innovations in traditional chemical products/processes – most of them, admittedly, relatively long ago – originated in Europe. Thus, having gradually evolved into its present position over a long period of time, the industry possesses some intrinsic strengths. Nevertheless, future developments could critically endanger this position. In terms of the main challenges to its future, the chemical industry in Europe is likely to develop in the following way.

Globalization. The European chemical industry began globalizing its distribution before the turn of the century. A little later, it established foreign production facilities, at first sporadically but then very extensively. After setbacks at the end of the First and Second World Wars, when many patents, brand names and plants were confiscated, the industry continued with this internationalization programme. Today, the world presence of German, British, French and Swiss chemical companies is probably unparalleled in any other major industry. This world-wide network will continue to represent an asset that potential new competitors are unlikely to be able to undermine – especially if European manufacturers learn to co-operate better with local suppliers at their sometimes very costly overseas manufacturing facilities.

Europe '92. Increased standardization of product specifications under single-market legislation cannot fail to have an effect on many subsectors of the chemical industry. It will, for example, mean less product differentiation for different countries, due to deregulation in user industries such as building materials and building equipment. Resulting price competition and cost pressure have already induced many manufacturers in such consumer-goods industries as detergents or adhesives to begin to standardize their product specifications and to restructure their logistics supply chains. A key feature of this process is the concentration of manufacturing plants, made more attractive by the elimination of delays at national borders.

The effects on industrial chemicals, though different, are no less pronounced. An attractive option would be the concentration of chemical synthesis activities in fewer plants – which is, however, blocked by Brussels legislation restricting, for instance, the transportation of certain types of chemicals. This makes an entirely different scenario conceivable for the single market, with a considerable increase in the number of 'swap' arrangements between European suppliers, designed to minimize shipping distances and costs. Central distribution warehouses with 'Euro-logistics points' might also play a role. These would be run by professional independents or joint ventures of several suppliers with the shared aim of minimizing logistics costs and distributing the cost of safety equipment over as many products and suppliers as possible. Quite apart from distances between producers and customers, more stringent product recycling requirements on manufacturers within the single market could give additional impetus to developments of this kind.

Many of today's European suppliers are already continental players, and most of the strengths that will be demanded by the European market are part of their intrinsic make-up. Hence, they should be able to cope with whatever restructuring is needed in their European production bases and distribution systems.

Eastern Europe. The highly industrialized Eastern European countries can be expected to focus on strengthening their basic chemicals industry. Consequently, as in the past, they seem likely to be exporters in this area rather than importers. Nevertheless, as customer industries develop and – at least initially – require substantial support in applications technology, Western European suppliers should be in an excellent position. The same applies to specialist sectors of the chemical industry, particularly pharmaceuticals: demand for high-quality medicines, which is known to rise sharply as prosperity spreads, is bound to take off in the countries of Eastern Europe as well.

Environmental regulations. In certain countries, particularly the German-speaking ones, the European chemical industry has a competitive advantage in the field of environmental protection: investments made decades ago as a result of progressive legislation have prepared companies for the future demands of the European Community. Roughly 10–15 per cent of all capital investments made by the European chemical industry in the last five years has been in environmental protection. If stringent legislation is pushed through, competitors will find it difficult to catch up. The overseas chemical industry will face an even more difficult situation if general international agreements set universal

standards for environmental protection in the industrialized countries. (The chance of this actually happening is
slim, however, as shown by the stubborn resistance of
Great Britain to environmental legislation following Central
European standards – e.g. on the disposal of dilute acid.)

On the whole, early investment does seem to have given
most European chemical companies a clear edge in the area
of environmental protection.

Innovation. Until the Second World War, Europe's largest
chemical companies (Bayer, Hoechst, Ciba-Geigy, Sandoz,
Hoffmann La Roche, ICI and Rhône-Poulenc) were the
'world's pharmacy'. From their laboratories came thousands of newly synthesized pharmaceuticals every year. In
a similar way, many European chemical companies long ago
began cultivating the crop-protection business on the basis of
their own inventions. Today, these 'life science businesses'
are important sources of earnings – in many companies, even
the principal one. They also act as a buffer if problems befall
the traditional chemical sectors.

The Europeans' traditional pattern of research – product innovation in the classical chemical sectors – has
more or less outlived its usefulness. For decades, major,
economically-important innovations have been sadly lacking. In far more promising areas of innovation (e.g. research
into process development) as well as in new methods of
innovation (e.g. molecular-biological investigation of the
mechanisms of disease), Europe has clearly fallen behind. The dearth of suitably qualified chemical engineers,
molecular biologists and genetic engineers, which is only
slowly being corrected, has certainly contributed to this
situation, as has restrictive legislation (e.g. on genetic
engineering). Meanwhile, many European chemical and
pharmaceuticals companies have set up relevant research
departments in Japan and the US. Even so, in the face of
the inherent competitive advantages of their Triad-based

rivals Europeans are likely to lag behind for a long time to come.

Information technology. The chemical industry has traditionally been one of the major customers for the suppliers of information hardware and software. However, these early and substantial investments tend to be geared to the conventional uses of information technology, mainly for administrative support. Furthermore, the adoption of those EDP applications at such an early stage has necessarily left the chemical industry with an IT patchwork of stand-alone solutions that will not readily admit 'migration strategies' to more modern, core process-related applications. In technology-related IT applications, all evidence suggests that the European chemical industry is certainly not ahead of its American competitors, mainly because integrated IT concepts (e.g. reflecting logistics processes) are non-existent.

Electrical/Electronics Industry

In Europe, the two main sectors of the electrical industry, conventional electrical engineering and electronics, and their subsegments face the challenges of the future with varying degrees of readiness.

☐ *Conventional electrical engineering* – including power stations and power generation, power distribution, metering and installation devices, drives, electrical household goods and electrotechnical industrial equipment – is marked by a broad range of very mature products, long life-cycles, and well-established customer relations. For the majority of products, key factors of success are manufacturing costs, economies of scale, continuous improvement, containment of development costs, and good contacts among the public authorities, industry and the trade. Networks between European industry and skilled trades and these customer groups are very close, and foreign companies find them relatively difficult to break into. National standards and industrial norms also contribute both to securing a high level of quality in the industry and to consolidating a relatively stable market.

Weaknesses are apparent, however, in the industry's international expansion into the US and Japan. In line with the conservative outlook of customers back home, the focus on cost and innovation also seems under-developed.

More serious threats to the industry may emerge if European markets become less partitioned as a result of harmonization of standards and cross-border mergers and acquisitions. And considerable problems may also arise as utilities, hitherto mainly state-owned, embark on international sourcing.

☐ In the *electronics industry,* the pace at which products are changing as a result of continuous redesign and rapid innovation is depressing the value added that can be captured by any individual product. This means that, even with increasing unit volumes, the profits – as well as employment – created by today's products will also shrink. Thus, one of the main tasks for management will be to exploit aggressively the opportunities for new businesses that emerge as a result of the cost/benefit leap with each technological innovation in the electronics sector. Reaching world-class productivity will be crucial in this context, since inefficiencies absorb funds urgently needed for building the new businesses.

Productivity is the main area in which weaknesses are evident. Here, European suppliers trail the world-class manufacturers, particularly in the Far East, in stand-alone products by as much as around 50 per cent. In the product businesses, where life-cycles are short, Europeans suffer from excessively long development times and strong functional specialization, which works against design-to-cost and manufacturing-oriented design. Moreover, many of the European companies are small by international comparison and development expenditure is often fragmented over too many areas.

With regard to the challenges of internationalization, environmental protection, innovation and information technology, the industry's prospects can be roughly outlined as follows:

Globalization. The electrical industry has traditionally had a very international orientation, yet its foreign manufacturing bases (predominantly in newly-industrializing countries) and its traditional export orientation are hardly enough to guarantee survival in the increasingly globalizing sectors of the business such as telecommunications and automation systems. In contrast, the traditionally strong power generation and distribution business, including suppliers, is of world standard and should benefit from the effects of globalization.

In the electronics industry, efforts must be concentrated on the specific strengths of each individual company. This will require identifying those areas in which a company can be a major European or global player. In many cases, companies will need to seek critical mass through alliances or acquisitions. This particularly applies to areas such as large telecommunications systems, in which development costs can be amortized only in the European or global market.

Europe'92. The European single market opens up a larger

market for the electrical engineering industry's traditional product areas (installation technology, plant technology), but it will also demand that the large number of local, sub-optimal manufacturing facilities be restructured. An example is the large number of cable-manufacturing plants throughout the EC, which will require a substantial consolidation of capacities. In the conventional product sectors, many small, sub-optimal manufacturing facilities in countries like Spain or Portugal, once necessary to meet local content requirements, will become redundant as parent companies tailor activities according to European standards. Far-reaching alliances, such as those between AEG and Siemens in traffic engineering, or ABB and Alsthom in power-station engineering, will also play a significant role.

Eastern Europe. The European electrical industry will profit in this market from the demand for consumer durables and capital goods, but mainly from infrastructural projects. Historical links, geographical proximity and similarities in standards will all have a positive effect on business in this area.

Environmental protection. This could hold a great deal of potential for the European electrical industry. European legal initiatives and directives go further than those in any other part of the world, and the electrical industry offers an impressive range of relevant products and systems in the power-engineering and installation-technology fields. ABB, CGE, GEC, Siemens and AEG have a clear lead in this sector.

Innovation. While the electrical industry's innovative capacity in its traditional business appears to be well developed, in electronic products and systems it is distinctly poor. The industry will have to redirect its R and D activities. Electronics manufacturers in particular will have to seize aggressively new business opportunities and push ahead with innovation. Higher productivity and correspondingly higher profits are needed to enable manufacturers to exploit new opportunities related to, or even within, core business areas and to pursue these in international markets. Creating small, entrepreneurial business units and learning from customers and competitors should stimulate this process.

Information technology. The electrical industry is feeling the force of the IT/S revolution both as a supplier and a user. As a supplier, the industry faces considerable problems with its Japanese and American competitors, who have distinct advantages in both product range and costs. The Europeans look unlikely to catch up with their lead in the near future. As a user, the European industry suffers both from the diversity of systems architectures and from insufficiently user-oriented hardware configurations.

On the whole, the electrical industry will have to make extensive structural changes in order to master the challenges of the future and to maintain something like its current international standing. In view of the difficulties in major sectors of this key industry, it seems imperative to improve the operating environment. In the European electronics markets, for instance, competition should be stimulated, including encouragement of investments by foreign companies. Support to users applying new electronics technologies also seems appropriate. Finally, more flexible working hours and greater workforce mobility (e.g. through retraining programmes) should be actively promoted to facilitate the necessary restructuring process.

The Company of Tomorrow

Of the three key European industries outlined above, the chemical industry is probably the best equipped to strengthen its position in future competition, in spite of its problems in innovation management. The automotive and electrical engineering industries, by considerably reducing costs, making some structural changes, and systematically improving their products, should be able to maintain their position. In contrast, as things look today, the electronics sector will hardly be able to avoid losing market share and value added. In all three industries, the trend is toward much smaller workforces being needed to generate a given amount of value added. The fate of agriculture, where fewer and fewer people are producing more and more, is becoming increasingly applicable to industry as well.

However, years of experience in consultancy tell me that intrinsically 'bad' industries do not exist. Excellent companies in troubled industries are still noticeably more successful than weak players in the high-potential industries. Industry scenarios like the ones outlined above, therefore, can do no more than alert individual companies to opportunities and risks, and their own specific need to adapt.

A picture of European industry by the year 2000 could look something like the pattern in Table 5. Compared to market positions today, improvements can be expected by banks, insurance companies, the retail trade, consumer goods, utilities and environmental technology. As in the automotive industry, the chemical industry and conventional electrical engineering, the emergence of major fault lines can be expected in mechanical engineering, aerospace engineering and construction, but on the whole these sectors should be able to hold their positions. Apart from the electronics sector, the most likely to come under real threat will be shipbuilding, mining, pulp and paper. Naturally, developments within each industry will vary considerably between different countries and different companies; the starting points of individual companies and their capacity for change differ too greatly to permit easy generalization.

European Industries by the year 2000
Anticipated position in international competition*

➕ ➕➖ ➖

Stronger	Steady	Weaker
• Utilities	• Conventional electrical engineering	• Data systems technology
• Environmental technology	• Chemicals	• Office communications
• Consumer goods	• Automotive engineering	• Consumer electronics
• Banking	• Aerospace	• Mining
• Insurance	• Materials	• Shipbuilding
• Retailing/wholesale	• Software	• Pulp/paper
• Media	• Textiles/clothing	
• Tour operators	• Construction	
• Plant engineering	• Mechanical engineering	
• Pharmaceuticals	• Steel	
	• Transportation	
	• Telecommunications	

* In terms of global market shares for Europe-based companies, reative to status in early 1990s

Table 5 © McKinsey & Company, Inc.

Company-specific 'cyclicality' will always be more important than industry-specific cyclicality, which means that it will be the performance of management in building the 'company of tomorrow and the day after' that will make all the difference. What should this company look like? I can see five major trends:

1. Polycentric organization with a newly-defined corporate centre.

2. Concentration on 'core processes'.

3. Strengthening the liabilities side of the balance sheet.

4. 'Empowerment of the front line'.

5. Adaptive companies.

1. Polycentric organization. The notion of the corporate centre as the 'brain', 'headquarters' or 'central command post', with the operational units (factories, branches, subsidiaries) as 'arms and legs', 'henchmen' or subordinate outposts, is less and less in keeping with the times. Rising cost pressure and a change in values and attitudes are prompting this change. With the experience of corporate raider activity in their minds, more critical and more sophisticated shareholders are asking questions about how much the head office actually contributes to corporate performance and profit. In the wake of the emancipation of employees, who have, metaphorically speaking, 'come of age', the move toward decentralized responsibility is gaining momentum.

Corporate centres, some of which are still of gigantic proportions with 10,000 and more employees, are being put to the test. Traditionally, these head offices are responsible for central control, legal obligations such as preparing and publishing the balance sheet, and for operational tasks that promise synergy, such as research, development or central purchasing. A new role will have to be found in which, typically, much smaller centres will make a leadership contribution with *proven* added value. Developments at ABB, where the head office today consists of only 100 employees, could set a precedent in this area.

According to Professor Horst Albach, a corporate centre should perform only those functions that make the company as a whole more efficient and that create confidence in the company. He sees the modern head office as a 'spider in the corporate web', dealing with the major tasks that shape the future of a company, such as the development of a corporate vision, strategy and personnel. A head office defined in this way has no omnipotent claim to leadership and will rarely intervene in day-to-day business operations.

A further trend is for a number of centres to serve different businesses or functions on a global basis. Within this kind of framework, for example, the centre for communications engineering could be located in the US, for microelectronics in Japan, for 'white goods' in Italy, and for automation systems in Germany. Similarly, certain research areas could be located in the US (biotechnology) or Japan (new materials). The organization at Hoechst, for example, where biotechnology research is located centrally in Massachusetts and global business areas such as resins or rubber are located at Celanese in New York, is a good case in point. The picture is similar at Bertelsmann, where world-wide responsibility for the music business is located in the US.

2. *Organization around 'core processes'.* An organization that concentrates its efforts on crucial value-added activities and outsources everything upstream and downstream of those activities is increasingly becoming the target model. This may mean that, in the future, as much work as possible, even that of whole functional areas, will be contracted out or spun off into small, independent units. In the extreme, a company may contract with thousands of former employees and hundreds of small and mid-sized companies which previously were corporate affiliates. This could break major companies up to such an extent that 50–60 per cent of today's workforce is released to become either self-employed or to work for small suppliers.

In making the transition from today's all-embracing company to a set of smaller units with the same or higher sales, companies concentrate on their indispensable 'core functions' (e.g. engine construction in car manufacturing), combined with detailed analysis and optimization of the associated micro-business systems. Werner Seifert, while head of Swiss Re, for example, went through every last detail of his insurance agents' acquisition practice to find the most efficient standard procedure. And I myself remember from my time with Deutsche Shell over thirty years ago that car drivers – who then still preferred to save money by putting only a few litres of petrol into their cars at a time – were consistently greeted by entrepreneurial Shell pump attendants with the words, 'Shall I fill her up?' Shell gas stations in those years boasted above-average sales growth.

Such structures and processes can trim down a traditional line organization considerably and replace it with sophisticated internal and external networking. The Japanese have had an unusually successful history in this area – Toyota produces over four million vehicles with a workforce of only 80,000. But Europeans, too, even if they do not refer to it as such, are traditionally very strong in horizontal networking and should, therefore, have what it takes to break up their large group structures.

3. Strengthening the liabilities side of the balance sheet. Companies have traditionally directed their attention towards the asset side of the balance sheet. They would determine which product areas should be expanded or contracted, which market segments pursued more intensively or neglected, which channels of distribution serviced more or less intensively. As a result, the liabilities side of the balance sheet was often neglected. It is here, however, that both human resources and technical and market infrastructure – the basis of a company's know-how and goodwill – are to be found. Strategic plans can be converted into reality only if these resources are available in the necessary quality and quantity.

4. 'Empowerment of the front line'. When, some twenty years ago, I presented a new management organization for

VARTA Batterie AG, majority shareholder Dr Herbert Quandt asked me how my plans would affect the lead caster in the factory, the lab tester in the development office, and the salesman in the field. This showed the great importance attached by this industrialist to the front line. Any new organization that failed to have an influence in that area would be of little use to him.

The excellent companies of the future will do everything to strengthen the front line as far as possible. From my own experience, I know that sales executives at Shell, both in the office and in the field, had greater discretionary powers in setting prices for heating oil and lubricants and also more generous expense accounts than those from competing companies. It was also obvious that these sales executives identified far more strongly with their company than was the case amongst competitors.

Skilled workers on the production side who are constantly on the lookout for new ways to improve products and processes can be an invaluable asset. The same applies to laboratory staff, technical assistants and young graduates working in development. Companies that manage to create genuine front-line empowerment and that constructively shape interaction of the front line with customers, suppliers and internal functions, enjoy a unique benefit. Departments that receive the feedback from such activities tend to be much stronger than others. At Toyota and Hitachi, each employee makes an average of 1.5 suggestions for improvement each year, 15–20 times more than in European companies. Elliott Jaques' concept, according to which an individual's scope of responsibilities should be determined by his or her operational and strategic powers of imagination, suggests a theoretical starting-point.

Recruiting and systematically developing the right executives is an indispensable part of the success of transnational, flexible corporate organizations. In addition to impeccable

professional qualifications, candidates should essentially
have a good knowledge of foreign languages, and be familiar
with foreign cultures and the mentality of foreign employees and colleagues, as a result of periods of study
or work abroad. With the effective 'half-life' of managers' specialist knowledge shrinking all the time, the
company has to provide systematic further training tailored
to clear career perspectives.

In leading European companies such as IBM Europe,
Unilever and Siemens, it has been standard practice for
some time to initiate their junior executives into management responsibilities in a targeted manner, and increasingly
to ensure a balanced composition of management committees. Many other European companies, however, still
have considerable deficits in this area, especially at the
top-management level. A good international mix at the
boardroom and subordinate management levels in Central
European countries tends to be underdeveloped. Most management boards of German-speaking companies are almost
exclusively made up of nationals of their home country;
one laudable exception is Nestlé, where six of the eleven
board members are not Swiss.

If two-thirds of the managers at the first and second levels
do not speak any foreign languages and only 5 per cent
have done any extended tours of duty abroad, this does
not help international competitiveness. Similarly worrying
is the lack of IT know-how at senior management levels
– due to the fact that electronic data-processing experts
are on average under the age of 45, i.e. under-represented
in European top management.

5. *The self-regulating, adaptive company.* The picture on
the horizon is of a company that nurtures consensus with
ongoing self-regulation. Increasing decentralization represents a significant step in the right direction, but must be
accompanied all the way by 'democratization'. The change

in values in society puts new demands on management accountability within the corporation. And on employees' lists of priorities, meaningful tasks rank at least as high as material benefits. Better training and a wider range of interests mean that employees have become more independent and self-confident, and therefore demand more sensitive guidance. This includes serious objective-setting, systematic skill development and relaxation of the boundaries between professional and private life.

The emergence of much smaller corporate centres will be a clear sign that change is taking place. But top managers in these centres will still need the support of highly-qualified, though very small, staff teams. And top managers will have to learn how to employ the skills of these teams more effectively than in the past. Again, politics is one of the fields that can teach us many things in this and related areas – such as how to cultivate relationships with customers, suppliers, opinion-leaders, universities, academic institutions and the press.

The most important factor of all in achieving the aim of self-regulation, however, may well be a new understanding of the role of management. While it is now almost commonplace to declare the days of 'command and control' to be over, this attitude must become reality in a much more radical way than many people imagine today. The role of management, whether at the top or at subordinate levels, is not to exert power but to establish frameworks and game rules, and to allow creative scope for employees to attain their objectives. The number of management levels also needs to be reduced to a considerable degree – as hierarchies crumble, many middle-management levels will also lose the reason for their existence.

The management capacities released in the process will be a valuable asset, either for (co-operative) leadership of a growing number of smaller, decentralized units, or for taking on specialist operational tasks. It is one of the characteristics of the new self-regulating organization that a career does not mean advancing through ever-larger areas of responsibility with ever-broader spans of control over more and more subordinates. A specialist career – involving new and varied tasks, or growth of competence and capabilities in one's traditional field – is accepted as a valid alternative to the traditional managerial career path.

Jürgen Schrempp, head of DASA, adds a further interesting viewpoint: companies can cope with the rapidly changing environment only if, as he puts it, *every* employee takes external change into account in whatever he does. The objective therefore has to be the 'natural' management of chaos at all levels. Webasto AG, the leading mid-sized supplier of automotive components, is one of the pioneers of social innovations of this nature. Instead of 'who is our manager' or 'which team is going to manage us', the Webasto question is 'how are we going to manage ourselves?' For many companies, this is no doubt still very much a pipedream. For the emancipated employee, however, it is a model well worth striving for.

VIII

Germany – A Model for Europe?

This is a book about Europe. But in many places, where examples are drawn from particular industries and companies, it is also a book about Germany. The main reason is, of course, a personal one: my own experience of life and work in Europe has been primarily in Germany. Yet there are some objective reasons too. The Federal Republic plays a prominent economic role in both the Triad and Europe. Of the big industrialized countries, it has the highest export quota in the world, with exports accounting for around 22 per cent of gross national product. In 1992, the old German Länder generated roughly 25 per cent of the European Community's gross national product. Thirty-five of the 'Top 100' European industrial companies are German.

Given such economic weight, could Germany serve as a model for the rest of Europe? As recent developments have made only too clear, I would suggest that, if the answer is yes, it can only be a very qualified yes.

A number of factors initially appear to speak *in favour of* Germany as a model for the rest of Europe. The first and perhaps most important is that the two essential features of Eurocapitalism – 'unity in diversity' and 'social solidarity' – are especially well developed there. The social dislocations brought on by reunification might seem to suggest otherwise. And this general malaise was certainly compounded, in turn, by Germany's faltering economy and strained capital markets. Remember, too, that no other industrialized nation has ever been expected to absorb such a burden so suddenly, in so short a time, and with so little disruption to its international standing. Post-war reconstruction, both in Europe and Japan, faced none of these contraints. In a sense, the real issue is not whether the social underpinnings of Germany's economic strength will hold together, but rather why – given the unprecedented strains to which they are being put – they have held so well.

Unity in diversity has been a key factor of the German economic region since its establishment with the German Customs Union, or *Zollverein*, in 1834. In 1858, Prussia was the dominant partner, containing half the *Zollverein*'s population and producing 80 per cent of its total output of coal and iron. Nevertheless, in spite of the sharp economic divide between north and south, differences in religion, and a wide range both of cultural traditions and regional loyalties, in time a real sense of unity grew out of the diversity. Today, unity has again taken on new meaning – and has to prove itself all over again – with diversity captured in a federal political structure and a multipolar economic structure.

In terms of a model for Europe, the German tradition of social solidarity and balance may be even more pertinent. This long historical tradition can be traced back in modern times to the social legislation of Bismarck in the late 19th century. His abhorrence of the ideology of socialism led him to make social policy a central element of national policy. Statutory provisions on health, accident and old age insurance, and the like, served as an example for the rest of Europe. Bismarck was the first European statesman to consider it the responsibility of government to resolve the acute social divisions created by the industrial age. From these beginnings grew a strong social state, which even before the Wall came down spent 28 per cent of its national budget on social welfare and education. Former US ambassador Vernon Walters was so impressed by this German model that he never gave up trying to find out how the Germans managed to 'work the least – and still be the best off'.

The relationship between government and private enterprise is also worth attention. In the West German economy the state plays a prominent role, with expenditures totalling 46 per cent of GDP in 1990. This placed it midway between the extremes of France, Italy and Sweden, where public expenditure accounted for 50, 53 and 61 per cent of GDP respectively, and Great Britain, with only 42 per cent. For the whole of united Germany, the government share in GDP has since caught up with French and Italian levels at around 50 per cent, being second only to Great Britain. A basic difference persists, though, and concerns the areas where the state operates. In Germany, for example, it plays a much stronger role in the production of public goods than in Great Britain, but a lesser role than in Italy or France in those areas where private companies are more efficient and less expensive suppliers.

Finally, the idea of Germany as a model for Europe might also be supported by the more aggressive approach that country, compared with many of its neighbours, has taken to the challenges of the future such as environmental protection. The first Ministry of the Environment at the local state level was established in Bavaria in 1972, followed by the Federal Environment Office in 1974, the first environmental information system (UIS) in Baden-Württemberg in 1983 and the Federal Environment Ministry in 1986. The increasing number of environmental laws introduced since 1974 has also set a good example: the Federal Air Pollution Act (1974), Technical Regulations on Air (1974), the Sewage Emissions Act (1976), Chemicals Act (1980), Hazardous Materials Ordinance (1986), Waste Act (1986), Technical Regulations on Hazardous Waste (1990) and the Packaging Ordinance (1991). Top management, too, is increasingly taking the environmental issue on board, as shown, among other things, by explicit allocation of environmental responsibilities to members of the management team and by repeated publications and speeches on related subjects by business leaders.

With such an array of exemplary characteristics, what speaks *against* looking to Germany as a model for Europe? The simple answer: history – and not just the catastrophe of national socialism. Germany took longer to find its national identity than did France or Great Britain. When in 1871 a large nation state was eventually formed at the centre of Europe, under the leadership of Prussia and at the expense of excluding Austria, it initially presented a threat to the equilibrium of the region. According to historian Gordon Craig, this central position is a perpetual problem that Germany will always have with its neighbours, if not the whole world. In contrast to its neighbours, Germany has always been susceptible to swings of mood, from excessive nationalism at one end of the scale to radical denial of national interest at the other.

European neighbours, moreover, have shown little enthusiasm for making the German model their own. The Nazis' idea that Germany should be the cure for the world's ills still rings mockingly in the ears of many of them. As recently as 1992 and 1993, embittered British, Italian and

French comments on the German Bundesbank left no doubt about European aversion to *de facto* dependence on Germany's national monetary policies. The behaviour of the French in connection with German reunification (as late as December 1989, *after* the fall of the Berlin wall, Mitterrand and his cabinet colleagues paid an official visit to the government of East Germany), Margaret Thatcher's brainstorming session with historians on the 'Germans in Europe', and the active disquiet of other EC member states about Germany's 'hasty' recognition of Slovenia and Croatia – all this reflected much the same kind of deep-seated suspicion.

Another historical development that is far from exemplary is the strict division between the liberal arts and the sciences which evolved in nineteenth-century Germany. This division, according to philosopher Hermann Lübbe, has been responsible for much of the country's susceptibility to irrational romantic movements and for its aversion to technology. It prevented the type of objective discussions held in other countries on the 'ethics of technology' from being conducted in Germany.

Beyond these historical and cultural concerns, there are two other present-day issues that challenge the case for Germany's relevance as a model:

☐ Germany's perceived lack of attractiveness as a location for industry.

☐ The experience of reunification, which places Germany in a unique position and poses a severe test to the resilience of the German economy.

A Location Put to the Test

In mid-1992, the German current affairs magazine *Der Spiegel* as well as *Business Week* in the US announced, under almost identical headlines, that the exodus of German industry had begun. Around the same time, the *Frankfurter Allgemeine Zeitung*, along with another major daily, the *Süddeutsche Zeitung*, dedicated a whole series of articles to the observation that the Federal Republic had lost its appeal to both domestic and foreign companies. To this day, the subject has kept recurring at frequent intervals. There are, in fact, many reasons to doubt the quality of Germany as an industrial location. Much of the discussion to date, however, has been conducted on too emotional a level. A few facts may help.

The chief weakness of Germany as a location for business appears to be poor adaptability of industry and society. The post-war period, up to the start of the Seventies, was marked by a generally very successful economic policy, a moderate social policy and economically sustainable wage settlements. From 1972/73 on – that is, after the fall of the dollar and the oil crisis – government and industry had great difficulty in keeping the economy on an even keel. Confidence that vigour and resilience were still alive did return eventually with the remarkable economic recovery enjoyed from the mid-Eighties to the beginning of the Nineties, and for that boost to morale alone, the Europreneurs in Germany and elsewhere deserve a hearty cheer. Even so, from the vantage point of the approaching mid-Nineties, it is obvious that several long-term trends in economic, social and wage policies are open to severe criticism. Some economic structures are being preserved artificially, and some regulations pass all reasonable bounds.

Between 1987 and 1991, for example, the coal and ship-building industries together received a total of over DM50 billion in government subsidies, while the goverment spent less than DM1 billion per year in supporting such future-oriented areas as communications engineering and information technology. Despite all the lip service paid to the importance of modern communications and information technology, everyday reality is quite different: even in Munich's new airport only six public telephones have been installed in each of the departure halls, and mobile phone service is still plagued by inadequacies and insufficient geographical coverage.

The much-acclaimed 'social safety net' is now very tightly – and expensively – woven. Germany is at the top of the world league in holidays, with a statutory minimum of thirty days paid leave a year. At DM42 per hour (1992), our wage costs in manufacturing similarly rank among the highest in the world. (By comparison, at the current exchange rates the equivalent in Japan at the time was DM30, and in the United States DM25.) At the same time, industry has become grossly over-regulated. In one case, it took seventy-three months to get permission to build and commission a new chemical production plant, a procedure which generally takes only thirty months in Japan. Regulations on shop opening hours are among the strictest in Europe. The American Chamber of Commerce in Germany only recently complained about the uncooperative stance of the German authorities toward American investors trying to locate facilities in Germany.

Education and training take too long (40 per cent of students are over 24, most students spend an average of over fifteen semesters at university, and every third student drops out.) In relation to the masses of students there are too few professors. Many courses of study are not sufficiently geared to the needs of industry, and the

working life of the individual is shortened by early retirement. Indeed, the German model suffers from the structural problem that, by international standards, we start
working late and retire early.

The negative effects of these rigidities are making their
mark in the steep decline in Germany's position in high-tech
markets. Germany's international position in the watch
and camera industries, as well as in microelectronics,
consumer electronics, office communications and manufacturing automation is insignificant. In the period from
1985 to 1989, Germany was responsible for 11 per cent
of the new chemical entities discovered world-wide in the
field of pharmaceuticals – just beating Italy and France at
10 per cent, and far behind the United States and Japan with
24 per cent and 27 per cent respectively. In basic research,
too, Germany is losing its lead. While the country was
awarded twenty-seven Nobel Prizes in physics, chemistry
and medicine between 1901 and 1930, in the period from
1961 to 1990 the figure dropped to eight.

As gloomy as such an overall picture may be, it must be
seen in perspective. Germany still possesses many strengths
as a business location. For example:

☐ its cultural and educational heritage;

☐ its skilled and well-trained workforce;

☐ its consistently high-quality products, particularly in
machine tools, production control-systems, chemicals,
telecommunications, power engineering and automotive
engineering;

☐ its proven ability to adapt to international market conditions, coupled with its history of reliability as an
international business partner, especially valued in plant
engineering;

☐ its sound, though improvable, infrastructure of roads, railways, telephone networks and hospitals, as well as its
competent, if not particularly cost-effective, public administration;

☐ its underlying social consensus – despite recent disruptions
– and its still relatively high level of working discipline.

Most of the strengths listed here can be had only in return
for a comparatively high tax burden and labour costs. To
make this arrangement work, therefore, special insistence
must be put on manufacturing only high-quality, high value-
added products and systems.

Germany's attractiveness as a location for industry is
a complex issue that does not lend itself to simple, one-
dimensional answers. A fair judgement requires detailed
information and careful analysis. At the *microeconomic
level*, for example, it is important to understand what
decision-making processes companies apply in choosing
locations, and which locational factors have the most weight
for various types of companies and investments. Also at
issue: the possibilities for an individual company to adapt
to locational factors (or to influence these factors), the extent
to which investment calculations should take into account
less easily quantifiable features of a location, such as leisure
opportunities, worker motivation and supplier reliability, in
addition to hard numbers on payback or ROI.

On the *macroeconomic level*, relevant questions include
the phenomenon of clusters of industry activity forming in
certain locations. What are the motives behind it? How
can it be initiated and influenced? Why do locations gain
or lose appeal in the longer term? What political, social and
institutional influences are at work in this process?

Two examples may help to illustrate how a more differentiated approach can throw new light on the question of

location. First, it is important to set the locational problem in the proper context. By its very nature, any decision on an operating location is a decision about a long-term investment. The implications such a decision has for the quality of the location can be assessed realistically only if all the relevant investment flows are considered individually.

The total volume of investments initiated in Germany in 1991 came to DM635 billion. Of this total, only a portion is geographically mobile – namely private investment in expansion and, to some extent, private building investments. And experience suggests that even these investments are in part predetermined by the wish to take advantage of shared scale in existing locations. My estimate is that this leaves only around DM170 billion of investment by German companies freely available for location decisions. Another relevant stream of investment comes, of course, from abroad: in 1991, non-German companies made direct investments of around DM270 billion outside their home markets, of which only DM1.2 billion flowed into the Federal Republic. On the whole, the bulk of funds available annually for location-related investments is too small to trigger a noticeable change.

Secondly, the public debate on location quality should not single out individual items from a complex web of factors and weight them at will. For example, to 'prove' the declining appeal of Germany as a location, reference is often made to the fact that the balance of direct foreign investment in the Federal Republic is negative (by DM22 billion in 1992). But this number is not especially helpful, since not all German investment abroad constitutes a vote against the quality of locations at home. In fact, two-thirds of such investments are made with a view to developing or servicing foreign markets. Distribution-oriented direct investments in foreign markets have become an integral component of global corporate strategies, since they help to bypass trade restrictions, avoid currency risks and reduce transport costs.

Moreover, drawing the balance of incoming and outgoing direct investments is misleading on two counts. German industry's commitment abroad is certainly not too high; it is more likely to be too low. For one thing, the accumulated total of German direct investments abroad by the beginning of 1992 amounted to DM259 billion, less than 2.5 per cent of the total German capital stock. Compared with other industrialized nations, German companies are still under-represented in many interesting markets in terms of both exports and direct investments. What is more, Japan's negative foreign investment balance has traditionally been higher than that of Germany; none the less, it would never occur to anyone to start talking about the exodus of Japanese industry. Instead, Japan's engagement in foreign markets is praised as forward-thinking and exemplary. Many foreign companies invest in Germany directly through their German subsidiaries. Strictly speaking, Opel's new factory in Eisenach should be counted as an investment by General Motors, in other words a foreign investment. The real investment of the ten largest foreign companies resident in Germany comes to over DM7 billion. Many foreign affiliates evidently feel very much at home in Germany.

Quite apart from a balanced consideration of macroeconomic indicators, the German debate on location quality also fails to take microeconomic factors into account – as, for example, newly-emerging *industry clusters*. Where market and sales motives lead OEMs to invest abroad, suppliers will follow. New production concepts introduced by car manufacturers will induce suppliers to set up nearby. In Wales and Ohio, whole clusters of production facilities for the automotive and supply industries have formed according to this pattern. Similarly, the presence of more than

600 automotive suppliers, including Michelin and Bosch, no doubt encouraged BMW's recent decision to set up a 2,000-man assembly plant in South Carolina. In general, for every new job in the manufacturing sector, approximately two further jobs are created in associated sectors up- and downstream.

The formation of *regional clusters* is also important, though more difficult to explain in strictly economic terms. Japanese companies feel particularly at home in Wales, Alsace, Spain and Holland. In Germany they are attracted to Düsseldorf and the immediate vicinity. In Spartanburg, South Carolina, BMW is in the best of German company: Hoechst, Bosch, Bertelsmann and Adidas are also located there. No other American state has managed to attract such a high level of German interest.

A third form of locational cluster formation is the *corporate cluster*. Decisions in favour of a particular location often develop a certain dynamic force of their own. A few years after the decision to invest, say, in a development and design centre, a pilot plant is set up, ultimately followed by a full-scale manufacturing facility, including logistical and distribution infrastructure. The reverse process, from distribution presence via manufacturing to development, is less likely to happen, although distribution is far and away the function most often established abroad.

While large locations involve a risk of long-term commitment and, therefore, high switching costs for the company concerned, the location itself stands to benefit in its competition with other sites. The more investment projects can be attracted to a location, the higher the likelihood that clusters will form as part of a natural, self-reinforcing process.

All said, concerns about the attractiveness of individual industry locations in Germany and elsewhere in Europe – while often shrill and exaggerated – must be taken seriously.

However, it would be in the interest of all concerned if the debate could be conducted on a more rational level.

Finally – whatever the significance of foreign investments – the essential turn for the better must be effected 'from within' the German economy. We need some far-reaching changes, and in particular I have four in mind:

☐ *New labour arrangements.* McKinsey calculated seven years ago that an increase in flexible part-time work alone holds an employment potential equivalent to 1.5 million additional full-time jobs. At present, no more than 15 per cent of employees in Germany work part-time, compared – for instance – with 33 per cent in the Netherlands.

☐ *New products.* Ground lost for various reasons in traditional fields of industrial activity must be compensated for through innovative products and services. The over 300,000 highly qualified jobs created in the dynamic American software industry over the past ten years are impressive evidence. Had the telecopier not only been invented in Germany but also turned into a marketable product there, supplies to the European market alone would have secured some 10,000 jobs. Today, vast potential exists in fields like new materials, genetic engineering, as well as in medical, transportation and energy technologies.

☐ *New markets.* German industry is excessively focused on the Western European markets, which absorb over two-thirds of its exports. In the growth markets of South-East Asia, German companies are vastly under-represented. If German presence in that region were comparable, say, to that of Japanese companies in Europe, the employment effect in Germany could be at least 400,000 jobs.

☐ *New companies.* A lot of vigour in an economy emanates from newly-founded companies. In Germany, we have had an upward trend lately, with start-ups numbering hundreds of thousands since the early Eighties. But we are still short on technology- and science-based break-through operations. A pattern of new businesses more like that in the US could be expected to produce hundreds of thousands of additional jobs.

Reunification – A Historical Challenge

The reunification of the old and the new German *Länder* is a historically unique situation. Yet it is becoming increasingly apparent that what was politically the right thing to do was economically wrong. No national economy has ever been subjected so abruptly or so uncompromisingly to international competition as the new *Länder*, the former East Germany.

Monetary union at parity certainly did not help industry in the new *Länder* exploit its comparative advantage. Nor did wage adjustments that took no account of productivity levels. Wages in the new *Länder* have now reached 65–70 per cent, but productivity only 38 per cent of levels in the former West Germany. Average unit costs are 70 per cent higher.

Extremely poor management of expectations by politicians has played a part in these drastic developments. Unrealistic prospects for the future in the East ('a blooming landscape in five years' time'), together with the illusion in the West that reunification could be had for free, explain why 65 per cent of subsidies in the East still go into consumption and three-quarters of this is borrowed money.

An immediate action package is urgently needed to forestall irreversible damage – that is, the permanent de-industrialization of Eastern Germany. Take an analogy with corporate practice: imagine that one company acquires another, which is 25 per cent of the original company's sales volume in size. When the acquisition is complete, it becomes apparent that bankruptcy would have been a more appropriate fate for the company purchased, as neither its products nor manufacturing plant nor management nor management systems are competitive. What would the buyer do? He would install crisis management straight away. He would set up a task-force of his most talented people and put integration at the top of his agenda, not spend months talking about short-, medium- and long-term solutions. He would pragmatically channel his energies into what could realistically be done, to prevent lasting damage to the core business.

By the same token, any meaningful action package for Eastern Germany should consist of a two-prong drive: creating new opportunities for entrepreneurs (that is, stimulate demand for East German products), and putting those entrepreneurs in a position to exploit such opportunities, i.e. to meet the new demand.

On the demand side, financial incentives to encourage the huge pent-up demand for private housing construction could be a powerful stimulus. So could innovative, large-scale infrastructure projects in the new *Länder*. And, perhaps of most immediate urgency, it seems imperative to prop up demand from Eastern Europe, once the main customer of East German industry.

On the supply side, the overriding need is for a dismantling of bureaucratic rigidities. Generous government assistance should encourage new start-ups; industry and public institutions in east and west should co-operate in massive-skill building efforts; new ways – such as flexible collective bargaining agreements and employee investment schemes – should be found to contain the cost of labour until production reaches competitive levels. And far-reaching deregulation should attract investment and entrepreneurial initiative.

Such measures could help to direct the ill-fated discussion about additional sources of finance into more constructive channels. Experience to date has not been overly encouraging. But if successful, this approach could be the starting point for a new model of European, and in particular Eastern European, regional development.

Germany – A Model on Probation

Reunification represents a challenge of epic proportions. The problems and setbacks that have accumulated so far are at the same time symptomatic of the problems of Western Germany as a business location. 'Social benefits' and 'rules and regulations' do seem to have overshot their optimum. An overdose of any medicine can be dangerous, and this applies here too. 'Never having had it so good' could easily curdle into rigidity, paralysis and inflexibility, with vested rights divorced from performance. We have too little experience of 'less for everyone' or of 'tightening our belts'. Yet this is the only solution. This is where the main challenges lie – and also the most important task for politicians.

The German poet Heinrich Heine once said that the Germans had a past and a future, but no present. It was also he who said that thinking of Germany kept him awake at night.

If we apply this to the issues raised by the location problem and reunification, it is fair to say that there will be a serious question mark over Germany's future unless it concentrates more on its present. By the same token, however, its many specific strengths make it possible to master the present – permitting cautious optimism (and sleep).

The German dilemma can perhaps be best illustrated by the results of an opinion poll taken in spring 1991, when Germans were asked what they would most like to be if they could choose a different nationality. The majority went for Swiss. I am not sure whether the respondents were aware of it, but in Switzerland the working week is over forty-two hours, holiday entitlement is around twenty-three days per year, and three-shift operation is not uncommon. Clearly, the quality of life at any location must be earned by the quality of its economy.

In my opinion, once European Germany has overcome its current problems (and it has to reckon with a time scale here of between five and ten years), it may well be a source of inspiration and stimulation within Europe. The question of whether it constitutes a model to be copied by other nations will be irrelevant in a united Europe.

IX

Europe 2000 – A Dream

This book was written at a time when the fate of Europe yet again hung in the balance, when countless numbers of politicians, cultural experts and economists were wondering whether there was still a future for the notion of one Europe in the light of the changing world. Certainly, we know that we need to strengthen Europe in view of all the major challenges facing us. And we are coming to realize that regulations, laws, commissions and congresses will not do it. Instead, we have to redefine – and become reacquainted with – the great European art of achieving unity in diversity. Perhaps a glance back to the turn of the century, when something like a European national consciousness existed, may help.

As Stefan Zweig, in his *The World of Yesterday – Reminiscences of a European*, has written:

It is perhaps difficult to describe to the present generation the confidence in the world that imbued us young
people after the turn of the century. Forty years of
peace had fortified the economic organism of the countries, technology quickened the pace of life, scientific
discoveries lent pride to the spirit of that generation.
A revival began that was felt almost equally in every
nation of our Europe. The cities became more beau-
tiful and more populous with every year that passed.
The Berlin of 1905 was no longer like the Berlin I had
known in 1901. The city of imperial residence had become
cosmopolitan, and was surpassed in turn in marvellous
fashion by the Berlin of 1910. Vienna, Milan, Paris,
London, Amsterdam, every return to them astonished
and gladdened the heart. Streets were broader and more
magnificent, public buildings more monumental, shops
more luxurious and tasteful. Everywhere there was a
sense of how wealth was growing and spreading. Even
we writers noticed it in the number of copies sold of
what we wrote which multiplied by three, by five, by ten
in the span of this decade. The bicycle, the automobile,
the electric railways had shrunk distances and given the
world a new sense of spaciousness. Inventions, discoveries followed one after another in rapid succession,
and each time the latest became public property in the
wink of an eye. For the first time, the nations shared
common emotions wherever there was common ground.
When the Zeppelin rose into the skies on its maiden
voyage, it was felt all over Europe, and Europe mourned
the airship's crash together. Vienna rejoiced when Bleriot
flew the English Channel. For the first time, there was
a sense of community in Europe, a European national
consciousness was developing.

The present day is comparable with that time in as far as countries are increasingly beginning to discover and cherish their European identity alongside their national one. At the same time, they set great store by retaining their cultural differences, their regionalism. In his visionary epilogue on 'Bohemia on Sea in the year 2006', written before the collapse of the Communist bloc, Hans Magnus Enzensberger[1] outlines how Berlin, Prague, Ramstein and Bucharest, despite the revolutions that will by then have swept Eastern Europe, have retained an independence which remains unaltered over the years. In addition, he sketches an absolutely credible picture of some Europe-wide changes that will have taken place by then – automobile-free inner cities, demilitarized zones and a self-assertive independence from the US.

Luigi Barzini too, in his classic work *The Europeans*,[2] describes how the flexible Italians, the mutable Germans, the quarrelsome French and the imperturbable British want to preserve the peculiarities of their countries in the teeth of every move towards European unification. German engineering, Italian design, French style, English consistency and Dutch cosmopolitanism may provide the perfect economic combination, without undercutting the cultural independence of any of these peoples.

The visions of a Jean Monnet and Jean Rey gave stimulus to the modern vision of Europe: Monnet described the Common Market as a process, not an outcome; Rey compared the building of Europe to the building of a Gothic cathedral – the first generation knows full well that it will not live to see the work completed, but it will keep on steadily working on it. In the last thirty years, Europe has enjoyed an extraordinary success story that few would have

[1] Hans Magnus Enzensberger, Böhmen am Meer, in *Ach Europa*, Frankfurt 1987.

[2] Luigi Barzini, *The Europeans*, New York, 1983.

expected. Industry has started to integrate, while national cultures have remained largely independent.

It is clear, however, that the 1989 revolutions have cost the concept of Europe its original *raison d'être* – that is, the containment of Soviet imperialism and the integration of the Germans into a peaceful, democratic alliance. The need for two Danish referendums on Maastricht and the very close call on the French vote were not the first indications of this. With the easing of pressure from the East and the reunification of Germany, which was too rapid for many Europeans' taste, the traditional concept of Europe '92 and, above all, Maastricht – with its single currency, defence and foreign policies – became the spectre of a centripetal power. Because people are naturally sceptical of the idea of political centralization, the huge costs of the European Commission, as well as crazy notions like that of harmonizing 10,000 different industry standards, have become a thorn in the flesh of voters. They all remember, in spirit if not in letter, Franz-Josef Strauss's classic comment that the Ten Commandments needed 273 words, the American Declaration of Independence 1,324, but the unified standard for European tractor seats 1,559.

All this has contributed to European reservations about relinquishing national sovereignty. Europeans have not necessarily wanted to strengthen the nation state, but they have not wanted to lose their self-determination either. Nor have they wanted to pursue apparently irreversible developments, such as the single currency, without a safety net. The lack of exit clauses suits neither national politicians nor industrial leaders. It is to be hoped that the near-collapse of the European Monetary System in 1993, with the ensuing relaxation of the exchange rate mechanism, will prove a healthy shock – reactivating the process of consensus-building and clarification of resolve within the Community.

In the present situation, I can envisage three scenarios

for Europe 2000: deepening relationships and a cautious, organic expansion into a Federal State; increased prominence for the CSCF Conference – that is, a Europe consisting of a free-trade zone and a loose confederation of thirty-two or more countries; or a relapse into individual nationalism, including a gradual retreat from current cross-border ties.

My conviction is that the way is clearly mapped for the first option, since many economic processes are irreversibly moving towards a unified Europe. Though no blueprint of the desired model exists (the United States of America is inappropriate for reasons of cultural and social history), it is hard to believe that the enormous momentum generated by the world's largest market, with some 350 million consumers and a strong industrial and scientific base, will dissipate. The European market – fairly homogeneous despite its considerable regional differences – is far bigger in many segments than the market in the US; its industrial experience base is unrivalled throughout the world. Integration will always show benefits greater than the costs incurred by individual countries. But to achieve all this, Europeans will need to develop a secondary regional identity in addition to their primary national identities.

There is a further point in favour of the first scenario: the professional Europeans in Brussels have learned, through the public debate over the Maastricht Treaty, that too much centralization will be rejected by the citizens, who want a more prominent, workable principle of subsidiarity and expect sensible checks on EC processes. Against this background, the picture of a unit of twelve plus seven members is quite conceivable, with not only strong political leadership, but also political infrastructures, such as a capital in Brussels (or Strasbourg), a major institute for reconstruction finance, such as the EBRD, in London, and an independent central bank in Frankfurt, Paris, Luxembourg or Amsterdam. This Europe will maintain its traditional ties with the US

– since, in the last analysis, its living conditions are similar
– and it will make outstanding contributions to the reconstruction of Eastern Europe.

The social contract responsible for the high level of social solidarity in Europe will have further reduced the
divide between northern and Southern Europe by the year
2000. It also ought to enable the Europeans to take a lead
in overcoming the world-wide North–South conflict. At a
minimum, the traditional links with former colonies should
have left the Europeans with an obligation to help these
countries in an enlightened manner.

It is quite conceivable that this Europe may consist of
fifty to seventy regions, and that these regions will be in
competition with one another to attract investment and
provide sophisticated infrastructure, while preserving their
own cultural identities.

Perhaps this optimistic scenario is too much the wishful
thinking of a convinced European. Perhaps it is a dream.
And perhaps the direct pressure that forced Europe into
action in earlier phases is now lacking. Whichever scenario
comes true, however, the following nine trends are likely
to be very much in evidence:

1. Europe will become an immigration zone and, thus, will
   have to be on the very front line in resolving the North-
   South conflict. For a region that has, over many generations, seen hundreds of thousands of Italians, Poles,
   Irishmen, Germans and Englishmen emigrate to the New
   World without itself ever being the target of much immigration, that is a major readjustment.

2. Europe will have to reconsider the burdens of a social
   safety net which in parts is too close-woven and too expensive. It will also have to find new ways to achieve
   lasting   reductions   in   its   notorious   double-digit

unemployment. Europe suffers more than any other industrial region in the world from the fact that it cannot supply enough jobs for people wishing to work.

3. Europe will have to make major infrastructural investments, particularly in transportation, the energy industry and urban development, and it will need far fewer administrative and regulatory constraints to make this possible.

4. Europe will have to make drastic cutbacks in the role of the state, with its sometimes substantial stakes in industry – for reasons of budget as well as managerial and entrepreneurial ability.

5. There will still be considerable structural differences among regions, despite great progress with regional development programmes. The equivalent of the Italian Mezzogiorno will live on in the east of Germany, the south of Spain and the north of England.

6. Europe will have to undertake gigantic steps to solve the environmental problem, particularly in Eastern Europe, including the potential of more Chernobyl-style catastrophes.

7. Political détente will reduce Europe's Cold War levels of defence spending, but it will have to prove itself able to address regional conflicts.

8. In order to be competitive with the US and Japan, Europe will have to anticipate, or at least keep up with, the

discontinuities that are becoming a fact of life in virtually all technologies.

9. Europe will see a tremendous upsurge in the demands on its capital markets, which in the longer term will mean high interest rates and/or considerably higher savings.

All of this will be taking place against a geopolitical background that appears almost threatening. For nearly two generations, an unspoken political consensus between the Europeans and Americans could be taken for granted, and major technological developments often grew out of joint European-American military defence efforts. These links no longer exist in their old form. Europe will become less dependent on the US in the future. It will be able to develop certain technologies independently, and it has access to, say, Russian aerospace capacities or Japanese and Korean electronics expertise. It is quite possible that some element of political rivalry might develop from this situation, especially since the Europeans have occasionally been regarded as junior partners by the Americans in the past.

Moreover, the nine points listed above will probably induce Europe to turn in upon itself more. It will need to do so to be able to meet the demands it faces without risking its special strengths, above all its social solidarity. That such introspection may be a major problem in a world of increasing regional conflicts – and especially at a time when Islamic fundamentalism is growing on Europe's southern flank – is also obvious.

On the other hand, the Europeans have also realized that cheque-book diplomacy, as practised by themselves and Japan in the Gulf War, is no longer enough. The US, which will probably have even more cause than Europe to concentrate on its domestic problems, can no longer police the world and has no desire to do so. Burden-sharing will become an absolute necessity among the Triad regions.

Against this backdrop, what will be the responsibilities of European corporations? This is their big chance to shape their own future and that of Europe. In the last few years, business leaders have often transcended national borders more than the politicians have; they are selling their products all over Europe and serving their European customers via Europe-wide manufacturing and logistics networks. To gain economies of scale, leading entrepreneurs have had to operate internationally. They have had to act as statesmen in their regional environments. Naturally, this means that they also have demands to make on Brussels. As my colleagues from the McKinsey EuroCentre in Brussels had the opportunity to discuss with Jacques Delors, the top managers of twenty of the largest European companies have a short list of core concerns they want EC institutions to respond to: (1) full implementation of the unified single market; (2) reduction of uncertainty about future directives, allocation of power and competitive environments; and (3) strong support for major infrastructure projects and future-oriented technology projects.

European industry can be the pioneer and the locomotive of European unity. At the same time, I think it is quite possible that the leading European companies will enjoy another major growth wave before the year 2000, which will allow them to capture and expand international leadership positions, and that their share of the 100 or 500 biggest companies in the world may increase. In the same way, mid-sized companies and start-ups will be able to exploit important opportunities in the Europe of tomorrow, capitalizing on their own technological strength and new scientific breakthroughs. Given the right technology base, cost structure and marketing know-how, many of today's mid-sized companies can grow into large enterprises, and many of the small ones can become mid-sized with a European presence. It is evident that many companies have embarked on an irrevocably European course and that the old notion of trade following the flag is no longer true. The situation is now reversed: industry leads the way, politics follows – often hesitantly. Investments have been made in Europe, stakes planted in the ground, that can hardly be moved even if political problems do occur in the unification of Europe.

This does not, of course, mean that European business has already mastered the difficulties of integrating different cultures or that it has become competitive in technologically-sophisticated areas. As products become ever more commodity-like, European manufacturers will have to strengthen their systems, component and plant-engineering businesses dramatically. At the same time they have to reduce their costs significantly in order to survive in high-volume segments. This will probably include developing Eastern Europe as a low-cost manufacturing base, as the Japanese are doing in both the Asian 'Tiger' states and the People's Republic of China, and as the Americans are increasingly doing in Mexico.

Viewed in a traditional perspective, i.e. in light of the industrial experience curve, Europeans should have little to fear from international competition. One hundred and fifty years of industrial experience versus 120 years in the US and 100 in Japan, on average double the US number of people involved in industrial production and four times as many as in Japan – this might provide an excellent starting-point. If, however, you look at Japan's impressive marketing orientation, the Americans' powerful technology thrust, and the increasing financial burden of Europe's social costs, then you start to feel less optimistic.

Certainly, their strengths in international business, their long-term orientation, their social consensus, and the specifics of their management culture, will stand European companies in good stead. But they will indeed need all such strength they can muster for the major effort they will have to make to overcome their weaknesses in high-tech businesses, globalization, social costs and non-hierarchical decision-making. And with political organizations struggling with their own crisis of legitimacy, the business community will probably also have to address such issues of society as social values, attitudes towards work, the balance between the rights and obligations of the individual and of the state.

In my opinion, corporations have become the backbone of European society, whether they like it or not. They provide an environment within which people find continuity in consensus-based relationships. They bear the major share of social costs. And they are the place for innovation in technology, products, organization and people management, and so have a decisive influence on social change.

This may well mean that the learning process described in Chapter IV may be reversed – with politicians taking lessons from industry. For industry has shown that it can do a number of essentials right, for instance:

☐ give priority to results and 'getting things done';

☐ practise efficient decision-making processes and extensive, cross-border networking;

☐ achieve multi-cultural education and mobility of staff;

☐ integrate, and capitalize on, a broad variety of strengths;

☐ live the subsidiarity principle in everyday practice by empowering the front line, i.e. delegating responsibility and accountability;

☐ bring forth a group of visionary Europreneurs in large corporations as well as a multitude of European-minded owner-entrepreneurs in mid-sized businesses.

Meetings of European politicians should be complemented by regular meetings with outstanding Europreneurs to ensure that political and macroeconomic considerations are underpinned with microeconomic expertise. Such discussions may even result in joint European projects.

If politics learns from industry in this way, from companies and their leaders, then it might also be possible for some of my yet-to-be-fulfilled dreams about Europe to come true:

1. *Making transnational European education compulsory.* Every student would have to study for a year in a European country where his/her native language is not spoken, and every apprentice would have to spend a six-month period in a foreign company with a different language. (As far as I am concerned, this is *the* way to create the 'Europeans' of tomorrow.)

2. *Solving environmental problems.* Under a 'cradle-to-the grave' concept of product responsibility, compulsory recycling would be added to the design-production-sales chain. Energy policy would be geared to an efficient use of environmentally-friendly solutions (making the nuclear power stations in Eastern Europe safe, using efficient cogeneration plants and renewable energy sources). And advanced transport and traffic systems would reduce pollution and safeguard mobility.

3. *Relieving the Third World prosperity gap* by far-sighted, long-term investment in technologies suited to these regions, coupled with large-scale programmes to feed and train the people in developing countries.

Opinions on what will happen to Europe in the next decade vary widely. It will certainly not be a tranquil decade. There will be no calm and cosy future. Alexis de Tocqueville, otherwise so far-sighted, was wrong about that 150 years ago. In my opinion, however, Europe has all the qualities it needs to end the century as the pivotal force that it set out to be a hundred years earlier. In the process, Europe can become an exemplary region of economic drive, of balance between ecology and economy and between the social interests of its different population and age groups. It can be a region that leads the way towards constructive solutions to the North–South conflict.

I admit that the realization of this optimistic view sometimes appears to be moving further and further away. Many of my hopes could no doubt be dismissed as dreams of never-never land. But the time for bold ideas and concrete steps has come – in order to give Europe's role in world politics fresh momentum, and to help it live up to its true weight in world affairs.

It was important for me to show in this book that the Europreneurs have a decisive and indispensable contribution to make in this process, especially since they have learned – in the last generation particularly – to take account of far more than just sales, growth and dividends. The Europreneurs have, indeed, become statesmanlike businessmen and the partners of politicians. These great European 'corporate statesmen' are ready to take on more responsibility for the common good, as they have proved in various ways through their business practice, at the environmental summit in Rio, and by *ad hoc* support on political issues on many occasions. By giving their companies a very strong European direction, regardless of political difficulties, and steering their internationalist course without doubt or fear, they offer quite a sound model for the Europe of the future.

The traditional press conference after the management summit. From left to right:
M. Wössner, H. Maucher, H. Henzler, A Herrhausen, L Späth, M. Zach, R. Gut, E. Reuter. © B. Hüdig

Appendix

Third Stuttgart Top-Management Conference 1990 Mutual Dependence in World Economy 'The Stuttgart Declaration'

At the beginning of the Nineties, the quest for liberty and prosperity is on the advance. Among the most encouraging prospects are the decline of ideological antagonism and cold war, the opening of frontiers and the expansion of democratic and market-oriented structures.

We believe

☐ That this development is accompanied, and accelerated, by a movement towards free market economies and globalization of corporations, leading to an increasingly interdependent world economy,

☐ That the new interdependence holds immense promise and challenge,

☐ And that managing interdependence is a task of supreme importance for all parties involved.

I. Towards an Interdependent World Economy

1. At the root of the dramatic changes in today's world is the free movement of ideas and information, of people and goods, of currencies and financial assets. Exchange leads to increased division of labour; gains from trade fuel the development of an interdependent global economy.

2. In this system of interlinked economies, the sharing of resources implies a sharing of contingent risks, like environmental hazards, north–south conflicts, drugs and other social problems; and it also implies an erosion of national sovereignty in dealing with both opportunities and risks.

3. As economic interdependence replaces military deterrence, the world will be a safer and better place for mankind, where countries, industries, companies and individuals each have a stake in the well-being of the others – the major guarantee for civilized behaviour.

II. *The Promise and Challenge of Interdependence*

4. In contrast to the zero-sum game of ideological antagonism, global economic interdependence produces the benefits of the positive-sum game of 'competitive cooperation':

   – Wider choice for consumers from the best goods and services world-wide,

   – Gains from specialization and trade,

   – Welfare effects of increased competition,

   – Market adjustments to balance competitive inequalities.

5. In view of these remarkable benefits, the challenge is to defend the emerging interdependence against some very real threats:

   – Increased vulnerability of companies and countries to interruptions in higly complex exchange relationships,

   – A tendency to politicize economic issues unduly,

   – The dangers of bilateralism, from petty retaliation to outright trade wars,

   – The spread of 'voluntary' restraint agreements or even quotas in international trade.

6. Currency fluctuations, trade conflicts and persistent trade imbalances show that better tools are needed to strengthen the self-adjusting stability of increasingly interdependent world markets.

III. The Management of Interdependence

7. To manage an interdependent world economy, we need
   not only national laws and international agreements to
   safeguard free trade. We also need more effective informal co-ordination mechanisms which set the agenda
   in such a way that costly ruptures in international economic relations are minimized.

8. We must do our utmost to avoid protectionism as well as
   reciprocity – open or hidden.

IV. The following recommendations are made:

☐ *Governments* should enable their citizens to benefit from
market-driven economies by creating and further improving an environment conducive to private initiative and
private industry. Governments must develop a framework
to deal collectively with traditionally parochial affairs,
such as taxes, standards and codes, and laws governing
the flow of goods, services and assets.

In an increasingly interdependent business world,
binding rules in the areas of cartel laws, fair market
practices, intellectual properties and common environmental standards should be developed and enforced
through appropriate supranational bodies.

☐ *Corporations*, large, medium and small, should use the
emerging international networks, and should be committed to free trade, competition, and the long-term goal
of creation of wealth, while recognizing their social and
environmental responsibilities.

☐ *Governments and corporations* must induce and encourage developing, newly industrialized and developed countries to participate actively in the global market economy, especially as the Eastern countries move towards free economies and the Third World needs dramatic improvements of their standards of living.

Third Stuttgart Top Management Conference
20–21 April, 1990
'Neues Schloß' Stuttgart

HOSTS

Lothar Späth	Prime Minister of Baden-Württemberg
Edzard Reuter	Chairman of the Board of Management Daimler-Benz AG

PARTICIPANTS

Belmiro de Azevedo	President Grupo SONAE Portugal
Thomas J. Bata	Chief Executive Officer Bata Limited Canada
Carlo de Benedetti	Chairman and Chief Executive Officer Olivetti SpA. Italy
Bertrand Collomb	Président Directeur Général Lafarge Office France

Hiroaki Fujii	Honourable Ambassador Permanent Representative of Japan to the OECD France
Frigyes Hárshegyi	Executive Director National Bank of Hungary (Magyar Nemzeti Bank) Hungary
Hans Olaf Henkel	Vice President IBM Corporation IBM Deutschland GmbH FRG
Matias Rodriguez Inciarte	Executive Vice President Banco Santander Spain
Karlheinz Kaske	President and Chief Executive Officer Siemens AG FRG
Hilmar Kopper	Spokesman of the Board of Management Deutsche Bank AG FRG
André Leysen	Président du Conseil d'Administration Photo-Produits Gevaert Belgium
Gert Lorenz	Member of the Board of Management N V Philips Gloeilampenfabrieken Netherlands

Pale Marcus

President and Chief Executive Officer
Danisco A/S
Denmark

Helmut Maucher

President and Chief Executive Officer
Nestlé AG
Switzerland

Jacques Mayoux

Honorary President
Société Générale
Vice-Chairman
Goldman-Sachs
France

Klaus Oberländer

General Manager
VEB Schwermaschinenbaukombinat
'Ernst Thälmann', Magdeburg
GDR

Antonio Oporto

Executive Marketing Vice President
Instituto Nacional de Industria
Spain

François–Xavier Ortoli

Honorary President
Total–CFP
France

John Raisman

Deputy Chairman
British Telecom
United Kingdom

Edouard de Royère

President General Manager
L'Air Liquide
France

Anders Scharp   President and Chief Executive Officer
                                 AB Electrolux
                                 Sweden

Hugo Michael Sekyra   Chairman of the Board of Management
                                 Österreichische Industrieholding AG
                                 Austria

Jeffrey M. Sterling   Chairman
                                 P & O Steam Navigation Company
                                 United Kingdom

Björn Svedberg   President and Chief Executive Officer
                                 Telefonaktiebolaget L M Ericsson
                                 Sweden

Peter Wallenberg   First Vice Chairman of the Board
                                 Skandinaviska Enskilda Banken
                                 Sweden

Heinz Warzecha   General Manager
                                 VEB Werkzeugmaschinenkombinat
                                 '7. Oktober' Berlin
                                 GDR

PARTICIPANTS FROM MCKINSEY & COMPANY, INC.

Joel Bleeke
Director
USA

Christian Caspar
Director and Office Manager
Scandinavia

Fred Gluck
Managing Director
world-wide

Herbert Henzler
Director and Office Manager
FRG

Peter Kraljic
Director
FRG

Kenichi Ohmae
Director and Office Manager
Japan

Gérard Thulliez
Director and Office Manager
France

***

Hermann Schaufler
Economics Minister, Baden-Württemberg

***

Erik Belfrage
Personal Assistant to Dr Wallenberg

Gerhard Brodil
Personal Assistant to Mr de Benedetti

*PARTICIPANTS FROM STAATSMINISTERIUM
BADEN-WÜRTTEMBERG*

Lorenz Menz
Permanent Under-Secretary

Manfred Zach
Minsterialdirigent, Government Spokesman

Peter Boudgoust
Ministerialrat

Hartmut Reichl
Ministerialrat

Gerhard Willke

Index